Psy-Q

Ben Ambridge is Senior Lecturer in Psychology at the University of Liverpool. His article 'Why Can't We Talk to the Animals?' was shortlisted for the 2012 *Guardian*-Wellcome Science Writing Prize. *Psy-Q* is his first book for a general audience.

Psy-Q
Test Your Psychological Intelligence

BEN AMBRIDGE

P

PROFILE BOOKS

First published in Great Britain in 2014 by
PROFILE BOOKS LTD
3A Exmouth House
Pine Street
London EC1R 0JH
www.profilebooks.com

10 9 8 7 6 5 4 3 2 1

Typeset in 11.25/13.75 Chaparral Pro
Designed by Nicky Barneby @ Barneby Ltd
Printed and bound in Great Britain by Clays, Bungay, Suffolk

A CIP catalogue record for this book is available from the British Library.

ISBN 978 1 78125 2109
eISBN 978 1 78283 0238

FSC
Mixed Sources
Product group from well-managed
forests and other controlled sources
Cert no. SGS-COC-2061
www.fsc.org
© 1996 Forest Stewardship Council

The paper this book is printed on is certified by the © 1996
Forest Stewardship Council A.C. (FSC). It is ancient-forest friendly.
The printer holds FSC chain of custody SGS-COC-2061

Contents

Acknowledgements

I would like to thank Daniel Crewe, Nick Sheerin and Penny Daniel at Profile, Melanie Tortoroli at Penguin, Sally Holloway at Felicity Bryan Associates for their extremely helpful guidance, comments and suggestions, Matthew Taylor for copy-editing and Nicky Barneby for design and typesetting.

Preface: Psychology Is Everything

You've heard of your IQ; your general intelligence. But what's your 'Psy-Q'? How much do you know and understand about what makes you tick? And how good are you at predicting other people's behaviour . . . or even your own?

The aim of this book is to share the answers that psychology has come up with to explain how and why humans do all the things we do. But it is not some dry, dusty psychology textbook, filled – as most are – with details of long, boring experiments and byzantine theories. What you want to know is what psychology can tell you about you and your life. Well, I'm not going to *tell* you. Instead, I'm going to *show* you, via a series of interactive tests, quizzes, puzzles, games and illusions. Of course, we don't have everything figured out right now. But by the time you reach the end of this book, you will not only have the very best answers that science can offer, but will also have gained a powerful insight into your own psychology.

Notice that I used the word 'science'. As a psychology researcher, I'm first and foremost a scientist. Psychology derives its value from following the scientific method: we come up with theories and test them, using the most controlled experiments possible. Every study that we meet over the course of this book is drawn from the peer-reviewed scientific literature. And while scientists rarely reach a consensus on anything, the explanations and conclusions I give are based on my reading of the best evidence that is currently available, with no wild conjecture, no pseudo-science and absolutely no pop-psychology pap. So, while you'll encounter both cutting-edge studies and plenty of classics, there are very few from the period before psychology established itself as an experimental science, somewhere in the 1950s.

But *Psy-Q* doesn't just *describe* these studies; it *is* these studies. You'll measure your personality, intelligence, moral values, thinking style, impulsivity, skill at drawing, capacity for logical reasoning, musical taste, multitasking ability, susceptibility to illusions (both visual and mental) and preferences in a romantic partner. You'll learn how we as a species think, feel, see and respond to others. You'll be surprised, delighted, amazed, amused, frustrated, horrified and downright baffled. You'll turn psychologist and ask friends and family to complete the studies in order to compare your results. You'll run to your computer to complete online versions of the studies, many at the companion website (www.PsyQbook.com). And by the end of your journey, I hope you'll have begun to see that *psychology is everything*: there is literally no aspect of the human experience that cannot be investigated, in some way or other, using the methods of experimental psychology.

As for the route that you take through the book, well, it's up to you. Although I've tried to put these studies in some kind of logical order, mixing up sections of different types to keep things lively, feel free to navigate your own path between cross-referenced studies or to float around at random as the mood takes you; it's your book, your brain and your voyage of discovery. So, anchors away, let's set sail on your very own psych-odyssey.

The Raw Shark Test

Let's start with what is almost certainly the most famous psychological test ever: the *Rorschach Test*. To complete the test, simply write what you see in the space below each image, then turn the page to find out what your answers say about you.

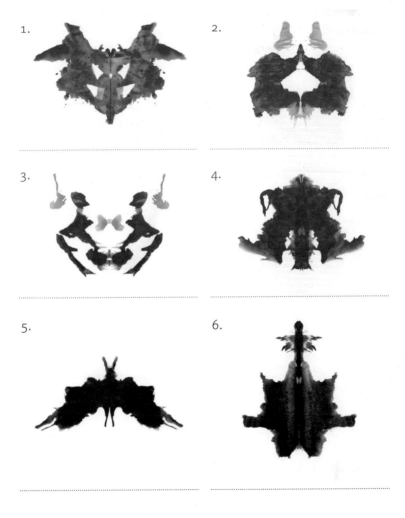

1.

2.

3.

4.

5.

6.

7.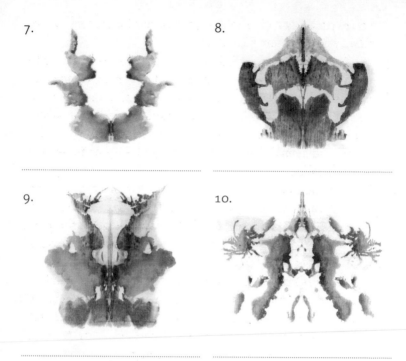

8.

9.

10.

ANSWERS

1. The first card is really just a warm-up, and has fairly obvious responses that don't actually say anything much about you. Is it a bat, a butterfly or a moth? It doesn't matter.

2. Now we're getting into it. Most people will say that this looks like two humans, or animals such as bears or elephants. But do you think they're fighting, holding hands or simply saying hello? If you said the former, this may indicate that you have angry or aggressive tendencies.

3. This one definitely looks like two humans, right (perhaps with love hearts or butterflies in between them)? If you didn't spot them, or took a long time to do so, this suggests that you may struggle with social interactions.

4. This card is often referred to as the 'father card', because whatever you say about it reflects your attitude towards your father. For example, if you saw a bear coming to devour you,

you're probably a bit afraid of your father (or all men, or authority figures more generally).

5. This is another 'easy' card, designed to give you a break, and to check that you're paying attention and not giving completely off-the-wall answers. If you didn't say something like *moth, butterfly* or *bat* (or the *Donnie Darko* rabbit), you've got issues.

6. Number six is a sex card. Oh, come on, use your imagination! If you said *animal skin* or *rug*, you might be trying to repress your sexuality.

7. The companion to number 4, this card is often called the 'mother card'. So what did you see? Two angels? Good. Two witches? Not so good. If you didn't see women at all, this may reflect some difficulty in getting close to the women in your life.

8. The last three cards are all full-colour in the original version, so you can be forgiven for struggling a little. Most people see some kind of four-legged animal. If you didn't, it may reflect a difficulty in coping with complex situations or emotions in which – as in this card – there is a lot going on.

9. Most people struggle to come up with anything much here (perhaps a person?), though if you drew a complete blank, it may reflect difficulties in dealing with situations where you have to think for yourself.

10. Again, there's quite a lot going on here, and no single 'typical' response. People sometimes see crabs, lobsters, spiders, snakes or insects. If you brought these parts together as one – for example, answering *an underwater scene* – this suggests excellent organisational skills. However, since test-takers know that this is the last card, psychologists are often on the look-out for conscious or unconscious attempts to send a 'take-home' message about one's current situation or mental state.

The *Rorschach test* – of which you have just taken a version – was published by the Swiss psychologist Hermann Rorschach in 1921. Rorschach may have taken his inspiration from *Gobolinks*, a nineteenth-century book of children's poetry based around inkblot people, animals and monsters (see Web Links and Further Reading to download this book for free). The theory behind the test is that, by asking patients to describe pictures rather than to talk about themselves directly, we can tap into subconscious thoughts and emotions that the patients may be unaware of, or even deliberately trying to hide (something we'll learn more about later in the section The Interpretation of Dreams).

Now, if you thought that the 'answers' above were a little flippant, you're right. Although these interpretations are based loosely on the conventional wisdom regarding this test, psychologists are divided as to whether or not the conventional wisdom is right, or whether or not the test tells us anything of value at all. So I figured I could say pretty much whatever I liked. I call the version with my interpretation scheme the *Raw Shark Test*.

This is not to say that today's clinical psychologists have abandoned the Rorschach test. Many still swear by it, and there exist detailed scoring manuals designed to overcome the apparent subjectivity regarding the interpretation of particular responses. Even the test's harshest critics concede that it can be useful for diagnosing schizophrenia (although one study found that it also diagnosed the disorder in almost one-sixth of apparently normal participants). Certainly the usefulness of the Rorschach test for the purposes I have used it here – assessing personality in (hopefully!) normal readers – is debatable, to say the least.

However, there is one pattern of responses that is particularly illuminating . . .

Web Links and Further Reading
Download *Gobolinks, or Shadow-Pictures for Young and Old* from: http://www.read.gov/books/young.html

A Dirty Joke

A patient visits a clinical psychologist who administers the Rorschach ink-blot test. 'Now tell me what you see,' says the psychologist, showing the patient the first card. 'A naked woman,' replies the patient. 'OK,' says the psychologist, 'let's try another one.' 'A couple having sex,' the patient responds instantly. 'Hmm,' says the psychologist, arching his eyebrows. 'Let's try the next one . . .'

This carries on through the whole set of ten cards, with the patient giving increasingly filthy answers. 'Mr Jones,' announces the psychologist, 'I'm afraid to have to tell you that you have an unhealthy obsession with sex.' The patient looks shocked. '*Me*?! You're the one with all the dirty pictures.'

Your Personality Profile

While the Rorschach test is of questionable value as a measure of personality, psychologists have developed a number of tests and questionnaires that are much more useful. Although there are many different ways to describe personality, perhaps the most widely accepted is the *Big Five* model, which attempts to capture personality in just five traits. Before we find out what these are, why not measure your own personality by taking the test below?

Below are phrases which describe people's behaviour. Please use the rating scale below to describe how accurately each statement describes *you*. Describe yourself as you generally are now, in relation to other people you know who are the same sex as and roughly the same age as you, not as you wish to be in the future. Please read each statement carefully and then tick the corresponding box (ignoring the numbers for now). It is important to be as honest as possible; remember there are no 'right' or 'wrong' answers.

In general, I . . .	Very Inaccurate	Moderately Inaccurate	Neither Inaccurate nor Accurate	Moderately Accurate	Very Accurate
1. Pay attention to details.	1	2	3	4	5
2. Have little to say.	5	4	3	2	1
3. Feel comfortable with myself.	5	4	3	2	1
4. Tend to vote for liberal political candidates.	1	2	3	4	5
5. Get chores done right away.	1	2	3	4	5
6. Dislike myself.	1	2	3	4	5
7. Procrastinate and waste time.	5	4	3	2	1
8. Respect others.	1	2	3	4	5

In general, I . . .	Very Inaccurate	Moderately Inaccurate	Neither Inaccurate nor Accurate	Moderately Accurate	Very Accurate
9. Feel comfortable around people.	1	2	3	4	5
10. Am very pleased with myself.	5	4	3	2	1
11. Make friends easily.	1	2	3	4	5
12. Don't like to draw attention to myself.	5	4	3	2	1
13. Believe in the importance of art.	1	2	3	4	5
14. Avoid philosophical discussions.	5	4	3	2	1
15. Accept people as they are.	1	2	3	4	5
16. Don't see things through to the end.	5	4	3	2	1
17. Have frequent mood swings.	1	2	3	4	5
18. Do just enough work to get by.	5	4	3	2	1
19. Am often down in the dumps.	1	2	3	4	5
20. Enjoy hearing new ideas.	1	2	3	4	5
21. Am the life of the party.	1	2	3	4	5
22. Would describe my experiences as somewhat dull.	5	4	3	2	1
23. Try to get back at others who have hurt me.	5	4	3	2	1
24. Tend to vote for conservative political candidates.	5	4	3	2	1
25. Carry the conversation to a higher level.	1	2	3	4	5
26. Keep in the background.	5	4	3	2	1
27. Rarely get irritated.	5	4	3	2	1
28. Don't talk a lot.	5	4	3	2	1
29. Panic easily.	1	2	3	4	5

In general, I . . .	Very Inaccurate	Moderately Inaccurate	Neither Inaccurate nor Accurate	Moderately Accurate	Very Accurate
30. Am always prepared.	1	2	3	4	5
31. Find it difficult to get down to work.	5	4	3	2	1
32. Have a vivid imagination.	1	2	3	4	5
33. Suspect hidden motives in others.	5	4	3	2	1
34. Have a good word for everyone.	1	2	3	4	5
35. Am not interested in abstract ideas.	5	4	3	2	1
36. Seldom feel blue.	5	4	3	2	1
37. Have a sharp tongue.	5	4	3	2	1
38. Do not enjoy going to art museums.	5	4	3	2	1
39. Often feel blue.	1	2	3	4	5
40. Shirk my duties.	5	4	3	2	1
41. Do not like art.	5	4	3	2	1
42. Am skilled in handling social situations.	1	2	3	4	5
43. Believe that others have good intentions.	1	2	3	4	5
44. Make plans and stick to them.	1	2	3	4	5
45. Know how to captivate people.	1	2	3	4	5
46. Am not easily bothered by things.	5	4	3	2	1
47. Insult people.	5	4	3	2	1
48. Make people feel at ease.	1	2	3	4	5
49. Carry out my plans.	1	2	3	4	5
50. Put other people down.	5	4	3	2	1

ANSWERS

The five personality traits are **Openness to experience, Conscientiousness, Extraversion, Agreeableness** and **Neuroticism** (referred to as a group by the acronym OCEAN). Before we find out your score for each of these traits, a quick health warning is in order. Psychologists are not in the business of categorising people as 'extroverts' versus 'introverts', 'agreeable' versus 'disagreeable' and so on. Since each of these traits forms a continuum, all we can meaningfully ask is whether an individual scores higher or lower than average for his or her particular age group, occupation, geographical region etc. That said, we can get a rough-and-ready rule of thumb simply by transposing the five scoring bands of the original questionnaire on to the possible range of scores for each trait: 10–17 = Low; 18–25 = Medium Low; 26–33 = Medium; 34–41 = Medium High; 42–50 = High.

To find your score for **Openness to experience**, add together your scores for

4	13	20	25	32	14	24	35	38	41

People who score highly for openness to experience appreciate adventure, novelty and variety. They are curious and creative, and enjoy the arts. They are more also likely to engage in risky sexual and drug-taking behaviour. Celebrities who might be expected to score highly on this measure include Jimi Hendrix and Kurt Cobain.

To find your score for **Conscientiousness**, add together your scores for

1	5	30	44	49	7	16	18	31	40

People who score highly for conscientiousness are organised and dependable. They tend not to act spontaneously, but make detailed plans and have the self-discipline to stick to them. Celebrities who might be expected to score highly on this measure include Stephen Hawking and Barack Obama (and, indeed, most scientists and politicians).

To find your score for **Extraversion,** add together your scores for

9	11	21	42	45	2	12	22	26	28

People who score highly for extraversion are the life and soul of the party. They are talkative, positive, assertive and full of energy. Celebrities who might be expected to score highly on this measure include Madonna and Oprah Winfrey (though some celebrities – think Michael Jackson and Lady Gaga – seem to adopt a flamboyant public persona to mask a more introverted personality).

To find your score for **Agreeableness,** add together your scores for

8	15	34	43	48	22	33	37	47	50

People who score highly for agreeableness are, quite simply, those people who everybody loves. They tend to be kind and co-operative rather than hostile and suspicious towards others. Women consistently score more highly on agreeableness than men. There are a great many websites discussing which celebrities are genuinely agreeable in person. Johnny Depp seems to have a good reputation, while the consensus is that Jennifer Lopez would probably score rather low for this trait.

To find your score for **Neuroticism,** add together your scores for

6	17	19	29	39	3	10	27	36	46

People who score highly for neuroticism are anxious worriers, who are likely to experience negative emotions such as depression and anger. Woody Allen has based his entire career on being a self-confessed neurotic.

But the point of this test isn't simply to discover which celebrity you most resemble. As we will see in later chapters, your scores for *openness to experience, conscientiousness, extraversion, agreeableness* and *neuroticism* predict a great deal about you, including what music you like (Stereo Types), whether you prefer to multitask or deal with things one at a time (Focus on Your Knitting), the types of words you use in your writing (I'll keep this one a surprise), your susceptibility – perhaps – to certain visual illusions (The Necker Cube) and even the levels of testosterone and oestrogen (sex hormones) that you were exposed to while in your mother's womb (Prescient Palmistry). Not bad for a two-minute checklist.

It's All Chinese to Me: Part 1

Don't look yet, but on the opposite page are ten Chinese characters. When I say "go", just glance and the page for a second or less, then turn over. Don't study the characters closely or try to remember them.

Promise?

OK, go!

It's All Chinese to Me: Part 2

弓　　戈　　重　　木　　手
尸　　廿　　月　　女　　疒

No cheating – turn over *right now*!

It's All Chinese to Me: Part 3

Below are twenty Chinese characters. This time, your job is to rate how much you like each one, on a scale of 1 (not at all) to 5 (very much). Write your score in the boxes below (labelled A–T). Although you may not have any particularly strong preferences, do try to use the whole of the scale (i.e., don't just put 3 for each one).

手	田	水	廿	山
A	B	C	D	E

戈	也	木	竹	广
F	G	H	I	J

在	重	金	難	女
K	L	M	N	O

月	弓	扌	卝	尸
P	Q	R	S	T

Now look at the next page to find out what this is all about.

A	B	C	D	E	F	G	H	I	J

K	L	M	N	O	P	Q	R	S	T

It's All Chinese to Me: Part 4

As you may have realised, some of these characters were ones that you had seen on the previous page, while others were new.

To find your total score for the **old, previously seen characters**, add up your ratings for **A, D, F, H, J, L, O, P, Q and T**.

To find your total score for the **new, previously unseen** characters, add up your ratings for **B, C, E, G, I, K, M, N, R and S**.

What did you find?

You preferred the old characters to the new ones, right? If you are anything like the participants who completed the original version of this study, your total liking score will have been around 30 for the old characters and 25 for the new ones.

Contrary to popular wisdom, familiarity breeds not *contempt*, but *content* (that's *content* as in 'happy' not *content* as in 'stuff that is contained'): you prefer something you've seen before to something you haven't, and – up to a point – the more you see it, the more you like it. This holds true even when the stimuli are presented subliminally: in the original version of this study each character was flashed up for just five-thousandths of a second, meaning that participants were unsure whether or not they'd seen anything at all, and certainly unable to consciously remember individual characters. Yet still they preferred the old characters to the new.

This effect is also seen with babies, who are born preferring sounds that they heard in the womb, whether their mother's voice or the theme tune to her favourite TV show. The same is true for both rats and chickens, which can easily be trained to prefer certain musical tones and even certain composers.

Psychologists call this the *mere-exposure* effect; but what causes it?

Many textbooks will tell you that the effect is due to an increased subjective feeling of familiarity ('Oh yes, I remember this one'), which we somehow misinterpret as liking. But this doesn't seem to be right, as the effect is seen even if participants report no subjective sense of familiarity at all, as in the study where they saw each Chinese character for just 0.005 seconds.

This leaves two more promising explanations. The first is *perceptual fluency* – the idea that visual processing is easier for things that you've seen before, and you like things that are easy. There is some supporting evidence for this idea, but it struggles to explain a related experimental finding: participants who are repeatedly shown the same (subliminal) stimuli report an overall improvement in their mood. If I ask you to do another form of processing repeatedly, such as solving the same set of maths problems over and over, you will probably find that it gets easier on each run-through; but I sincerely doubt that it will improve your mood.

The second explanation is based on classical conditioning. You're probably familiar with Pavlov's famous experiments, in which a dog that hears a bell every time food is about to be served comes to associate the bell with the food, and salivates whenever the bell rings. Robert Zajonc, a psychologist at Stanford University in California, argues that *mere-exposure* effects work in a similar way. The thing that we become familiar with (e.g., the Chinese character) is like the bell, and the 'feeling of liking' is like the salivation. What is like the food? Zajonc's answer is simply the fact that everything is OK and nothing bad is happening. So, in the same way that the bell comes to mean 'food is coming' – and hence causes salivation – the Chinese character comes to mean 'everything is OK', and hence causes liking, which, consequently, improves your overall mood.

Of course, advertisers have known about the mere-exposure effect for years. Why do you think companies are prepared to pay millions in sponsorship just for their name or logo to be seen, even though this type of advertising gives consumers virtually no information about the company or its products?

But if Zajonc's explanation of exposure effects as classical conditioning is correct, these sponsorship deals could easily backfire. What if a particular brand starts to be associated not with the feeling that everything is OK but with that sinking feeling you get when your team is losing? In this case, perhaps the old adage would prove to be right after all, and familiarity – in this case with the company logo – really would breed contempt.

Speaking of contempt . . .

Spot the Deference

What's the difference between a psychologist and a psychiatrist?

ANSWER

The (not particularly funny) 'joke' answer is either 'drugs' or 'about £30,000 a year'. But, of course, the joke answer doesn't make any sense unless you know the real answer.

Psych-ology is the study (*ology*) of the person, mind or soul (the *psyche**). *Psych-iatry* is the treatment or healing (*iatry*, from the Greek *iatros*, meaning 'doctor') of the same.

So, a **psychiatrist** is a doctor who specialises in treating patients with conditions such as depression, obsessive-compulsive disorder (OCD) or schizophrenia. This is done mostly through the use of drugs (hence the first 'joke' answer), which is why all psychiatrists are fully qualified medical doctors. Of course, the fact that doctors tend to be among the highest-paid of all professionals, particularly in the United States, is what gives rise to the second 'joke' answer.

A *psychologist*, on the other hand, is someone who studies people and their behaviour but does not necessarily offer any treatment. Now, some psychologists are qualified *clinical psychologists*, who have taken a psychology degree and a postgraduate clinical psychology training course, and treat the same types of patients as psychiatrists. Clinical psychologists generally do not use drugs but instead employ 'talking cures' such as cognitive behavioural

---

* *Psyche* is the Greek (and Latin) word for 'breath'. The idea is that man received a human soul (a spirit, an identity, a personality), when God breathed life into him (so, rather poetically, psychology is actually the study of the 'breath of life', the essence of humanity). The first letter of the Greek word *psyche* – Ψ – pronounced 'sigh', is often used to represent psychology in logos, badges etc.

therapy (CBT), which aims to show patients that their obsessive or compulsive thoughts are inaccurate or unhelpful.

But most psychologists are not clinical psychologists. There are other types of practising psychologists, such as *sports and exercise psychologists, occupational psychologists* and *educational psychologists*, who are hired by sports teams, businesses and education providers respectively to help improve performance. Beware, though: while all of the titles above – including *psychiatrist* and *clinical psychologist* – are 'protected terms' in most countries (meaning that you need a qualification to use them), anyone can call him or herself a 'psychologist' with no qualifications at all.* (In fact, there's nothing to stop *you* calling yourself a psychologist, particularly after you've tried out a couple of the studies in this book on other people.)

Most psychologists, however, are *academic psychologists*: lecturers and researchers who conduct the types of studies that make up this book. There are as many different types of academic psychologist as there are sub-branches of psychology: *developmental psychologists* (interested in children and learning), *health psychologists* (interested in, um, people's health), *cognitive psychologists* (interested in mental processes such as reasoning, memory, categorisation and so on), *forensic psychologists* (interested in criminal behaviour), *psychopharmacologists* (interested in the effects of drugs on the brain), *neuropsychologists* (who investigate how memories, concepts, thoughts, feelings and so on are physically instantiated in the cells of the brain) and psychologists who focus on addiction, obesity, ageing, language,† driving, animal learning, visual perception, human–computer interaction, intelligence, personality, sexual attraction, face recognition, pain, hearing and just about

---

* We also have *psychotherapists* (some of whom are Freudian *psychoanalysts*), who try to help patients 'talk through' their problems. In many countries, these terms are not protected, so a *psychotherapist* or *psychoanalyst* is not always a qualified psychiatrist or clinical psychologist.

† My research investigates how children learn their native language, which makes me part developmental psychologist, part cognitive psychologist and part psycholinguist.

anything else that humans (and, in some cases, animals) think, do or feel.

To return to the original question, though, the difference between a *clinical psychologist* and a *psychiatrist* can be considerable with regard to the approach taken when treating patients with conditions such as depression, OCD and schizophrenia. A somewhat unfair – though perhaps not entirely inaccurate – cliché is that the former are interested only in providing 'talking cures' (which some psychiatrists dismiss as having little proven effect), while the latter are interested only in prescribing drugs (which some psychologists dismiss as drugging-up patients to keep them quiet).

In short, if a clinical psychologist and a psychiatrist are assigned to the same case and disagree as to the best course of action, you're going to be waiting an awfully long time before one defers to the other (yes, to 'spot the deference'). In the meantime, if you want to annoy a psychologist, just call him a psychiatrist (and vice versa).

How Many Clinical Psychologists Does It Take To Change a Light Bulb?

One, but the light bulb has to want to change.

ANSWER

Professional Psychopaths

So, if a psych-*ologist* studies the psyche and a psych-*iatrist* treats it, what's a psychopath? Well, since the Greek word *pathos* means 'suffering' and *pathology* is the study of disease, we can work out that a *psychopath* is someone with a psyche that is suffering, diseased or disturbed (we'll find out shortly exactly what traits mark out someone as a psychopath).

In everyday life many people use the term jokingly to describe anyone who is controlling and egotistical; I'm sure you can think of a few examples from among the people you know. Actually, it may be less of a joke than you imagine: psychopathy is a continuum, meaning that people with at least some psychopathic personality traits are all around us. Below are listed twenty different jobs (in alphabetical order). Ten have the highest proportion of professionals with psychopathic personality traits; the other ten, the lowest. Your job is to sort them into the two lists.

Accountant

Beautician/stylist

Care worker

CEO

Charity worker

Chef

Civil servant

Clergy

Craftsperson

Creative artist

Doctor

Journalist

Lawyer

Media (TV/radio)

Nurse

Police officer

Salesperson

Surgeon

Teacher

Therapist

ANSWER

The ten professions with the highest proportion of psychopathic personality traits are: CEO, lawyer, media (TV/radio), salesperson, surgeon, journalist, police officer, clergy, chef and civil servant.

The ten professions with the lowest proportion of psychopathic personality traits are: care worker, nurse, therapist, craftsperson, beautician/stylist, charity worker, teacher, creative artist, doctor and accountant.

These findings come from a large online survey of psychopathic personality traits. So are a large proportion of CEOs, lawyers and policemen really psychopaths? It depends what you mean by 'psychopath'. Being a psychopath isn't all or nothing; most perfectly ordinary people have *some* psychopathic personality traits to *some* degree. So-called 'psychopaths' are just people who score highly for most or all of these traits, which include impulsivity, sexual promiscuity, superficial charm, high self-worth, low levels of fear, depression and stress, a lack of remorse or guilt, manipulativeness, a need for stimulation and the failure to accept responsibility for one's own actions.

In fact, most psychopaths – far from being murderers – are neither mad nor bad. In fact, the same personality traits that may lead to a life of violent crime in some people lead to great success for many others. It is not difficult to imagine how traits such as high self-worth, fearlessness and manipulativeness could lead to a seat in the boardroom for someone who is non-violent, highly intelligent and well educated, but a life behind bars for someone who enjoys none of these advantages.

Interestingly, because of their over-inflated self-opinion, psychopaths almost never identify themselves as such, or accept the label when it is given to them by others. Instead, they see traits such as impulsivity, charm and fearlessness simply as characteristics of highly successful people.

So relax. If you're worried that you may be a psychopath, you almost certainly are not one.

Web Links and Further Reading

Test yourself for psychopathic personality traits at www.wisdomof psychopaths.com. Two very readable popular books on this topic are Kevin Dutton's *The Wisdom of Psychopaths* and Jon Ronson's *The Psychopath Test*.

I Just Can't Wait

Congratulations! You have just won £1,000 in a lottery! However, this is a very unusual lottery, in that you have been offered the choice of receiving a certain amount immediately, or a larger amount later. (Don't worry, the lottery is government-backed, so there's no chance of the organiser going bust or failing to pay out.)

What would your choice be in each of the following scenarios?

(a) £100 now or £1,000 in five years
(b) £500 now or £1,000 in five years
(c) £750 now or £1,000 in five years
(d) £500 now or £1,000 in one year
(e) £750 now or £1,000 in one year
(f) £900 now or £1,000 in one year

ANSWERS

The first one (a) is pretty straightforward, isn't it? It certainly seems worth waiting five years to get ten times as much money. Doubling your money over five years (b) is probably worth it, but by the time we get to option (c) most people would take the money and run. What about with a one-year delay? Again, most people would say it's worth the wait to double your money (d), and – just about – for an extra £250 (e), but not when you sacrifice just £100 to get the money immediately (f).

The tendency to discount or undervalue rewards that are delayed until some point in the future is known as *delay discounting*. The original study – recently reprised for a marketing campaign (see Web Links) – was conducted with children, who were offered the choice of one marshmallow now or two in fifteen minutes. Only about a third managed to wait.

So what do your answers say about you? A review published in 2013 found that the more susceptible you are to delay discounting (in questionnaires such as this one), the more likely you are to . . .

- Become addicted to alcohol, cigarettes, methamphetamine and opioids such as heroin (as we will see later, in the section Cake Addicts)
- Become obese (particularly if you are a woman), and to suffer from binge-eating disorder
- Gamble to excess
- Suffer from Attention Deficit Hyperactivity Disorder (ADHD), depression and personality disorders such as psychopathy (see Professional Psychopaths)
- Start having sex at a young age
- Engage in criminal activity

And the less likely you are to . . .

- Eat breakfast
- Wear sunscreen

- Wear a seatbelt
- Exercise
- Go to the dentist
- Get yourself tested for various types of cancer
- Do well at school

It is really quite remarkable that we can predict all of these different behaviours on the basis of a simple questionnaire that does not ask, directly, about any of them. But when you think about it for a minute, it turns out that these behaviours, while very different on the surface, have something important in common: going to the dentist, studying, exercising, dieting and generally abstaining from sex, drugs and rock 'n' roll all involve giving up an immediate reward in the anticipation of a larger reward in the future. All involve accepting some short-term pain (in the case of a visit to the dentist or physical exercise, quite literally) for a long-term gain, such as keeping one's own teeth and not suffering from obesity.

If people are sad, they become even more likely to give in and plump for the smaller reward now in an attempt to boost their mood. Showing people pictures of attractive members of the opposite sex and depriving smokers of their cigarettes have the same effect, presumably because people have used up all their willpower controlling their urges. Similarly, delay discounting increases when people are asked to perform some complex task at the same time as weighing up the different options, as the concurrent task uses up both willpower and processing resources.

The good news is that there are also ways to help people play the long game. One effective technique involves directly stimulating a part of the brain involved in self-control (this isn't quite as drastic as it sounds, as it can be done non-invasively using electromagnets). Changing the 'framing' of the problem also proves effective.* For example, if we rephrase '£750 now or £1,000 in a year' as '£750 now and £0 in a year or £0 now and £1,000 in a

---

* Keep an eye out for another framing effect in a later section (I can't tell you which, as then you won't fall for it).

year', the first option starts to look a bit less attractive, as it's clear that you'd be giving up not only £250 altogether, but also £1,000 on a future date. Naming an actual date (e.g., £0 now and £1,000 on 1 September 2015) increases this effect still further. Finally, increasing participants' blood sugar levels seems to increase their ability to resist short-term temptation in the lottery game, presumably because they already feel relatively satisfied.

You may be asking yourself whether or not these techniques would work outside the lab. Try for yourself. You can try the date-naming technique by thinking about your pension. What would you rather have: (a) £30,000 each year until __/__/__ (enter your retirement date here) and £0 each year thereafter or (b) £25,000 each year until __/__/__ (enter your retirement date here) and (with a well-run plan!) £10,000 each year thereafter? If the answer is (b), but your current situation looks more like (a), then you have some difficult decisions to make. A more pleasant exercise is to try out the blood-sugar technique next time you go shopping. You might well find that, ironically, the best way to ensure that you fill your trolley with healthy food rather than junk is to treat yourself to a chocolate bar before you head to the supermarket.

Web Links
This video shows children completing a delay-discounting study as part of a marketing campaign for sweets: www.youtube.com/watch?v=JPtIe Zooq-4. You can find plenty more videos of this type by searching for 'delay discounting' or 'delayed gratification'.

Take It or Leave It?

Congratulations! You've won another lottery prize.

But again, it's a lottery with a twist: you must share the prize, £10, with another winner, and he gets to choose the split. Your only choice is whether to accept the offer – in which case the money is split between you according to the proposed offer – or to reject it – in which case you both get nothing. The other person can make only a single offer, which you must accept or reject. There can be no negotiation, and no second offer. Your choice is simple: Take it or leave it.

Which of the following offers would you accept or reject?

(a) £8 to you, £2 to the other person
(b) £5.01 to you, £4.99 to the other person
(c) £5 each
(d) £4.99 to you, £5.01 to the other person
(e) £3 to you, £7 to the other person
(f) £2 to you, £8 to the other person
(g) £1 to you, £9 to the other person

ANSWER

Before finding out what most people do, let's think about what we'd expect if people generally act rationally, doing whatever is in their own best financial interests (as is assumed under most theories of economics). Clearly, the rational strategy is to accept any offer that is greater than zero. Even the worst offer above boils down to a choice between getting £1 and getting nothing at all. So you should take it, right?

In fact, almost everyone rejects the £1/£9 split, and a majority the £2/8 split. That is, most people are prepared to forgo £2, just for the opportunity to punish the other guy for his unfair proposal: a classic case of cutting off your nose to spite your face.

By the time we get to £3 or above, most people grudgingly accept any unfair split (with no particular sticking point around the 50/50 point), and – of course – happily accept any split in their favour. When playing the role of 'proposer', most people make an offer of somewhere between 40 and 50 per cent (£4–£5), though we cannot tell how much this is due to a sense of fair play rather than a fear of leaving with nothing.

Although the offers that people will accept don't seem to vary much between different societies (or between adults and children), we do see some interesting differences in the offers that people *make*. American university students (the usual participants) are among the most generous in the world, offering – on average – something very close to a 50/50 split. People from smaller, more traditional societies tend to make less generous offers, with the Hadza of Tanzania and the Tsimane of Bolivia offering just 25 per cent. This gives the lie to the romantic notion that people who practise a simpler way of life are more caring and sharing; when resources are scarce, you take what you can get.

Looking across species – specifically at our closest cousins, chimpanzees – we see big differences in both the offers made and the offers accepted. The chimp version of the game uses two boards. Each board holds ten grapes, divided into two piles (say 5/5 on one board, 8/2 on the other). The apparatus is set up so that each chimp can only ever reach a particular pile. First, the proposer makes an 'offer' by selecting one of the two boards and pulling it part of the way towards both chimps (it is not possible for him to pull it closer). The other chimp has the same choice I gave you: he can accept the offer, by pulling the board the rest of the way or reject it, by leaving the board where it is, meaning that both get nothing.

In chimpanzee versions of the study (and in some human versions) the game is usually played over and over. In the original study of this type, the chimpanzees almost always made selfish offers throughout. In a more recent study the chimps started out making selfish offers, but gradually became fairer over time (though perhaps only because chimpanzees who were made un-fair offers typically threatened or spat at the proposer, which did not happen in the previous study).

But what is really interesting about chimpanzees is not what they *offer* but what they will *accept*: both studies found that, unlike humans, chimpanzees almost always accept even very unfair of-fers (e.g., 2/8 in favour of the proposer), albeit sometimes grudg-ingly (they were not pulling at random, as they invariably rejected offers of 0/10).

So, while it is debatable whether or not chimpanzees share hu-mans' sense of fairness, what is almost certain is that they show the more rational behaviour in the ultimatum game. Does this mean that chimpanzees are smarter than humans? . . .

Are You Stupider than a Monkey?

... Let's find out. Here is a memory test that a monkey can pass.*

On the opposite page –but don't look yet – the numbers 1–9 are printed in random positions, as shown on the left below:

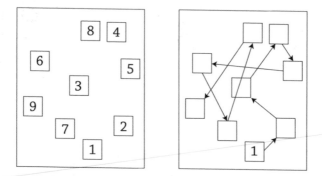

I'll be generous and allow you to look at this page for a second or two (the chimp needs only just over half a second). You will then turn to the next page, where the boxes (except for the first one) are blank. Using a pen, connect the boxes in order, as shown on the right above.

When you're ready, look across at the opposite page. Give yourself just two seconds before turning over.

---

* Actually, a chimpanzee. Technically, chimpanzees are not monkeys. However, I couldn't resist the temptation to use a line from *The Simpsons*. In the episode in question, the residents of Springfield are complaining because a new dialling code has been introduced for part of the city. Here's the phone company mascot, Phoney McRingring, speaking in an infomercial: 'But how will I remember all those numbers? Well, scientists have discovered that even monkeys can memorise ten numbers. Are you stupider than a monkey?'

Are You Stupider than a Monkey?: Training

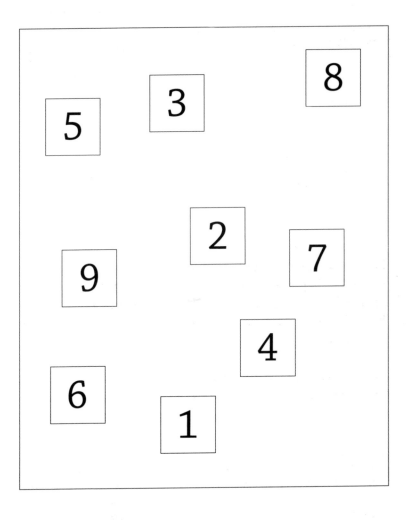

Are You Stupider than a Monkey?: Test

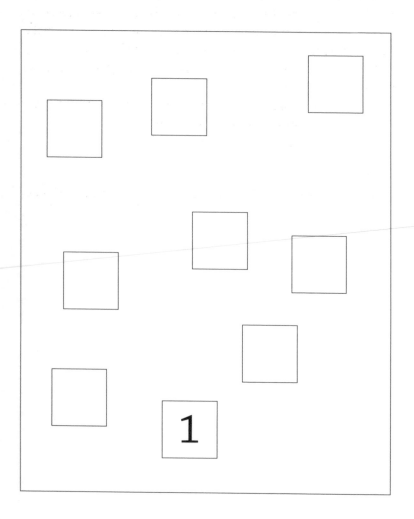

ANSWER

So how did you get on?

If you failed, never mind; this story actually ends relatively happily for our species. Although the original – very well-publicised – study showed that chimps outperformed humans on this task, a follow-up study that arrived with far less fanfare showed that, if humans – like the chimps – were given untimed practice runs, they could beat them quite easily.

So, yes, chimpanzees have excellent memories, but there's no evidence that they can beat humans just yet.

Now, what was my phone number again?

Web Link
Try the online version of this test at http://games.lumosity.com/chimp.html

A Straightforward Question

Backwards everything say professor the did why?

ANSWER

Psychology reverse of professor a was he.

The Tragic Tale of Kitty Genovese

Kitty Genovese was a twenty-eight-year-old bar manager who lived in Queens, New York. In the early hours of 13 March 1964, Kitty returned home from work. As she approached her apartment building, a man attacked her with a knife. Kitty screamed for help. The lights of the surrounding apartments came on as people rushed to their windows to see what was happening. Everyone witnessed the attack in progress, but no one called the police. Instead, her neighbours switched off their lights and went back to bed. Kitty's attacker pounced again. Again Kitty screamed, and again the lights came on as her neighbours rushed to their windows. This time, a man shouted out, 'Why don't you let that girl alone?' Frightened, the attacker ran off. But still nobody called the police. The attacker returned and stabbed Kitty for a third time, wounding her fatally. All in all, a total of thirty-eight neighbours witnessed the attack, which unfolded over thirty minutes, yet not one of them came to her aid, or even called the police.

A version of this story is told to virtually all students of psychology from high-school to degree level; the version above is based on an introductory lecture that I attended as a first-year undergraduate student. The tragic tale is typically used to illustrate the phenomenon of *bystander apathy* caused by *diffusion of responsibility*: because there were so many people who witnessed the attack and so *could* have called the police, nobody thought it was his or her own responsibility to do so.

The problem is that this story – while a good teaching aid – is largely inaccurate with regard to both the bystanders and their apathy.

First, nobody knows where the widely cited total of thirty-eight eyewitnesses comes from: the police found only six. Of the three who gave evidence at the murder trial, only one reported seeing a man beating (not stabbing) a woman (an incident that might have been dismissed as a 'mere' domestic squabble, particularly in 1964). Crucially, the final attack (there were probably only two – not three, as in some accounts*) took place inside a stairwell, out of the line of sight of the apartment windows.

Second, the few witnesses that there were *did* intervene. One shouted at the attacker, causing him to run off (and – for all that the witnesses knew – give up on the attack). Several residents have claimed – including in a sworn affidavit – that they *did* call the local police station, despite the fact that the police were often hostile to callers (the 911 emergency number system did not yet exist in 1964). All in all, there seem to have been few bystanders and little apathy.

Despite the inaccuracies of the Kitty Genovese story, a great deal of follow-up experimental research has confirmed that by-stander apathy is a real phenomenon: people really are less likely to help a stranger when part of a large group. However, this is not necessarily due to diffusion of responsibility (which is typically the only explanation presented along with retellings of the Genovese story). For example, when in large groups, people are less likely to notice such incidents at all, are less likely to perceive situations as emergencies ('If it's a real emergency, why does nobody else look worried?'), are anxious about doing the wrong thing and being judged by others, and are more likely to think – quite justifiably, in many cases – that one of the other people present is better quali-fied or able to help.

So next time you see somebody in trouble, with no one coming to their aid, offer to help; if not for their sake, then for your own. It's probably either a genuine emergency or a psychologist investi-gating bystander apathy: yours.

---

* The third attack was probably added as an embellishment, following the *rule of three*, a writing principle which holds that stories, titles, slogans, jokes and so on are often most effective if they consist of three parts, with the final part particu-larly surprising or significant (e.g., *Goldilocks and the Three Bears; The Three Little Pigs; I came, I saw, I conquered; New York, Paris, Peckham*).

The Necker Cube

This is a Necker Cube (named after its Swiss inventor, Louis Necker).

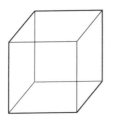

What's special about the Necker Cube is that just by looking at and thinking about the cube in a different way, you can make it flip. That is, you can make it look as though this (shaded) side is at the front (with the rest of the cube extending backwards in space towards the top right of the page) . . .

. . . or as though this (shaded) side is at the front (with the rest of the cube extending backwards in space towards the bottom left of the page).

People vary in how quickly they can mentally flip the cube, and whether they find this mental flipping easy or difficult.

Cover up the two shaded cubes, and see how many times you can flip the Necker Cube in thirty seconds (time yourself with a stopwatch; there's probably one on your phone).

ANSWER

How did you get on? Most people can get the cube to flip somewhere between twice and ten times in thirty seconds. Were you at the top or bottom end of this range? And what does this say about you?

Although the idea is controversial, some psychologists have claimed that your cube-flipping rate can predict your personality type. The idea is that extroverts – people who are the life of the party – tend to get bored quickly and so rapidly flip the cube for something to do. On the other hand, introverts – people who prefer to be at home with a good book – don't get bored so quickly, and so don't flip the cube as rapidly (remember, you can measure your extraversion by completing Your Personality Profile).

Although it's debatable whether or not your flipping rate can predict your personality type, there's good evidence to suggest that it can actually predict something far more surprising, which we'll measure later: a trait that is not so much mental as physical (though I won't say any more now, so as not to spoil the surprise).

Meanwhile, an online experiment to discover once and for all whether or not extroverts really are faster flippers than introverts is still running. Why not take part at . . .

Web Link
www.bbc.co.uk/science/humanbody/mind/surveys/neckercube/

Anchors Away

Ahaaa, me hearties. Here's one to try on all ye shipmates.

Find a few friends, and ask them to make a guess at some obscure percentage. For example, you might ask them to guess the percentage of United Nations member countries that are in Africa, the percentage of Germans who play the piano, or the percentage of Brazilian students who get the top grade in their high-school English exam. The question can be about anything you like, and there's no need to know the correct answer yourself (though stick to percentage questions, in order to ensure that the number is always somewhere between 0 and 100). You will probably get a wide range of answers, but note them down anyway.

Now find a new batch of friends and repeat the experiment. This time, engage them first in a bit of light-hearted banter about facts and figures, and throw in some real or fabricated percentage statistic with a high number. It can be anything you like, as long as it is completely unrelated to the test question (perhaps something like 'According to this *Psy-Q* book I've been reading, 83 per cent of statistics are made up on the spot'). Note down their answers, and compare them with the first group.

What did you find?

ANSWER

Did you find that the second group gave higher answers than the first? If so, you have found an 'anchoring effect'. This is the term given to the finding that hearing a number – even if it is known to be totally irrelevant to anything – 'anchors' subsequent estimates to similar values, or at least to values broadly on the same scale. Our brains seem to have great difficulty flipping from one frame of reference to another, even when the two are completely unrelated. For example, in the classic study of anchoring effects, which used the 'UN members in Africa' example, people's judgements were affected by the spin of a wheel of fortune: participants who spun a 10 normally guessed around 25 per cent, while participants who spun a 65 typically guessed around 40 per cent. (The actual answer is around 28 per cent.)

Anchoring effects also arise in intuitive mathematics. The 'wheel-of-fortune' researchers, Amos Tversky and Daniel Kahneman, conducted another study in which they asked high-school students to estimate the answer to a maths problem within five seconds. One group saw

$$8 \times 7 \times 6 \times 5 \times 4 \times 3 \times 2 \times 1 =$$

while the other saw

$$1 \times 2 \times 3 \times 4 \times 5 \times 6 \times 7 \times 8 =$$

The second group gave much lower answers than the first (of course, the two answers should be identical), because the lower numbers at the start of the problem anchored their frame of reference to relatively low numbers. (The answer is 40,320, by the way.)

Be on your guard for other cognitive biases – they will pop up again in this book.

But, for now, let's set sail again, and continue our Psychodyssey. Y'aaaaaar. Anchors away!

A Shocking Experiment

Picture yourself as a typical middle-aged, middle-of-the-road kind of guy – perhaps a teacher, a salesman or a labourer – living in a small American city (if you know it, New Haven, Connecticut) in the early 1960s.

You respond to an advert in the newspaper asking for participants in a study of learning and memory being conducted at the prestigious Yale University, in return for $4.50 (perhaps about $35 in today's money). When you arrive, the experimenter hands you a cheque, and tells you that – as in all experiments – the money is yours simply for turning up, no matter what happens during the study. He then introduces you to another volunteer and tells you that you will be participating together in a study of the effects of punishment on learning. He explains that one of you will be the 'teacher' and the other the 'learner', and invites each of you to draw a slip of paper from a hat. Yours says 'teacher'.

The three of you then move on to an adjacent room, where the experimenter straps the learner into an electric chair and applies an electrode paste 'to avoid blisters and burns'. He also attaches an electrode to the learner's wrist and explains that this is connected to a shock generator in the next room. The learner looks worried and asks 'Are the shocks dangerous?' The experimenter replies, 'Although the shocks can be extremely painful, they cause no permanent tissue damage.'

Leaving the learner strapped into the chair, you and the experimenter proceed into the room with the shock generator. The experimenter explains that you will first be given a sample shock. He attaches the electrode and presses the third button for a 45-volt shock. The red light next to the button comes on, the blue 'voltage energizer' light flashes, the dial on the voltage meter leaps to the right, and a buzzer sounds. OUCH!

The experimenter then explains the learning and punishment

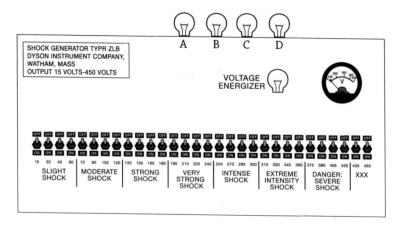

task. You are first to read out a list of word pairs (e.g., *cat* + *table*, *book* + *jug*, *house* + *bag*) and then test the learner on his ability to remember the second word of each pair (from a choice of four) when given the first. For example, if you say *cat*: [A] *book*, [B] *house*, [C] *table*, or [D] *jug*, the correct answer would be [C] *table*, because this was paired with *cat*. Because you can't see or hear the learner, he makes his choice by pressing a button, which lights up one of the four bulbs – A, B, C or D – on the top of the shock generator. The experimenter gives you the following instructions:

Administer a shock to the learner each time he gives a wrong response. Move one level higher on the shock generator each time the learner flashes a wrong answer. Always announce the voltage level before administering a shock. When you get to the bottom of the list, repeat it over again, and continue giving shocks until the learner has learned all the pairs correctly.

Regardless of how much you know – or think you know – about this study, you may like to pause to think about how high you would go before refusing to continue with the experiment. Before conducting the study, the researchers took a straw poll of psychology students, who guessed that only about 1 per cent of participants would continue to the highest possible level: 450 volts (or 'XXX').

The experiment begins, and the learner isn't doing well. In fact, he's only getting about one in four right. Still, you don't hear him say anything or make any other sign of protest, so you carry on with the experiment. After receiving the 300-volt shock, the learner bangs on the wall. You carry on with the next word list, but no answer appears on the response panel. You turn to the experimenter and ask what to do. He says:

No response counts as a wrong answer. Increase the shock level one step every time the learner fails to respond correctly. Allow 5–10 seconds before considering no response as a wrong answer.

You administer a 315-volt shock, and the learner again bangs on the wall. You tell the experimenter that the other volunteer obviously doesn't want to carry on with the study. He says: 'Whether the learner likes it or not, you must go on until he has learned all the word pairs correctly. So please go on.' Reluctantly, you move on to the next word pair. Again, no answer appears on the response panel, but neither does the learner bang on the wall after receiving the shock. You ask the experimenter if the shocks are dangerous. He replies: 'Although the shocks may be painful, there is no permanent tissue damage, so please go on.'

You carry on: 330 volts, 345 volts, 360 volts. Still no response. You tell the experimenter that you want to stop. He says: 'Please go on.' You protest that you really do want to stop now. He says: 'The experiment requires that you continue.' You protest some more. He says: 'It is absolutely essential that you continue.' You refuse. He says: 'You have no other choice. You must go on.' You refuse. To your overwhelming relief, the experimenter halts the study. He then takes you next door, where the learner gets up from his 'electric chair', smiles and shakes your hand. He is an actor, and the shocks were a hoax. Phew!

Why do good people sometimes do terrible things? Is 'I was only following orders' a valid excuse? Because most people have heard about Stanley Milgram's famous study – which was designed to answer exactly these kinds of question – second- or third-hand, much of what is widely 'known' about both the findings themselves, and what they tell us about human nature, is wide of the mark.

For starters, when psychology students learn about this experiment, they are often told that almost all participants were willing to give lethal shocks, simply because someone in a white lab coat (actually it was grey) told them to. The usual conclusion is that even good people unthinkingly and passively go along with whatever authorities tell them to do, however evil; and it is this depressing aspect of human nature that has enabled all kinds of atrocities.

But these popular retellings typically gloss over a number of important details of Milgram's studies, and risk leading us to precisely the wrong conclusion.

First, it is simply not true that all – or even nearly all – participants obeyed the experimenter. Even in the version of the experiment described above, over a third did not. But this was a rather extreme version of the study, designed to maximise obedience. When the learner was placed in the same room as the teacher, 60 per cent of participants disobeyed the experimenter. When the learner, teacher and experimenter were all in different rooms, with the experimenter delivering his instructions via telephone, over three-quarters of participants disobeyed, often giving only the lowest possible shock, while insisting to the experimenter over the telephone that they were following his instructions to the letter.

Second, participants did not believe that they were giving lethal shocks. All were told beforehand – and reminded, if they asked – that the shocks were painful but not dangerous. As Milgram himself points out, participants 'assume that the discomfort caused to the victim is momentary, whilst the scientific gains resulting from the experiment are enduring'.

This relates to the third point missed by most textbook summaries. Participants did not give shocks simply 'because someone in authority told them to'. Most genuinely believed that the 'punishment and learning' experiment served a worthy purpose, and that both volunteers had an obligation to the experimenter, having both signed up, taken the cheque and drawn lots to allocate the 'learner' and 'teacher' roles (of course, this draw was rigged).

This suggests that the moral that we should take from Milgram's studies is not that people do bad things because they unquestioningly obey authority but, rather, one that is perhaps even more unpalatable. Alex Haslam, a Professor at the University of Queensland in Australia, argues that Milgram's studies suggest that those who follow orders to commit atrocities do so because they believe in both the legitimacy of that authority ('we have made a commitment to do what the experimenter tells us') and the higher cause ('I agree with the experimenter's goal of making scientific discoveries about learning'). If Haslam is right, then the unpalatable truth is that soldiers who commit atrocities under order do so not *despite* being good people but *because* they are – in their own minds – good people; and good people follow orders from a legitimate authority, particularly one with whose goals they agree.

Mission to Mars

Congratulations! You have been selected to take part in the first manned mission to Mars. As you step out of your spacecraft, a Martian approaches you and says:

Pabikutibudogolatudaropipabikutibudodaropigolatupabikugolatudaropitibudopabikugolatutibudodaropi

pabikudaropitibudogolatupabikudaropigolatutibudotibudopabikugolatudaropitibudopabikudaropigolatu

tibudogolatupabikudaropitibudogolatudaropipabikutibudodaropipabikugolatutibudodaropigolatupabiku

golatupabikutibudodaropigolatupabikudaropitibudogolatutibudopabikudaropigolatutibudodaropipabiku

golatudaropipabikutibudogolatudaropitibudopabikudaropipabikutibudogolatudaropipabikugolatutibudo

daropitibudopabikugolatudaropitibudogolatupabikudaropigolatupabikutibudodaropigolatutibudopabiku

Which of the following pairs are words in the Martian language (before you give up, you should know that eight-month-old infants have passed this test):

golatu and *daropi*

OR

tudaro and *pigola*?

ANSWER

The words are *golatu* and *daropi* (*pabiku* and *tibudo* are also words).
Tudaro and *pigola* are not words. Here is the Martian speech with
the breaks in between words:

pabiku/tibudo/golatu/daropi/pabiku/tibudo/daropi/golatu/pabiku/golatu/daropi/tibudo/pabiku/golatu/tibudo/daropi/pabiku/daropi/tibudo/golatu/pabiku/daropi/golatu/tibudo/tibudo/pabiku/golatu/daropi/tibudo/pabiku/daropi/golatu/tibudo/golatu/pabiku/daropi/tibudo/golatu/daropi/pabiku/tibudo/daropi/pabiku/golatu/tibudo/daropi/golatu/pabiku/golatu/pabiku/tibudo/daropi/golatu/pabiku/daropi/tibudo/golatu/tibudo/pabiku/daropi/golatu/tibudo/daropi/pabiku/golatu/daropi/pabiku/tibudo/golatu/daropi/tibudo/pabiku/daropi/pabiku/tibudo/golatu/daropi/pabiku/golatu/tibudo/daropi/tibudo/pabiku/golatu/daropi/tibudo/golatu/pabiku/daropi/golatu/pabiku/tibudo/daropi/golatu/tibudo/pabiku/

The eight-month-olds who completed the original study figured
this out. That is, after hearing the 'Martian' speech steam, and
subsequently being given the choice of what to listen to, they
chose the combinations that are NOT words (*tudaro* and *pigola*)
over those that are (*golatu* and *daropi*). Presumably, having already
figured out which are the words, the infants were bored of them.

How can you figure out that *golatu* and *daropi* (and *pabiku* and
tibudo) are words whereas *tudaro* and *pigola* are not? The answer
is that every time you hear *go*, it is always followed by *la*, with *la*
always followed by *tu*. The same is true for the sequences *da+ro+pi*,
pa+bi+ku and *ti+bu+do*. (Check if you don't believe me.) However,
the same is not true for *tudaro* or *pigola*. While *tu* is sometimes
followed by *da+ro* (in fact, eight times), it is just as often followed
by *ti* ... or *pa* ... Similarly, *pi* is followed just as often by *go+la* as it
is by *ti* ... or *pa* ...

'So what?' you may say. 'Just because *go* is always followed by
la+tu, this doesn't mean that *golatu* is necessarily a word. It could
just be a coincidence.' If you were to say this, you would be *technically* right, but almost certainly wrong in practice. If *golatu*
were not a word, it is spectacularly unlikely that *go* would *always*
(twenty-four times out of twenty-four) be followed by *la+tu* just

by chance. To help us see why, I've switched the Martian words for English words with the same structure:

golatu = goal/keep/er
daropi = das/tard/ly
pabiku = pa/cif/ist
tibudo = time/ta/ble

Things that are words, like *goal+keep+er* (the equivalent of *go+la+tu*) appear twenty-four times, because *goal* is always followed by *keep+er*. Things that are not words, like *er+das+tard* (the equivalent of *tu+da+ro*) occur only eight times (the eight occasions on which *goalkeeper* happens to be followed by *dastardly*).

pacifisttimetablegoalkeeperdastardlypacifisttimetabledastardlygoalkeeperpacifistgoalkeeperdastardlyti
metablepacifistgoalkeepertimetabledastardlypacifistdastardlytimetablegoalkeeperpacifistdastardlygoalk
eepertimetabletimetablepacifistgoalkeeperdastardlytimetablepacifistdastardlygoalkeepertimetablegoalk
eeperpacifistdastardlytimetablegoalkeeperdastardlypacifisttimetabledastardlypacifistgoalkeepertimetabl
edastardlygoalkeeperpacifistgoalkeeperpacifisttimetabledastardlygoalkeeperpacifistdastardlytimetableg
oalkeepertimetablepacifistdastardlygoalkeepertimetabledastardlypacifistgoalkeeperdastardlypacifisttim
etablegoalkeeperdastardlytimetablepacifistdastardlypacifisttimetablegoalkeeperdastardlypacifistgoalke
epertimetabledastardlytimetablepacifistgoalkeeperdastardlytimetablegoalkeeperpacifistdastardlygoalke
eperpacifisttimetabledastardlygoalkeepertimetablepacifist

But you knew that, right? After all, you're smarter than an eight-month-old, aren't you?

Carrot or Stick?

Tommy 'Top Gun' Taylor and Peter 'Pontius' Pilot are both very experienced teachers at the flight school.

Tommy's strategy is to shower trainee pilots with praise for every smooth landing, and punish them for every poor landing by shouting at them, or making them run laps of the airfield.

However, Tommy is worried that his teaching methods don't seem to be working. Although his trainee pilots almost always manage a better landing after a telling-off, they also almost always perform a worse landing immediately after being praised for a good one.

Tommy decides that the stick is better than the carrot, and resolves to stop praising pilots for good landings, but to increase the punishment for poor landings. But when he tells his colleague of the plan, Peter just sighs and says, 'It doesn't make any difference.' Is Peter right, or is he just an old cynic?

ANSWER

Peter is almost certainly right. The reason is that pilots' landings – like most things that show a degree of variability – are subject to a phenomenon known as *regression to the mean*. While a few landings will be terrible and a few will be outstanding, most will be somewhere in between – close to the average.* So, after a terrible landing it is virtually inevitable that the next one will be better, simply because almost all landings are better than terrible. Similarly, after an excellent landing, the next one will generally be worse, simply because almost all landings are worse than excellent.

So the pattern that Tommy notices – better performance after bad landings, worse performance after good landings – would happen anyway, even if he wasn't there. If you're not convinced, try throwing darts randomly at a dartboard. If you hit a 1 or 2, it's almost certain that the next score will be higher. If you hit the bullseye or a treble 20, it's almost certain that the next score will be lower. But the carrot and stick don't come into it, as you can produce this pattern simply by throwing the darts blindfolded.

Regression to the mean is a real problem when designing psychology experiments. Often we want to find out whether we can improve people's performance on a particular task with some type of training. But we may often be kidding ourselves, with improvement among the worst-performing participants being due not to our carefully planned training, but simply to regression to the mean.

Not that this problem is restricted to flight schools and psychology studies. The failure to take into account regression to the mean is one reason why people believe in demonstrably useless treatments such as homeopathy (we will meet another reason, *confirmation bias*, in **Card Trick**). Illnesses come and go of their own accord. So if you feel at your absolute worst on Monday, you'll

---

* 'mean' is simply a more precise term for what we refer to in everyday speech as 'the average'. (Technically, there are several different types of average, of which the [arithmetic] mean is just one.)

probably feel a lot better by Friday, whether or not you took a homeopathic remedy on Tuesday. But if you did, you probably credited the improvement to the pill.

In short, regression to the mean is absolutely everywhere. So if you hated this section, never mind, the next one will be better, *honestly . . .*

Liar, Liar

How good do you think you are at determining whether or not somebody is lying? Let's put a number on it. If you had to judge the truthfulness of 100 statements – 50 truths and 50 lies – how many do you think you'd get right altogether (i.e., what is your predicted percentage accuracy score)?

ANSWER

Now, obviously I don't know anything at all about you. Neverthe-less, I can say with confidence that the number you should have written is very close to fifty; perhaps fifty-five if you're lucky.

When it comes to detecting liars, most people think they're pretty good. But studies have consistently shown that almost no-body is any good at all, including those whose job it is to catch liars for a living. A 2006 review brought together 108 experi-mental studies, consisting of over 16,000 participants. The gen-eral public (in practice, mostly students) had an accuracy rate of 54 per cent (where 50 per cent equals chance performance), with detectives (51 per cent) and police officers (55 per cent) no better. People who were supremely confident in their judgements were no better than those who were unsure. Accuracy did not improve with age, experience or education; neither were there any differ-ences between men and women.

So why do we think that some people are good at detecting liars when, actually, they're not? There seem to be two statistical quirks at play. One is that although people don't vary much in their lie-detection ability, they vary quite a bit in their *credulity*; i.e., how likely they are to believe or disbelieve people in general. Let's imagine 50 per cent of all statements are lies (which is generally how it works in experimental studies). Someone who disbelieves everyone might *look like* a great lie detector because he catches all the liars, but only if we conveniently forget the fact that he's false-ly accusing all the truth-tellers as well. In reality, his 'hit rate' is 50 per cent; exactly the same as someone who accepts everything he's told. The second statistical quirk is that, although lie detec-tors do not vary much in their ability, *liars* themselves vary much more. So anyone who sees a constant parade of very poor liars (a policeman, for example) is in danger of kidding himself that he is a genius at detecting deception, when, in fact, a liar with even the most basic competence would have him stumped.

Is there *anyone* who can detect a liar? In keeping with the old adage of 'to catch a thief . . .', a recent study found that, the better you are at lying, the better you are at detecting lying in others. Indeed, the 2006 review found that criminals, with 65 per cent correct guesses, were one of the very few groups that outperformed the public at large.

But take heart. Even if you are not a criminal, there are some reliable cues to deception that you can look out for, provided that the liar is in a real-life, high-stakes, emotionally charged situation (rather than, say, a psychology experiment). One good example is television appeals for 'missing' relatives, who have, in some cases, been murdered by the appealers. Genuine appealers are more likely than fakers to express concern and hope, and to avoid brutal language (e.g., saying 'taken from us', rather than 'killed'), and are less likely to make speech errors, to shake their heads and to look away.

Of course, in everyday life, the lies that we are trying to spot are far more mundane. While, on balance, this is obviously a good thing, it does make lie detection far more difficult: the more mundane the lie, the easier it is for the liar to keep his cool and avoid giving off signals of deception. So is there *anything* you can do to catch liars in everyday circumstances?

In the first – and, so far, only – study of its kind, participants were asked to deliver a package to a 'secret agent'. They were then interviewed about the drop-off by either a 'colleague', to whom they were to tell the whole truth, or an 'enemy spy', to whom they were to lie about the *location* but tell the truth about everything else (including the fact that they had indeed delivered the package to an agent). As part of the interview, participants were asked to draw a picture of the drop-off. Amazingly, only two of out of the sixteen liars included in their drawings the 'secret agent' who received the package, as compared to twelve out of fifteen truth-tellers. The reason is that, when told to lie about the location of the drop-off, the liars tended to pick a location that they knew well, so that they'd be able to sketch it easily. The drawback with this otherwise excellent strategy is that their mental picture of this location did not, of course, include the 'secret agent'. D'oh!

So if you want to know where your partner *really* was on that suspicious night out, you could do worse than get him to draw the gathering, and see whether or not he includes everyone that he says was there. And if your insurance company asks you to draw a picture of the accident, for God's sake don't forget to include the other car!

Lyer, Lyer

Which of the two lines below is longer, A or B?

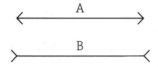

ANSWER

For this section, you can find the answer yourself: Get hold of a ruler and measure the two lines. Amazing, isn't it?!

Although this illusion has been known about for over a hundred years – having been first pointed out by Franz Müller-Lyer in 1889 – psychologists are still undecided as to precisely what it means.

One of the most fascinating things about this illusion is that, no matter how hard you try, you cannot make it go away. Even after you have measured the lines, B looks longer.

Stop for a minute to think just how weird this is. Your brain is what decides, on the basis of the input that it receives from the visual system, that the second line is longer. But your brain already knows that the lines are the same length; so why is it overruling itself? What does it even mean for a brain to overrule itself?

The philosopher Jerry Fodor argued that the only feasible explanation is that the brain contains a number of 'modules' – self-encapsulated systems that are sealed off from higher-level thought processes. No matter how much we may *know* that the lines are the same length, we cannot get that information to the vision module, a sealed off 'black box' that takes its input only from the eyes and keeps shouting 'B is longer'.

The opposite view is that vision is not 'sealed off' from the rest of our cognition at all. On the contrary, vision, like most brain processes, is susceptible to our prior expectations, and even to cultural influences. On the face of it, this sounds crazy; how could cultural influences affect something as basic as whether one line looks longer than another?

But maybe it can. In the 1960s, a team of psychologists and anthropologists showed the Müller-Lyer illusion to volunteers from sixteen different societies from around the globe and measured their susceptibility to the illusion. The researchers came up with a clever way of putting a number on just how susceptible people are to the illusion: they showed each person lots of different versions of the illusion, and measured how much *longer* Line A had to be than Line B for each person to say that they *looked* the same. For example, in the version of the illusion shown below, Line A is actually about a fifth longer again than Line B, but to me – and probably you – they look about the same.

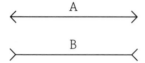

The findings were rather surprising. American students – the population that had supplied the participants for almost all previous demonstrations of the Müller-Lyer illusion (and, indeed, most psychology studies of any kind) were extremely atypical. American students proved more susceptible to the illusion than any other group studied, including South Africans (both students of European descent and Zulus), Suku people from Angola and Bété people from the Ivory Coast. San foragers of the Kalahari Desert were exceptional in the opposite direction; they did not experience the illusion at all.

This suggests that the Müller-Lyer illusion may be susceptible to cultural influences; but what kind of cultural influences? The researchers suggested that the differences observed may be due to the fact that the environments of modern societies contain many 'carpentered corners', such as the perfectly square corners of buildings, whereas the environments of more traditional foraging societies do not. So when we in the West see part of a 'Line B' type configuration, it is generally in the context of the far side of a room (see opposite page).

In situations like this, the brain says to itself 'OK, that far wall *looks* narrower than the wall behind me, but *actually* it's just further away. So if I want to know the real length of that line, I have to mentally stretch it out a bit. In these real-world 3D scenarios this is a good thing. Otherwise, if – for example – we saw cows in the distance, we might make the mistake of thinking that they were

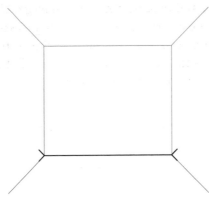

tiny.* The problem is that the brain performs the same mental stretching-out process when it encounters a similar configuration of lines and angles on a flat page.

When we see part of a 'Line A' type configuration, it is generally in the context of something much closer, like the near edge of a rug in the same room (see below). So the brain has learned from the 3D scenario that it does not need to mentally boost the length of the line (or not by much), and applies the same logic to a similar configuration when found in a 2D drawing.

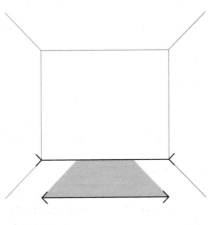

---

* Irish and UK readers might recognise this scenario from the TV series *Father Ted* (see http://www.youtube.com/watch?v=vh5kZ4uIUCo)

The idea is that because foraging tribespeople do not have much experience with the square corners of rooms and carpets, their brains are not tricked in the same way.

However, the story does not end here. A later study found that participants from Malawi were more susceptible to the Müller-Lyer illusion when the figures were drawn in red rather than blue, while for Scottish participants the colour made no difference. This suggests that at least some of the apparent cross-cultural variation observed in the 1960s study may be due in fact to biological differences: people with darker skin tend to have a higher density of retinal pigmentation, which reduces the detectability of edges, and hence the magnitude of the illusion.

Many debates in psychology can be characterised as *nature–nurture* debates. Are some people born more aggressive or more intelligent than others (*nature*), or do they become this way in response to influences in their environment (*nurture*)? Often it turns out to be a bit of both. And so it is with the Müller-Lyer illusion; differences in susceptibility to the illusion between different groups are probably due to both biological and cultural differences. The wider lesson is that we should not take studies conducted on American university students as being representative of the human race in general, even when we are looking at something as apparently fundamental as the perception of line-length.

Speaking of which, here is another line-length illusion.

The Line-Length Illusion

On the left is a line. On the right are three more lines: A, B and C. Your job is to decide which of these lines is equal in length to the first line. This illusion is even more powerful than the previous one, so I will give you a clue: I did a quick poll of seven students in my Psychology department, and all said 'A'.

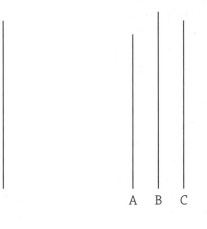

ANSWER

The correct answer is 'C'. I bet you got it right, didn't you?

This 'illusion' is based on Solomon Asch's famous conformity experiment from 1951. The classic version of the study was conducted with nine participants, all but one of whom were actually in league with the experimenter, and had been told to choose an incorrect line, but to all agree on the same one. The way this worked was that the experimenter asked each person in turn to state his choice out loud, with the real participant always the last but one. So by the time the real participant had made his choice, he (all the participants were male) had already heard seven others give the same – obviously incorrect – answer. To ratchet up the pressure even further, the experimenter had the confederates give the right answer on some trials, meaning that the real participant did not have the escape route of assuming that all of the others were crazy, or that he had somehow missed an instruction to always give an incorrect answer.

The question was this: would the participant go along with the majority to the extent of giving an answer that he almost certainly knew to be incorrect? On the whole, yes: about three-quarters of the time, people went with the majority verdict.

Then again, you probably already knew that didn't you? Like the Müller-Lyer illusion, the Asch conformity study is not only a staple of every university and high school psychology course but has been the subject of various radio and TV documentaries and reconstructions (see Web Link).

But here's what you might not know: the reason I knew you probably wouldn't fall for this trick (apart from the fact that it's hard to recreate the social pressure of the original without real-life confederates present) is that levels of conformity as measured by Asch's study have plummeted since the 1950s. In fact, one study conducted in the 1980s found only one incorrect answer in almost 400 trials (although this was conducted with maths, engineering and chemistry students, for whom an evening measuring lines probably constitutes a good night out).

Another interesting difference from the original Asch study is that this latter version was conducted in Britain. Whether Brits are less conformist than Americans is a matter of debate. However, a review which drew together the results from over 100 Asch-type studies conducted across seventeen countries found clear differences on the basis of the extent to which their societies value 'individualism' versus 'collectivism' (as measured by questionnaire studies). Countries in which questionnaire respondents place a high value on pleasure, creativity and curiosity (such as the United States, Britain and Germany) show low levels of conformity on the Asch test. Countries in which questionnaire respondents place a higher value on behaving appropriately, maintaining the status quo and avoiding anything that might disturb the traditional order (such as Japan, China and Zimbabwe) show higher levels of conformity.

Indeed, 'conformity', a term that has rather negative connotations in the West (e.g., 'giving in', 'going along'), might not be quite the right word for what participants in more collectivist societies are doing. As the authors of this cross-cultural review point out, in societies where it is considered impolite to disagree with others in public, participants who endorse the majority view might be thought of as showing tactfulness or sensitivity to others, rather than a desire to humiliate them in public over something so trivial as the length of a few lines.

One of the most interesting findings to come out of this review was a significant – though small – gender difference (we will focus on the wider issue of psychological gender differences in Men are from Mars . . .). Setting aside studies with mixed-sex groups – in which participants may have had obvious ulterior motives for either agreeing with certain group members or for striking out as individuals – all-female groups showed significantly more conformity that all-male groups; and there was no sign of this effect diminishing over the years.

Does this mean that women are stupider, weaker or more easily manipulated than men? Not at all. Perhaps, like the members of collectivist societies, women are simply the 'grown-ups', who are more interested in maintaining harmony within the group, while men, like the members of individualist societies, are the five-year-olds who always have to be right.

Web Link
Many different versions of the Asch study can be found on YouTube. Here is my favourite: http://www.youtube.com/watch?v=TYIh4MkcfJA

A Barking-Mad Test

Draw a dog.

Yes, that's it. Just draw a dog. Don't worry, this isn't a lie detector test *à la* Liar, Liar. Just draw a dog; the best dog you can.

ANSWER

OK, now we will rate your drawing. Score one point for each of the following features.

DOG POINT SCALE

1. Head present
2. Neck present
3. Neck 2-dimensional – must flow into head or body
4. Eyes present
5. Eye detail – lashes
6. Eye detail – pupil
7. Glance – eyes focused/in same direction
8. Nose present – any indication
9. Nose present – 2-dimensional
10. Mouth present
11. Lips 2-dimensional
12. Hair or spots – any indication
13. Hair I – scribble closely conforming to body – includes spots
14. Hair II – more than just scribble or on circumference
15. Ears present
16. Ears in proportion – length greater than width
17. Legs present – any indicator
18. 4 Legs
19. Legs engaged in activity – or lying down
20. Legs in proportion – length greater than width
21. Legs 2-dimensional
22. Some distance between front and rear legs
23. Legs in perspective
24. Crotch-like indicator for legs
25. Legs in proportion – taper off from top
26. Digits present
27. Feet – any indication
28. Feet – 2-dimensional
29. Details of toes correct

30. Trunk present
31. Trunk in proportion – length greater than width
32. Head not more than ½, nor smaller than ¹⁄₁₀, of body width
33. Length of face greater than width
34. Tail present
35. Tail – 2-dimensional
36. Tail shaped
37. Motor coordination lines
38. Motor coordination junctures
39. Head outline – good contour
40. Trunk outline – deviation from oval form
41. Collar or leash

The *Draw-A-Dog Scale* is a real psychological test, used to measure children's cognitive development. The average score for five-, six- and seven-year-olds is 14, 18 and 22 points respectively, with boys and girls showing similar performance. So if you didn't manage to beat this, you should be asking yourself some serious questions.

The logic behind this test, and the more widely used Good-enough-Harris *Draw-A-Person Test*, is that it provides a relatively pure measure of cognitive development that is unclouded by other factors. For example, more traditional IQ tests based on language, maths or logic are affected by factors such as children's ability to read or understand verbal instructions, and – as such – are more a measure of education level than of pure cognitive development.

But the *Draw-A-Person Test* also has a darker – and more controversial – cousin: the *Draw-A-Person Screening Procedure for Emotional Disturbance*. As its name implies, clinicians use these drawings to identify children who are emotionally disturbed. Some people have claimed that individual errors or distortions represent specific problems (e.g., that children who miss out eyes are unwilling to interact with the world around them). Although there is little evidence for such specific claims, some studies have found that, when taken as a whole, drawings can help to distinguish normal and disturbed children. One scoring criterion, for example, is whether children draw fists, claws, guns or knives. Drawing monsters instead of people and writing swear words are both cause for concern, as is drawing unusually huge or tiny people. That said, this is an inexact science; even the study that provides perhaps the strongest support for this test found that drawings could correctly classify only around 63 per cent of children as normal versus potentially disturbed.

So if some of your child's drawings are a little bit – ahem – colourful, don't start calling the doctor just yet. But if – like the *Simpsons* bully Nelson Muntz – she draws 'a robot with guns for arms, shooting a plane made out of guns that fires guns', you should probably run for the hills.

Your Perfect Partner

How important to you are each of the following characteristics when choosing a partner?

Before you fill in the questionnaire, ask yourself this: would your partner – if you have one – give similar or very different answers? If you would like to find out, there is a second copy of this questionnaire on the next page (please don't look at each other's answers).

Please give each characteristic a rating between 1 – completely unimportant – and 4 – very important.

You

1. Good sense of humour ....
2. Ambitious and hard-working ....
3. Similar taste in music, films, books etc. ....
4. Good looks ....
5. Outgoing/sociable ....
6. Neat and tidy ....
7. High earning potential ....
8. Wants children ....
9. Similar politics and religion ....
10. Few previous sexual partners ....
11. Similar attitude to yourself re: smoking and alcohol ....
12. Cheerful ....

Finally, would your idea partner be:
(a) the same age as you, ...
(b) older or ....
(c) younger. ....
If (b) or (c), by how many years ....

Your Partner

Please give each characteristic a rating between 1 – completely unimportant – and 4 – very important.

1. Good sense of humour ·············
2. Ambitious and hard-working ·············
3. Similar taste in music, films, books etc. ·············
4. Good looks ·············
5. Outgoing/sociable ·············
6. Neat and tidy ·············
7. High earning potential ·············
8. Wants children ·············
9. Similar politics and religion ·············
10. Few previous sexual partners ·············
11. Similar attitude to yourself re: smoking and alcohol ·············
12. Cheerful ·············

Finally, would your ideal partner be:
(a) the same age as you, ·············
(b) older or ·············
(c) younger. ·············
If (b) or (c), by how many years ·············

ANSWERS

Although all of the characteristics listed above probably have some influence on people's choice of partner, for our purposes in this section, most were red herrings. We are actually interested in your answers to just five questions. You can compare the importance ratings given by you and your partner for these five key characteristics by filling in the table below. You should also fill in the gender of each person.

	You	Your Partner
Gender	Male / Female	Male / Female
Ambitious and hard-working		
Good looks		
High earning potential		
Few previous sexual partners		
Ideal age gap	.... years older/ younger	.... years older/ younger

How did your ratings compare? The cliché, of course, is that men choose partners who are younger, good-looking and have had few sexual partners, while women choose older, ambitious high earners.* But is any of this true?

The answer is an emphatic 'yes'. While psychology studies often show that many of our 'common-sense' intuitions are entirely wrong, this is one cliché that is basically true.

When over a thousand Americans were given a questionnaire similar to the one you have just completed, men really did place

---

* Although most of the research discussed here was conducted with heterosexual male and female participants, the study described at the end of this section found that gay and heterosexual men actually give very similar answers (e.g., both tend to rate good looks as relatively important in a partner), as do lesbians and heterosexual women (e.g., both rate good looks as relatively unimportant).

more importance than women on youthfulness, good looks and chastity, while women placed more importance than men on ambition and earning potential, as well as preferring older partners. (If you're impatient to find out exactly what counts as 'good looks', take a peek at the later section What's in a Face?)

I know what you're thinking: surely there is no culture on earth that places a higher value on physical attractiveness in females and on earning potential in males than *America*? There must be some cultures in which older women are prized for their wisdom and have their pick of good-looking virgin toyboys?

Nope. Or, at least, if such societies do exist, they were not represented among the thirty-six other cultures that were also included in this survey. In every single group, good looks were rated as more important by men than women, with high earning potential showing the opposite pattern. Sex differences were not quite so apparent with regard to ambition and hard work, but, nevertheless, only three cultures failed to show the predicted pattern: Spain, Colombia and South African Zulu (in the latter case, perhaps because Zulu women traditionally build the family home and perform other strenuous tasks, such as fetching water). The issue of previous sexual partners is complicated by cross-cultural differences. In many of the societies studied, it is considered important for *both* partners to remain virgins before marriage, often for religious reasons. Nevertheless, in every country where a significant gender difference *was* observed, virginity of a partner (this questionnaire asked about the importance of the partner having *no* previous sexual partners) was more important to males than to females.

With regard to age differences, in every country men preferred women younger than themselves, with the biggest preferred age gaps observed in Zambia and Nigeria (six to seven years) and the smallest, by far, in Finland (about five months). In every country, too, women preferred older men, with the biggest preferred gap in Iran (five years) and the smallest in French-speaking Canada (just under two years). On average, men like women who are 2.66 years younger than themselves, while women like men who are 3.42 years older.

So why do men like attractive young virgins, while women like older, ambitious hard-workers? Most people are at least vaguely familiar with the theory of *parental investment and sexual selection* put forward by the biologist Robert Trivers in the 1970s. The idea is that having a child is very 'costly' for females, who must invest not just nine months of their lives but all of the effort, discomfort and missed opportunities that go along with it. If the child does not survive, all of this investment is wasted. So it is very important, from the female's point of view, to choose a sexual partner who is willing and able to protect, feed and generally provide for the child, in order to ensure its survival. In the modern world, this basically translates into someone ambitious with high earning potential, which usually means someone older.

For men, creating a child involves only a few minutes of effort, usually entirely pleasurable. So, in purely evolutionary terms, if one particular child does not survive, very little investment has been wasted. This means that there is no particular incentive for men to look for women who will be able to protect and provide for their young. A better strategy (again, speaking in purely evolutionary terms) is to mate with a large number of women who are young and fertile. How can men tell who is young and fertile? By looking for youthful traits such as smooth skin, shiny hair, big glossy lips, and so on. So – the theory goes – men find these traits attractive purely because they are indicators of youthfulness and fertility.

But why do men historically value not only youthfulness but also virginity? Well, generally speaking, men's investment in their children does not end at the point of conception; most invest time and resources in caring for their children after they are born. What is an absolute disaster, in evolutionary terms, is pouring all of this investment into *another man's* offspring rather than your own. Before paternity tests came along, the only way for a man to be sure that a child was his own was to mate only with women who were demonstrably virgins.

Now, you might think that all of this was true way back in the days of Fred and Wilma Flintstone but has no relevance to the world of today. If a woman has a good job, why does she need a high earning man to provide for her children? And if she is using contraception, the merits of the man as a potential father are irrelevant anyway; she may as well just have sex with the best-looking man possible. Similarly, if a man is using contraception, why would he be attracted to women who show signs of fertility?

These objections misunderstand how evolution works. The idea is not that men today consciously pursue women who are more fertile. Men pursue women who they find physically attractive. It is just that – thanks to evolution – the women who men happen to find physically attractive are those who look young and fertile.

But are we really such slaves to evolution, unable to overrule our genetic impulses? Are we really still stuck in the caveman era? Well, yes and no. On the one hand, recent surveys of this type show that women place more importance than they used to on physical attractiveness, while men place more importance than they used to on earning power. On the other hand, differences remain. A large internet survey published in 2007 found that men still ranked 'good looks' and 'facial attractiveness' as more important than did women, while women ranked dependability, honesty and kindness (and also humour) as more important than did men. *Plus ça change, plus c'est la même chose.*

Let us end, however, with a heart-warming finding from the same survey. Despite these differences, all groups – men and women, gay and straight – placed intelligence, humour, honesty and kindness among the top six most important traits. Awww!

Digital Love

TRUE or FALSE? Married couples who met online are more likely to be dissatisfied with their relationship, and to eventually split up.

ANSWER

False. A 2013 study of almost 20,000 Americans (the largest ever study of its type) found that married couples who met online and offline reported almost identical satisfaction scores. On a scale where 1=Extremely Unhappy and 7=Perfect, the average satisfaction scores were 5.64 and 5.48 for the couples who met online and offline respectively. So, if anything, the couples who met online were *more* satisfied with their relationship.* Similarly, the percentage of couples who had split up by the end of the survey period (seven years) was slightly *lower* for the online (5.96 per cent) daters than for the offline ones (7.67 per cent).

But does it make a difference precisely where you met? For offline daters, not at all. So you can all forget those *Is He Mr Right, or Just Mr Right Now?* coffee-table magazine questionnaires that tell you that if you met in a bar or club, your relationship is doomed. Online couples who met in virtual worlds had a slightly higher break-up rate, but otherwise there were again no differences.

As you would expect, by far the most popular way of meeting online was through dating websites. This raises the question of whether some are better than others, a question no doubt at the forefront of the minds of those who commissioned the survey: marketing executives at one of the leading online dating sites. To their credit, this company clearly did not put pressure on the researchers to fudge the data, as no difference between the different dating sites was found.

So, if you are single, the lesson is simple: get out there and meet someone. It doesn't matter how or where, offline or online. Indeed, if marriage is your goal, you will be interested to know that – at least on the basis of this survey – over a third of all marriages now begin online.

---

* Technically speaking, this difference is statistically significant (see the section The Tea Test). However, statistical significance does not always translate into practical significance. It would be difficult to argue that a difference of 0.16 points on a 7-point scale translates into a meaningful difference in marital satisfaction.

St Valentine's Day: Massacred?

Read the description below (adapting it to your own gender), and then answer the questions that follow.

Nick/Nicole is a twenty-year-old student at your local university. His/her subject is English, and s/he is considering doing a minor in history as well. S/he lives with room-mates in a four-bedroom house near the university. S/he has a part-time job working at the University Welcome Centre, and one of his/her favourite things to do is try new kinds of food. S/he also likes to watch TV, tries to go to the gym a couple of times per week and loves to go see his/her favourite bands play live concerts. Nick/Nicole is single. Today is Valentine's Day.

1. What do you think s/he will do this evening? Take a few minutes to write a short description of Nick/Nicole's night. Please write at least five lines.

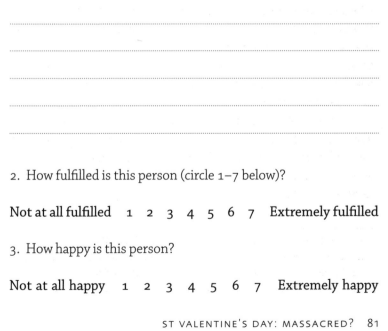

2. How fulfilled is this person (circle 1–7 below)?

Not at all fulfilled   1   2   3   4   5   6   7   Extremely fulfilled

3. How happy is this person?

Not at all happy   1   2   3   4   5   6   7   Extremely happy

ANSWER

Of course, since they are fictional characters, your answers tell us nothing about Nick or Nicole. But they tell us a lot about you.

Single people who think that their single status is relatively permanent tend to say that single Nick/Nicole is happier and more fulfilled (around 5/7) than do those who see their single status as temporary (around 4/7), and are more likely to describe a fun evening. **Coupled people** who think that their coupled status is permanent tend to say that single Nick/Nicole is less happy and fulfilled (around 4/7) than do those who see their coupled status as temporary (around 5/7), and are more likely to describe a depressing evening.

If we change the story so that our hero has a partner, the results flip around. Now, permanent couples and temporary singles portray Nick/Nicole as happier than do temporary couples and permanent singles. In short, whether they are single or in a couple, people who see their current status as permanent and unchangeable tend to see it as something that is desirable for others. Conversely, people who see their current status as one that they will soon put behind them tend to see it as undesirable for others. In other words, as the authors of the study put it, 'The way I am [or soon will be] is the way you ought to be.'

Have you noticed how, whenever somebody buys a new phone, computer or car, they invariably try to persuade everyone else to get the exact same model, regardless of whether or not it fits their needs or budget? Then the would-be buyer counters that the other person is an idiot for not getting the deal that *he* plans to get. There it is: *The way I am is the way you ought to be.* This can be pretty annoying. So why do we do it? In many cases, the answer is that the culprit is experiencing something called *cognitive dissonance*, and is trying to convince himself that his decision – whether to stay in a relationship or to buy that particular phone – is indeed the best one.

The term *cognitive dissonance* was coined by Leon Festinger, who, in 1959, conducted a classic demonstration of the phenomenon. Participants completed some extremely tedious tasks (such as turning pegs on a board) and were then paid either $1 or $20 to convince a new potential subject that the tasks were fun and interesting. The idea was to cause the original participants to experience the discomfiting state that arises when our situation, actions or publicly stated convictions (e.g., saying 'the task is fun') contradict our beliefs ('the task is boring'): *cognitive dissonance*. Later, the participants were asked to rate the task. Those who had been paid $1 to lie about it rated it as less boring than those who had been paid $20. Festinger agued that the participants in the $1 group reduced their cognitive dissonance ('The task was boring, but I said it was fun') by convincing themselves that the task wasn't actually that bad. The $20 group had a much easier way to escape from their cognitive dissonance ('The task was boring, but I said it was fun . . . *but only because they paid me a lot of money to do so*').

So, cognitive dissonance arises whenever our situation, actions or publicly stated convictions (e.g., 'I'm in a couple, and that's great') are placed in some conflict with our inner beliefs (e.g., 'Being single on Valentine's Day sounds fun'). The Nick/Nicole effect – i.e., the finding that people deem their own current or anticipated relationship situation to be the better one – arises because it's much easier to change our beliefs ('actually, being single on Valentine's Day is probably depressing') than to change our situation ('Honey, you're dumped'). If our situation is one we cannot change (e.g., having just bought an iPhone), and we come to hold a conflicting belief (e.g., 'that Samsung seems a much better deal'), our only option is to change our belief ('actually, Samsungs aren't so great') or live with the cognitive dissonance.

This is why customer feedback questionnaires drive me mad. If you have already spent a lot of time and money on a meal, training course or university degree, and begin to experience a conflicting belief ('Hmmm, this really isn't very good'), you are far more likely to change your belief ('Actually, all in all, it's been pretty good') than to tolerate the cognitive dissonance and give low scores on the questionnaire. So if your restaurant is getting bad reviews, you could always try jacking up the prices: few people will be able to admit to themselves that they paid £200 for a terrible meal.

The Tea Test

New psychology students at university are often horrified to discover that they are required to take a course in statistics, and to learn to run statistical tests themselves. So why do we put them through it? What's the point of statistical testing? What, in fact, *is* statistical testing?

In order to explain, I'd like to take you back to my childhood. When I was growing up, in the south-east of England, a common refrain in our household was 'Cup of tea please, Ben; and milk in first.' To this day, my mother swears blind that tea tastes better if the milk is added before the tea, rather than after, and continues to sip suspiciously any cup of tea that she is offered in order to check that her rule has been followed. Although my mother usually detected my attempts to trick her into accepting milk-in-last tea (perhaps because of my guilty expression), I was generally rather suspicious of her claims that she could actually tell the difference.

A noted biologist, Sir Ronald Fisher (1890–1962), had a similar experience with a colleague named Dr Muriel Bristol-Roach, and was similarly suspicious. Rather than just muttering under his breath and refusing to make the tea, Fisher sat down and devised a statistical test that could be used to settle the question once and for all: *Fisher's exact test.** Fisher gave Bristol-Roach eight cups of tea, telling her that the milk had been added before the tea in four, and after in the others, and asked her to say which was which.

That's all very well, but where does statistical testing come into it? Well, say that our taster got four cups right and four cups wrong (i.e., a 50 per cent success rate). Would you want to con-

---

* Confusingly, another commonly used test is actually called the *tea test* – well, *t-test*, but it's pronounced the same – though that test was invented for a different beverage-related purpose: quality control at the Guinness brewery in Dublin.

clude that she can tell the difference between milk-in-first and milk-in-last tea? Of course not; it's easy to see that someone who simply flipped a coin for each cup could expect to get half of them right by sheer chance alone. Now, what if she got five right and three wrong? Again, we wouldn't want to say that she can tell the difference, because our coin-flipper would have to be only slightly luckier than average to get the same result. What about six right and two wrong? Seven right and one wrong? All eight right? How many cups does our tea taster have to identify correctly before we conclude that she really can tell the difference and didn't just get lucky?

The point of Fisher's test* is to answer this question. It turns out that the probability of getting all eight correct by chance alone, using the coin-flipping method, is 1 in 70,† or 0.014 (i.e., 1 divided by 70). Scientists call this a p (short for probability) *value*. Now, we can never *entirely* rule out the possibility that a particular result – such as getting all eight cups correct – is down to chance alone; our coin-flipper could just have been *extremely* lucky. Instead, scientists have agreed on a rule of thumb, known as $p<0.05$: if (a) the probability of a particular result (e.g., getting all eight cups correct) happening by chance alone is less than 1 in 20 (i.e., 0.05) and (b) this result then happens, then we accept that the result almost certainly didn't happen by chance alone. That is, we accept the result as *statistically significant*.

---

* Incidentally, although these tales of tea-tasting suggest a rather genteel character, there was a darker side to Fisher. He was an enthusiastic advocate of eugenics, the idea that people with less desirable traits should be discouraged from having children, and was dismissive of the idea of a link between smoking and lung cancer (perhaps, cynics noted, because he not only enjoyed a smoke himself but was also funded by the British Tobacco Research Council). Even more controversially – to put it mildly – Fisher argued that different races differ in their innate intellectual abilities, and that documents such as the *UNESCO Statement of Race* constituted nothing more than ill-informed – if well-intentioned – efforts to 'minimise the real differences that exist'.

† Why 1 in 70? Because there are 70 different ways to pick four cups from eight, and only one of these correctly gives you the four milk-in-first cups.

So, let's round off our tea-tasting example. The story goes that Dr Bristol-Roach did, in fact, get all eight cups correct. Because the probability of getting all eight correct by chance alone – 1 in 70 (p = 0.014) – is clearly less than our cut-off of 1 in 20 (i.e., $p<0.05$), we accept that the result did not occur by chance alone, and that ... drum roll, please ... she actually can tell whether or not the milk was added first.* Score 1–0 to my mum.

Now that you know this, you can try your own tea-tasting challenge at home. Don't like tea? Well, maybe you would like to find out whether you can tell Pepsi from Coke, diet drinks from regular, brand-name groceries from supermarket own-make equivalents, or even – just for the grown-ups – red wine from white wine (surprisingly difficult if both are chilled). Just remember: with eight drinks, you need to get them all right to significantly beat chance. If you're particularly thirsty and up the number of drinks to ten, you only need to get 9/10 correct (though you'll also need a lot of cola and a strong bladder).

Finally, it is important to be aware that this idea of testing whether apparently meaningful differences between groups could have arisen by chance alone – which is done as a matter of course in all sciences – has not entered public consciousness. Newspapers are *always* reporting as meaningful tiny differences between groups that are *extremely* likely to have arisen by chance alone. Worse still, I have seen newspaper articles in which a researcher's claim that – for example – a minuscule increase in crime rates is 'not statistically significant' is portrayed as the special pleading of a boffin who is determined to hide the truth. In fact, the truth is that if an 'increase' in crime rates is not statistically significant, there's no reason to think that crime rates have actually changed at all.

---

* Not all psychology experiments are as simple as Fisher's tea test; more complicated experiments need more advanced tests (you can try out two of the most commonly used on the companion website). But no matter how complex the test, the goal is always the same: to investigate the likelihood of an experimental effect as big as the one we observed (e.g., 8/8 cups correct) occurring by chance alone.

So, yes – as the cliché goes - there are lies, damned lies and statistics. But the damnedest lies are told not when statistics are used, but when they are ignored.

Further Reading and Web Links
David Salsburg's book *The Lady Tasting Tea: How Statistics Revolutionized Science in the Twentieth Century* provides a detailed account of how the work of Ronald Fisher, and contemporaries such as Karl Pearson, laid the bedrock for modern-day statistical testing.

The companion website (www.Psy-QBook.com) contains two bonus online sections that outline – and let you try out – more complex statistical tests that can be used to investigate questions such as whether women smile more often than men.

Reading and Righting

Quick, what does this sign say?!

How cmoe it's not taht hrad to raed wehn all the mdilde lretets of a wrod are jebumld up?

ANSWER

If you found that sentence very difficult to read, you are probably 'over-reading' it. If you go through slowly sounding out each word letter-by-letter, you will come up with nothing but garbage. If, on the other hand, you skim-read the sentence, just glancing briefly at each word, you will be able to read it surprisingly easily.

What's going on here? Most people think that when we read, we do so by mentally sounding out each letter – *c, a, t* – and then joining these sounds together to recognise the word (*cat!*). While this is indeed how begnining-readers usually start out, most adults have long since largely abandoned this strategy, at least for nomral everyday reading (we keep it in reserve for reading foreign, new or very unfamiliar words). What takes its place is a process of whole-word recognition that is highly automated and extremely fast. It generally takes less than a fifth of one second to recognise a word. How can we recognise words so quickly? The answer seems to be that we do not, as you might imagine, read by matching the word on the page on to an exact template stored in our heads:

Printed Word   Template

Instead, the template that is stored in our heads seems to contain just (a) the relevant letters and (b) tags indicating their approximate positions.*

---

* At least, according to one recent model. If there is one thing you will never get psychologists to agree on, it is a model of visual word recognition.

At first glance, this seems a bit odd. Wouldn't it make more sense to store an exact template of ecah word? Well, maybe, but good luck trying. Consider a relatively long word like *happiness*. Even though this word isn't that long in the grand scheme of things (it's certainly no *antidisestablishmentarianism*), you have pretty mcuh no chance of storing the *exact* position of each letter (quick, what number position is the *e* in?). All you can store is some very rough positional information ('it's quite near the end'). This means that when you encounter a jumbled up word such as *sotp*, it's actually a pretty good match for your 'stop' template, and is therefore recognised relatively easily, particularly if you're given a bit of context such as a sentence, or – say – a road sign with a distinctive shape.

To prove the point: did you notice the four words that were jumbled up in this passage?*

———

THE EDN

———

* *Beginning, normal, each* and *much*

Prelude or Requiem?: Part 1

Q: Why couldn't Mozart find his best friend?
A: Because he was Haydn

Sorry, one more:

Q: What is Mozart doing right now?
A: Decomposing

Look, I'm sorry, all right? But I can't introduce this section by telling you what it's about, or it won't work, so you'll have to make do with lame jokes instead.

Anyway, let's get on with it. For this section, you will need a recording of Mozart's sonata for two pianos in D major (K.448). There are plenty of versions on YouTube, and on free streaming services such as Spotify, but do try to find one with both movements if possible. This next part is optional, but you may like to also find a recorded relaxation exercise. Again, these are relatively easy to track down online, but it's important that you find one that does not include any music, but just talks to you soothingly ('focus on your breathing, feel yourself sink deep into your chair' . . . you know the type).

First, listen to the Mozart piece for ten minutes. Don't read, check your emails or watch any video that accompanies the music; just sit and listen. When the ten minutes are up, turn the page and complete the test shown.

Prelude or Requiem?: Part 2

This test involves imagining what a piece of paper that has been first folded and then cut will look like when unfolded again. Look at the practice problem below.

Practice 1

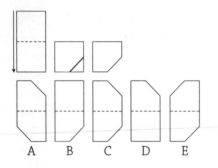

The top half of the picture shows the folding and cutting process. First, the long thin piece of paper is **folded** from top to bottom as shown by the arrow. Next, this folded paper is **cut** – in this case by having the bottom right corners snipped off – as shown in the middle part of the top half of the picture (cuts are indicated by **bold lines** —). The right-hand part of the top half of the picture shows the final **folded and cut** paper. Your job is to imagine what this paper will look like if unfolded again, and to choose the correct option (A–E) from the bottom half of the picture (dashed lines - - - show the fold or crease). For this example, **C** is the correct choice. If you don't understand why this is, you should go through this explanation again. When you are happy that you understand how the test works, have a go at the second practice item.

Pactice 2

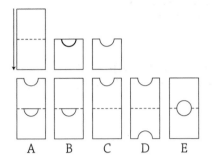

A   B   C   D   E

This one is a little trickier because the cut is on the folded side, but it should be relatively easy to see that **E** is the correct answer.

Now you know how it works, please proceed to the test proper, which consists of six items. Note that, unlike the practice items, some of the test problems have two or even three folds. Don't forget to record your chosen answer for each item, either by circling your response in the book or by making a note elsewhere.

1.

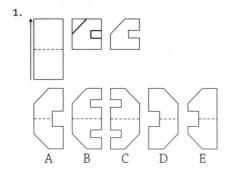

2.

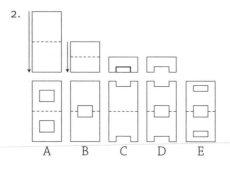

3.

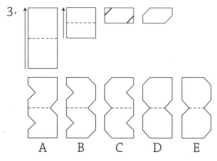

4.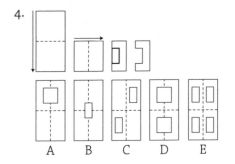

A   B   C   D   E

5.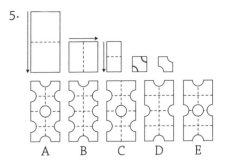

A   B   C   D   E

6.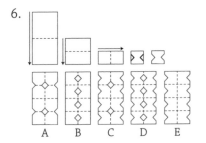

A   B   C   D   E

Phew, difficult isn't it?!

Before we see how you got on, we're going to try another six. But first, I would like you to spend ten minutes either sitting in silence or, if you prefer, listening to a relaxation recording. (It doesn't make much difference either way.)

Done?

OK, now please turn over to Part 3 to complete the second and final batch of six puzzles.

Prelude or Requiem?: Part 3

1.

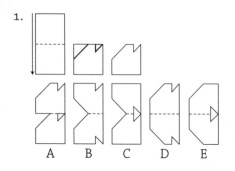

A   B   C   D   E

2.

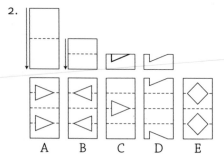

A   B   C   D   E

3.

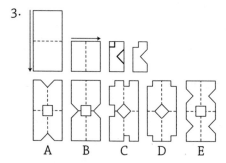

A   B   C   D   E

4.

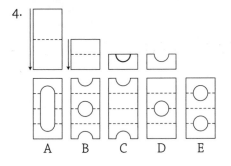

A   B   C   D   E

5.

6.

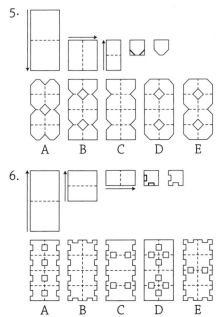

A   B   C   D   E

Now turn the page to find out how you did.

ANSWERS

Mozart set: B, A, C, D, A, D
Silence/relaxation set: C, A, E, E, B, D

When this study was conducted under test conditions (with quite a few more paper folding and cutting problems, as well as some other tests of spatial reasoning), the same participants showed significantly better performance after listening to the Mozart piece than after sitting in silence or listening to a relaxation tape (there was no difference between the two).*

When this study was published, things went a little crazy. Although the experiment was conducted on adults (well, university students), and its authors made no claims regarding babies or children, the Governor of the US state of Georgia, one Zell Miller, decreed that free classical music CDs should be handed out to the families of every newborn baby in the state, in an attempt to boost children's brainpower. A self-styled Mozart-Effect™ guru named Don Campbell† made millions publishing CDs for children, infants and even unborn babies, as well as a book: *The Mozart Effect: Tapping the Power of Music to Heal the Body, Strengthen the Mind, and Unlock the Creative Spirit*. As the title suggests, Campbell's claims went way beyond visuo-spatial problem-solving. (Ironically, listening to Mozart did not seem to heal Mozart's *own* body; the composer suffered from many illnesses throughout his life including smallpox, bronchitis, pneumonia and rheumatism.)

Others have gone further still. An article in a British newspaper listed numerous attempts to find Mozart-effects including – deep breath – improving classroom behaviour, calming jostling pedestrians, keeping streets free of drug dealers, reducing violence and

---

* Neither did it make any difference whether participants did the Mozart version first, second or last. Just to be on the safe side, I avoided giving you the Mozart version last, to make sure that any better performance with this version couldn't be due simply to having had more practice at the task.

† Yes, Don Campbell registered 'Mozart Effect' as a trademark.

vandalism at railway stations, calming dogs and increasing yields of milk and eggs (for farm animals, obviously). All but the latter were apparently successful.

The Mozart effect has made its way into popular culture, with most people falling into one of two camps: those who think the effect is well proven and those who think it has been thoroughly debunked. As is often the case, the truth is rather more interesting, and somewhere in between.

The finding of a Mozart effect (at least, for mental paper folding-and cutting puzzles in adults) is generally well supported by follow-up studies. And it's not as if any old classical music will do; the effect disappears if you replace Mozart's upbeat ditty with a sad Albinoni adagio. Still, the idea that there is something special about the music of Mozart that makes people smarter is almost certainly untrue. The same follow-up study found that the Mozart effect is observed only for people who enjoyed the piece, and found that it made them feel alert and happy. If you're not a Mozart fan, sorry, but no Mozart effect for you. Another follow-up study by the same research team found that the beneficial effect remained if the Mozart sonata was replaced with another upbeat number (Schubert's Fantasia for piano) or even a Stephen King story (*The Last Rung on the Ladder*). In fact, participants who preferred the story to the sonata showed a bigger boost for the former than the latter.

So, to borrow a title from a review paper summarising the major studies in this area, should we sing a prelude or requiem for the Mozart effect? It depends. Listening to something that you like – Mozart if you like Mozart, Stephen King stories if you like Stephen King stories – peps you up, and so gives you a short, temporary boost, at least on a rather narrow range of spatial reasoning tasks. But there is no reason to think that it will make you smarter.

Or – if you are a chicken – lay more eggs.

Speaking of which, I don't know whether or not he played his music to them, but, as a matter of fact, Mozart used to keep chickens. Well, he did for a while, then his patience ran out and he killed them all. Why? He couldn't stand the way they used to run around going 'Bach! Bach! Bach!'

The Patient

Emergency! Scientists have found a new disease that is spreading around the country. The bad news is that the disease causes various types of cancer. The good news is that the disease is pretty rare: only one person in 10,000 has it. Since the disease has no symptoms, government scientists have developed a test to see who is infected. The test isn't quite perfect, but it gives the correct result for 99 out of every 100 people tested (i.e., 99 per cent).

In the week that the test is launched, one million people take it, including you. Disaster! The test says that you have the disease. But remember that the test isn't perfect. What is the probability that you actually do have the disease, given your test result?

(a) 99 out of 100 (i.e., 99 per cent)
(b) 98 out 100 (i.e., 98 per cent)
(c) 10 out of 100 (i.e., 1 in 10, or 10 per cent)
(d) 1 out of 102 (i.e., 0.98 per cent, slightly less than 1 per cent)

ANSWER

Almost everybody chooses the first answer, as they simply cannot see beyond the fact that the test is accurate in 99 per cent of cases. But this is incorrect. The reason is that it is necessary to take into account not only the accuracy of the test, but *the likelihood that you had the disease to begin with*. If you chose (d), perhaps because it seemed like the most unlikely answer and you suspected a double bluff, congratulations – you're right!

Before we dive headlong into the maths (which is actually pretty simple, though very counter-intuitive), let's try to understand – in simple terms – why the probability that you have the disease is much less than the 99 per cent that most people choose.

The thing to bear in mind above all else is this: *the disease is very rare to begin with*. So, before even thinking about the test, the probability that you are infected is 1 in 10,000. So while an incorrect test result is *quite* unlikely (odds of 1 in 100), it's much, much more likely than actually having the disease (odds of 1 in 10,000). As an analogy (based on a popular cartoon, see Web Links), imagine that you have a machine that tells you whether or not the sun will rise tomorrow, and this machine is 99 per cent accurate. It tells you that the sun won't rise tomorrow. What's more likely – that the sun won't rise tomorrow, or that this is the one time out of 100 that the machine has got it wrong?

Now, returning to the disease, let's walk through the maths to see why the correct answer is the unlikely seeming 1 in 102.

Out of the million people that took the test, only 100 are actually infected (because the disease affects 1 person in 10,000, and 1,000,000 divided by 10,000 is 100). Because the test is 99 per cent accurate and 1 per cent inaccurate . . .

- 99 people who DO have the disease will correctly be told that they are infected (100 × 99 per cent = 99)
- 1 person who DOES have the disease will incorrectly be told that s/he is NOT infected (100 × 1 per cent = 1)

This leaves 999,900 people who are not infected (1,000,000 – 100). Because the test is 99 per cent accurate . . .

- 989,901 people who DO NOT have the disease will correctly be told that they are NOT infected (999,900 × 99 per cent = 989,901)
- 9,999 people who DO NOT have the disease will incorrectly be told that they ARE infected.

So, how many people are TOLD that they have the disease? The answer is 10,098 (99 people who actually do plus 9,999 people who actually don't). And how many of these people actually do? 99.

So the probability that someone who is told that they have the disease actually has it is 99/10,098 = 0.0098 = 0.98 per cent = 1 in 102.

Don't worry if you find this confusing; so do most psychologists. In fact, the vast majority of statistical testing in psychology, and indeed almost all science, is based on exactly the faulty reasoning that leads most people to choose 99 out of 100 as the correct answer. For example, think back to The Tea Test. The statistical test tells us whether you can really tell apart milk-in-first and milk-in-last teas or whether you just got lucky. We said that if you got all eight cups right, it's very unlikely that you just got lucky.

What we failed to take into account, however, was the likelihood that a person can tell apart milk-in-first and milk-in-last tea (equivalent to the likelihood of having the disease) to begin with. For example, if we have reason to believe beforehand that only one person in a million can distinguish between milk-in-first and milk-in-last tea, we'd want to see a lot more than eight consecutive successes before we were prepared to believe that you were one of these extremely rare tea masters, rather than someone who just got lucky.

So why does psychology (and, more scarily, most medical research) use the wrong type of testing? One reason is that we often don't have the necessary information to use the right type (i.e., we don't know in advance how many people can distinguish milk-in-first and milk-in-last tea, or how many people have the disease; indeed, often, this is exactly what we're trying to find out). Another is simply that we psychologists are very set in our ways and don't like change.

Web Links and Further Reading
Here are some websites that work through similar examples:

http://www.cs.ubc.ca/~murphyk/Bayes/bayesrule.html
http://www.cs.ubc.ca/~murphyk/Bayes/economist.html
http://yudkowsky.net/rational/bayes

An excellent clear explanation is also given in Derren Brown's book *Tricks of The Mind*. You can do your own calculations automatically online at:

http://www.gametheory.net/Mike/applets/Bayes/Bayes.html

The use of frequentist statistics (as in the tea-tasting example) as opposed to Bayesian statistics (as described in the current section) is satirised in this cartoon:

http://xkcd.com/1132/

The Radiologist

Another patient has contracted the disease, and is rushed to the hospital with suspected lung cancer. An X-ray is taken and given to the radiologist – you guessed it: you. Your job is to provide a diagnosis. Small spots (about 3cm, or 1½ inches in diameter) are generally harmless 'nodules', but any spot larger than this may be a potentially cancerous 'lung mass'. Bearing in mind that the X-ray has had to be reduced in size to fit into the book, please inspect the picture and count up any potentially cancerous spots.

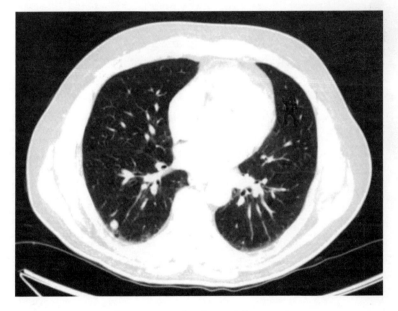

Done? Now turn the page to check your diagnosis.

ANSWER

Forget the cancer. *Did you spot the gorilla*?

This phrase has entered the popular consciousness, thanks to books by Richard Wiseman and by Christopher Chabris and Daniel Simons. Although Chabris and Simons created the 'invisible gorilla', this pop-culture phenomenon actually started with a lesser-known study conducted in the 1970s by a psychologist named Ulric Neisser. Participants watched a video of six people – three wearing black T-shirts, three wearing white T-shirts – passing a ball around a basketball court, and were asked to count the number of passes made by the white team. A few seconds after the start of the video, a woman with an umbrella strolls casually across the screen, right through the middle of the game. The participants were so caught up in their task that most failed to notice the woman entirely. This is hard to imagine just by reading about it, but if you watch the video (see Web Links), you will appreciate just how easy it is to miss the woman when you are focusing on the players.

The most famous invisible gorilla film was created almost by accident. Chabris and Simons started out by replicating the original woman-with-an-umbrella version (though with somewhat higher production values that Neisser's superimposed ghostly film), replacing the woman with a gorilla for some takes. At the end of their filming session, with some time and videotape to spare, they decided to see how far they could push it, by having the gorilla pause in the middle of the scene and thump his chest, rather than just strolling straight on through. To their amazement, they found that it made little difference. Most people still failed to notice the gorilla, even when he paused to thump his chest at the camera, and remained on screen for a full nine seconds. Nowadays, most people have heard of the invisible gorilla, but if you can find someone who has not (perhaps a young child), why not try showing them Chabris and Simons's film (see Web Links)? One reason that this updated version works particularly well is that the focus on the white team encourages participants to 'tune out' individuals wearing black: i.e., both the black team and the 'invisible' gorilla.

So, you have already seen the invisible gorilla, but have you heard the silent gorilla?

Participants who were asked to monitor a conversation between two women – and to ignore a conversation between two men taking place simultaneously – successfully tuned out male voices to such an extent that most failed to notice when a third man began repeating the phrase 'I'm a gorilla', and continued to do so for nineteen seconds. (Again, see Web Links to try the study for yourself.)

What these studies demonstrate is a phenomenon known as 'inattentional blindness' (or perhaps, in the latter case, 'deafness'). When we are very focused on paying attention to one particular aspect of a visual or auditory scene, we fail to notice things that would otherwise be quite obvious (as you can see for yourself if you try showing a friend either the invisible or silent gorilla videos). The drawbacks of inattentional blindness are obvious; for example, a driver who is looking out for cars at a junction may fail to notice a cyclist or pedestrian. The benefits are less obvious but, on balance, almost certainly outweigh the drawbacks.

Imagine, for example, if it were not possible for us to focus on one particular conversation while tuning out others. This limitation would make it almost impossible for most of us to go about our daily business, let alone attend any kind of social gathering. Or, to consider a less trivial case, imagine being operated on by a surgeon who was constantly being distracted by every tiny sound, sight and smell in the vicinity. I would plump for a surgeon who 'suffered' from extreme inattentional blindness every time.

Which brings us back to our X-ray. Did you spot the gorilla? If not, don't worry, you are in good company; 83 per cent of *real* radiologists also failed to do so.

Web Links and Further Reading
Watch Neisser's original video at: www.youtube.com/watch?v=wcjn-J1B7N0E The invisible-gorilla version is at: www.theinvisiblegorilla.com/videos.html The silent-gorilla version is at: www.pc.rhul.ac.uk/sites/attentionlab/auditory-gorilla/

The invisible-gorilla phenomenon is discussed in Robert Wiseman's *Did You Spot the Gorilla?* and Christopher Chabris and Daniel Simons's *The Invisible Gorilla*.

The Surgeon

What is wrong with this passage?

A boy and his father have been exposed to the disease. Sadly, the father
rapidly develops a tumour and dies. The boy survives, but desperately
needs an operation and is rushed to hospital. A surgeon is called. Upon
entering the room and seeing the patient, the surgeon exclaims, 'Oh no!
I can't do the operation. That's my son!'

If you have never encountered this puzzle before, try to figure out what is going on, before turning the page to find out the
answer.

If you are already familiar with this puzzle, turn the page to find
out what its solution tells us about our thought processes. Clue:
it's not what you think.

ANSWER

Nothing is wrong with the passage. The surgeon is the boy's mother.

If you've never encountered this puzzle before, and you got it right, congratulations! If you couldn't figure it out, don't worry, amazingly few people do.

A version of this puzzle has been doing the rounds since at least the 1970s. Usually, it's presented as a demonstration of the sexism inherent in all of our thought processes. Actually, though, psychologists who study language argue that this riddle tells us something interesting about the way we represent word-meanings.

One possible way in which we could represent word-meanings is as a kind of checklist of necessary features. For example, our meaning for *grandmother* might be:

• Has two X chromosomes (i.e., is genetically female)
• Has a biological son or daughter who also has a biological son or daughter

An alternative way of representing meaning is via a prototype: a general idea of the *type of thing* that this word represents. So our meaning for *grandmother* might be something more like 'a kindly old woman with grey hair, who has grandchildren who think of her as their grandmother'. The feminist parable has the first view of word-meanings in mind (being male is not on the 'checklist' for being a surgeon). But actually the second view of word-meanings seems to be more accurate. For example, most people would be happier to use the term 'grandmother' for (a) an old woman whose daughter subsequently adopted children than (b) a thirty-five-year-old egg donor who has no idea whether or not she even *has* any grandchildren.

So the fact that most people are stumped by this riddle doesn't mean that we're all sexists, just that we tend to interpret words as referring to prototypes, rather than by using checklist-style definitions (after all, the vast majority of surgeons *are* still men).

This story may have something of a happy ending. While still extremely low, the proportion of female surgeons today (around 20 per cent in both the United Kingdom and the United States) is far higher than it was when the above riddle started doing the rounds in the 1970s, and rising rapidly. Perhaps future generations will answer, 'Well, of course she doesn't want to operate on her own son', without batting an eyelid.

The Doctor

Yet another member of the public has been exposed to the disease, which has caused a cancerous tumour in his stomach. He is rushed to a doctor: you.

The patient will die very soon unless the tumour can be removed. However, it is impossible to get to the tumour to remove it, or to inject anything into it. There is a special type of ray that can kill the tumour from outside the patient's body. The problem is that if the ray is set to a high enough intensity to destroy the tumour, it will also destroy all the healthy tissue that it passes through along the way, eventually killing the patient. What is the solution?

ANSWER

This is a very hard problem, and few people are able to come up with the solution. I will give you the answer, but first I would like to tell you a fairy tale.

Once upon a time, there was a wicked king who lived in a huge castle. Everyone who lived in the kingdom hated the wicked king, and got together an army of a hundred brave knights, who agreed to attack the castle and kill him. Although the castle was well defended, the knights knew that, if they all attacked the castle together at exactly the same time, they could break down its defences and get inside. But the knights had a problem. Although there were lots of roads leading up to the castle, they were so narrow that only twenty men could pass along each road at any one time. The leader of the knights was very clever. He divided his men up into five groups and told each to approach the castle using a different road. As soon as the leader gave the signal, all one hundred knights charged towards the castle, arriving at exactly the same time. They were easily able to break down the defences and kill the wicked king, and everybody lived happily ever after.

Right, now back to the tumour problem. Actually, wait. You've already figured it out, haven't you?

This pair of stories is sometimes used by psychologists to investigate the role of *analogies* in problem-solving. Although the doctor's dilemma and the fairy tale having nothing in common on the surface (a castle does not resemble a tumour, or a knight an anti-cancer ray), the two problems have the same underlying structure. In exactly the same way as the knights can converge on the castle with enough manpower to overcome its defences, so the separate anti-tumour rays converge with enough power to take out the cancer. It is this underlying structure, rather than surface similarity, that is useful in an analogy. If, for example, instead of the fairy story I had told you about a patient who had a similar-sized tumour on his arm, which doctors easily removed using the same ray turned up to full power, it would have been of no help whatsoever.

So, next time you face a tricky dilemma, try thinking whether there is any familiar situation that is somehow analogous (in a later section, Can Psychology Save the World?, I do exactly this for the problem of global environmental disaster). Two further sections, At My Wick's End and Under Pressure, outline some further strategies for stimulating this kind of 'out of the box' thinking.

The Health Minister

Government statisticians and epidemiologists have been hard at work, and have calculated that the disease is expected to kill 600 people. Government scientists have also been hard at work, and have managed to come up with two alternative treatment programmes, which they present to the health minister: Uh-huh – you again.

Only one of the two treatment programmes can be adopted. Which do you choose?

- If you choose **Treatment A**, 200 people will be saved.
- If you choose **Treatment B**, there is a 1/3 probability that 600 people will be saved, and a 2/3 probability that nobody will be saved.

Time to make a new choice?

- If you choose **Treatment B**, there is a 1/3 probability that nobody will die, and a 2/3 probability that 600 people will die.
- If you choose **Treatment A**, 400 people will die.

present you with the corrected options:

But hold on a minute. Wouldn't you know it? The government scientists have messed up the maths. Rather embarrassed, they this dilemma, 70 per cent of people choose Treatment A. a rather unlikely punt on saving all 600. Indeed, when placed in better to be guaranteed that 200 people will be saved than to take I bet you chose A, didn't you? I think we can all agree that it's

ANSWER

ANSWER

This time Treatment B looks like the much better option, right? We can't condemn 400 innocent people to certain death when we have a chance to save all 600.

But do you know what? The government scientists didn't mess up the maths at all. They were just messing with your head. The choice you were presented with was exactly the same each time; all that was different was the way that the two outcomes were 'framed'. (We encountered a different type of framing effect earlier, in I Just Can't Wait.)

Let's look again. The text in bold shows how, for both Treatment A and Treatment B, the first framing can be flipped to give the second, or vice versa.

Framing 1	If you choose Treatment A, 200 people will be saved (i.e., 400 people will die).	If you choose Treatment B, there is a 1/3 probability that 600 people will be saved (i.e., a 1/3 probability that nobody will die), and a 2/3 probability that nobody will be saved (i.e., a 2/3 probability that 600 people will die).

F
L
I
P

F
L
I
P

Framing 2	If you choose Treatment A, 400 people will die (i.e., 200 people will be saved).	If you choose Treatment B, there is a 1/3 probability that nobody will die (i.e., a 1/3 probability that 600 people will be saved), and a 2/3 probability that 600 people will die (i.e., a 2/3 probability that nobody will be saved).

In the first framing, both courses of action are presented as *saving* people; i.e., as a potential gain. When faced with a potential gain, we become *risk-averse*, extremely reluctant to risk losing the gain that is within our grasp. (See Can't Stand Losing You for evidence that we hate losing something more than we enjoy winning that same thing.) Consequently, we take what looks like the safe option – saving 200 people for definite – rather than the gamble.

In the second framing, both courses of action are presented as *killing* people: i.e., as a potential loss. When faced with a potential loss, we become *risk-taking*. 'Screw it,' we think, 'if 400 people are going to die *anyway* (i.e., under Treatment A), then we might as well take a punt on being the hero and saving all 600 (Treatment B).'

At least, this is the traditional story, and most books leave it there. But a number of follow-up studies (including a 1998 meta-analysis of 136 studies and 30,000 participants) have suggested that at least part of the effect is due not to risk-aversion versus risk-taking, but to the ambiguous wording of the question. In the first framing of Treatment A ('200 people will be saved'), the fact that 400 people will die is not made explicit. In one sense, this is entirely the point. But the fact that these people were not mentioned might have caused some respondents to assume that what happens to them is unclear; maybe some will survive after all. If the wording is made more explicit (e.g., 'If you choose Treatment A, it is certain that 200 people will be saved, but it is also certain that 400 people will die'), respondents are split almost exactly 50/50 between Treatment A and Treatment B.*

None of this would matter if it were all just a bit of fun. But terrifyingly, both doctors and patients show evidence of framing effects when making decisions about treatments. Fortunately, the

---

* Note that, to the extent that there is a 'right' pattern of responses, a 50/50 split is it. In the long run, a 100 per cent chance of saving 200 people (Treatment A) and a 1/3 chance of saving 600 people (Treatment B) amount to the same thing: because 100 per cent × 200 = 200 and 1/3 × 600 = 200, if you re-enacted the scenario over and over enough times, you would save almost exactly the same number of people regardless of whether you always chose A or always chose B (or even went for a mixture of both).

rewording study mentioned above provides us with a helpful way to overcome these framing effects. It sounds obvious, but next time you hear about a contraceptive that is 95 per cent effective, a treatment that is 95 per cent safe or a dessert that is 95 per cent fat-free, take a minute to explicitly spell out the flip side: there is a 5 per cent (1 in 20) chance of pregnancy or something going wrong with the treatment.

And that tempting cake is 5 per cent *pure fat*.

Red or Black?

Unfortunately, your shockingly poor performance has got you sacked from your successive jobs as radiologist (how *did* you miss that gorilla?), doctor and health minister (I'm still not quite sure how you managed to land that job).

But things are looking up, and you have got a new job – one that is not quite so well paid, but not without its glamour: inspecting roulette machines in casinos, arcades and betting shops to check that they are fair.

Your boss gives you a reminder of the basics of the game: customers place bets on whether a ball spun around the roulette wheel will come to rest in a red or a black pocket (and/or on particular numbers). Provided they are well maintained, traditional wooden roulette wheels are always completely fair. Computerised electronic roulette machines, however, are a different story: there's always the risk that some enterprising hacker could have tampered with the software . . .

This is where you come in. You have received a report of a casino where some of the electronic machines are showing suspicious behaviour. You choose four machines, have twenty 'spins' on each and note down the results. Two look fine, but two give you cause for concern. Which two machines should you investigate further?

Machine A	Machine B	Machine C	Machine D
Red	Red	Red	Red
Black	Black	Red	Black
Black	Black	Black	Red
Red	Black	Red	Red
Black	Red	Black	Red
Black	Black	Red	Red
Red	Black	Black	Red
Red	Black	Red	Black
Black	Black	Red	Black
Black	Black	Black	Black
Red	Black	Red	Black
Black	Red	Red	Red
Red	Red	Black	Red
Black	Red	Black	Black
Red	Red	Red	Black
Red	Black	Black	Black
Black	Red	Red	Black
Red	Red	Black	Red
Red	Red	Black	Red
Black	Red	Red	Black

ANSWER

Machine B and Machine D look suspicious, don't they? Machine B has a streak of six blacks in a row, and ends with a string of eight reds, split up only by a single black, right in the middle. Machine D has a streak of five reds, and two streaks of four blacks. It's almost as if the machine has been programmed to lull gamers into a false sense of security, then wham! Just when you were expecting black ... it's red!

Machine A and C look much more honest, don't they? A good, healthy mix of reds and blacks, with no suspicious streaky behaviour.

So, if you said that Machines B and D should be investigated ...

... you're completely wrong.

B and D were actually generated at random. A and C are lists that I put together by hand, to have the *appearance* of randomness.

Why do most people get this wrong? The answer is that the human brain seems to be hard-wired to look for predictable patterns: so much so that it spots them even when there are none. Genuinely random patterns *look* 'streaky'. Unless there is anything to stop it, a random sequence will generally have a couple of streaks somewhere, just by chance. After all, a roulette wheel has no memory. So the fact that black has come up on the last three spins has no bearing on the likelihood of the next spin also coming up black. The lists that *look* random, but are not, were deliberately created to avoid having more than two reds or blacks on consecutive spins. While this is what makes them *look* random, it is actually the giveaway sign that they are not: it's pretty unlikely that no streak of three or greater should appear somewhere, in a sequence of genuinely random spins.

The method that people use for guessing which machines look random is a particular type of *heuristic*. Heuristics are the mental short-cuts that we use to make judgements when we don't have all the necessary information (or when we do, but don't know how to use it). For example, if we have to guess which of two people is a librarian given only their physical appearance, we are more likely to choose the one wearing glasses. Here, we are using a *represent-ativeness* heuristic. The person with glasses is more representative of our mental picture of a librarian. The same heuristic is what leads us to the wrong answer in the roulette machine problem. A string such as Red, Black, Black, Red, Black is a better match for our mental picture of what a random pattern looks like than Red, Red, Red, Red, Red, even though it is no more likely.

The same misconception turns up all over the place. For example, basketball fans and commentators often talk about players having a 'hot hand' streak when they just can't miss. Actually, when a group of psychologists analysed the performance of several teams they found that – exactly as for the roulette wheel – apparent streaks were just a consequence of random variation in performance.

Interestingly, some people have claimed – though Apple have always denied – that the iPod/iPhone shuffle mode is not, in fact, completely random. The conspiracy-theory version of this claim (which I am by no means advocating) holds that Apple deliberately over-play popular songs in the hope that others will overhear, and subsequently purchase them. The research discussed here suggests a more interesting possibility: hypothetically a manufacturer of music players might avoid true randomness because, paradoxically, purchasers would complain – when a few songs by the same band inevitably came on one after another – that the playlist wasn't random enough.

Finally, buses. You know when you wait half an hour for a bus and then three come along at once? Knowing what you now know, you might assume that this is just another illusion, and that a 'streak' of buses is actually no more common than you'd expect by chance alone. Actually, no; buses really do come in streaks. The reason is that, when a bus gets to a really busy stop, it has to wait ages for everyone to get on, giving the bus behind it a long time to catch up. The only solution is for buses to leave the stop after a predetermined boarding period, even if people are still trying to get on. Unsurprisingly, few bus companies have ever attempted this solution, presumably fearing that it would enrage customers.

So next time you're waiting for a bus, why not pass the time by trying to spot examples of apparent 'streaks' caused by random behaviour? What about the queue itself: are there streaks of gender, hair colour, shoe type? If you look hard enough, you're sure to find at least one.

Track the Attacker

We saw in **Spot the Deference** that *forensic psychologists* study criminal behaviour, which often involves helping the police track down suspects. Let's see how you'd get on in this profession. The map below shows a number of violent attacks for which the police believe that the same person is responsible (indicated by black dots). Draw an X on the map to indicate the area in which you think the attacker lives.

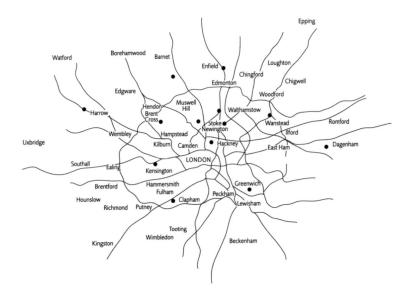

ANSWER

The attacker probably lives in the Stoke Newington area.

To figure this out, you need to know the two golden rules of offender behaviour. The first is the *circle rule*: most violent offenders live somewhere within a circle drawn to link the two crimes that are the furthest apart. To narrow this down further, we need to know the second golden rule: offenders typically do not travel very far to commit their crimes. You might think that it would make more sense for them to travel a long way from home, both to minimise the chances of being recognised and to throw a spanner in the works of these geographical profiling techniques. But by their very nature most violent criminals are impulsive and don't even think about being caught, let alone plan out their attacks in detail to minimise this possibility. To follow this second golden rule, all you need to do is put your X as close as possible to as many dots as possible, which places the suspect squarely in London's trendy Stoke Newington.

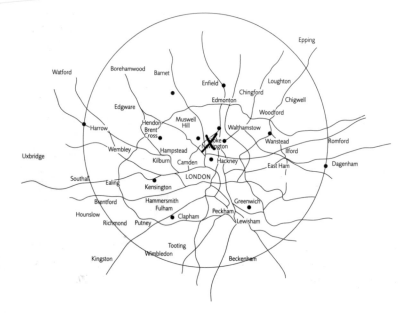

These 'golden rules' may seem obvious; perhaps you already had a hunch that he would live there or thereabouts. However, one study found that explaining these two seemingly simple rules to naïve volunteers significantly improved the accuracy of their predictions: so much so that they were as good as a formal mathematical algorithm used by many forensic psychologists.

Although it's undoubtedly useful, geographical profiling probably isn't what springs to mind when you think of a psychologist helping the police track down a killer. Admit it: you picture a detective who possesses such an instinctive understanding of the criminal mind that, given just a few seemingly insignificant facts, he can put together a picture-perfect description of the suspect. ('We're looking for a man who is thirty-three-and-a-half-years old, drives a 2007 Ford Mondeo and whose ex-wife worked for a bank, probably Barclays.') Of course, this is the kind of fiction that you only find on TV.

Or in the casebooks of the FBI. Yes, many detectives in the bureau's behavioural science unit consider themselves to be experts in using clues from the crime scene to build up a detailed profile of the killer. Malcolm Gladwell reports a famous case in which a profiler correctly described a bomber as wearing a double-breasted suit . . . buttoned. But, the odd fluke aside, most academic reviews have concluded that this is pure fiction. Although many offenders do have a consistent *modus operandi*, there is essentially no correlation between the details of the crime and the offender's background.

So, while I hope you had fun tracking the attacker, if you want to know what type of suit he prefers, sorry, but you're going to have to catch him first.

Web Link
If you would like to play amateur detective, the software package that the professionals use for geographical offender profiling – CrimeStat – can be downloaded for free from www.icpsr.umich.edu/CrimeStat.

Morality Play

I think we can all agree that serial violent attackers aren't particularly moral people. But most of our moral judgements are more subtle. Take the questionnaire below to measure your own moral values.

Below are listed eight fundamental moral principles. Your job is to decide how much you agree with each one. Please indicate your response to each question (strongly disagree, disagree, agree or strongly agree) by ticking the relevant box on the page opposite.

(a) If an action might harm an innocent person, it is never morally permissible to commit it.

(b) Rights and wrongs are not absolute but differ from situation to situation, and may be different for different people.

(c) The best way to decide whether an action is morally good or bad is to weigh up the likely positive and negative consequences.

(d) There are certain actions that are inherently immoral, whether or not anyone comes to any physical or psychological harm as a result.

(e) It is morally right to obey the laws of your country, whether or not you agree with them personally.

(f) It is immoral to carry out an action that exposes other people to small risks, even if both you and they stand to benefit greatly.

(g) It is more important, morally speaking, for society to protect individuals from harm than to be 'fair'.

(h) Lying is always immoral, no matter what the circumstances.

ANSWER SHEET

Question	Strongly disagree	Disagree	Agree	Strongly agree
a				
b				
c				
d				
e				
f				
g				
h				

To find out how to score your answers, please follow the instructions below.

If you ticked 'Agree' or 'Strongly agree' for Question (a), then please turn to page 138

If you ticked 'Disagree' or 'Strongly disagree' for Question (a), then please turn to page 150.

ANSWER

Sorry, the rest of the quiz was just a red herring. We are only interested in your response to Question (a).

Did you notice the switch?

First, you were asked whether you agreed or disagreed with the statement that 'If an action might harm an innocent person, it is **never** morally permissible to commit it.' You were then asked to justify the reasons why you agreed or disagreed with precisely the opposite statement: 'Even if an action might harm an innocent person, it is **sometimes** morally permissible to commit it.'

Perhaps you noticed the switch and assumed it was a misprint. Or perhaps you skim-read the second part and thought you were being asked to play devil's advocate and come up with possible arguments against your own position. If so, you are in the minority. In a slightly more sophisticated version of this study conducted at Lund University in Sweden, over two thirds of participants failed to notice at least one swap of this type. What is more, participants who failed to notice the swap generally offered convincing and apparently heartfelt arguments in support of a position that they had rejected just moments earlier.

Did people misunderstand the task, or notice the switch but decide to play along? It doesn't seem so. Even after the experimenters came clean about the deception, and asked participants whether or not, in retrospect, they had noticed anything odd about the study, the majority of participants confessed that they had not. (If anything, the figure quoted above is an underestimate, as it does not include participants who were 'wise after the event', despite having argued quite happily against their own previously stated position without so much as a word of complaint.)

As the authors point out, this study raises an interesting philosophical conundrum. For participants who did not notice the switch, which view is their 'real' one? It is tempting to say that it is the one that they ticked initially, before all of this experimental monkeying around. The problem here is that, since these participants generally ended up arguing so eloquently *against* this position, it would take quite some argumentation to convince them of the correctness of their own 'real' view. But in what sense is a person's view his 'real' view if we have to convince him of it in the face of his own counter-arguments? Neither does it seem very satisfactory to say that participants' 'real' view is the one for which they argued at the end of the study. This would mean either: (a) that when someone ticks a 'strongly agree' box, he actually means 'strongly disagree' and vice versa; or (b) that it is possible to genuinely alter someone's opinion on a topic of fundamental importance using nothing more than a cheap conjuring trick.

One way out of this paradox is to assume that people generally make moral judgements on the basis of intuition or emotional 'gut feelings', and any so-called logical arguments or reasons they might give after the fact are nothing more than self-justifying hot air (we saw in St Valentine's Day: Massacred? that there is often a disconnect between our inner and publicly stated beliefs). For example, most people strongly feel that it is morally wrong for a brother and sister to have sexual intercourse, but actually find it rather difficult to come up with any logical arguments to support this position (assuming – say – that both are infertile and that nobody else will ever find out). The problem with this suggestion is that, as the authors ask, if we really do have a moral 'spidey sense' of this type, wouldn't it have started tingling when the switch occurred?

A second way out of the paradox is to focus on our argumentative nature: we humans just *love* to argue. How often have you found yourself arguing with a family member over some trivial issue such as where to go on holiday, only to stop in your tracks and realise that you are both arguing just to win the argument, and could just as easily – in some parallel universe – be having exactly the same argument with the positions reversed. The same thing could be happening in this study. When given 'their' position and told to argue for it, people don't need asking twice. This is no doubt some of the story, but it still doesn't seem quite enough to explain why people failed to notice the switch.

This brings us to the third, and perhaps most satisfactory, possible escape from the paradox. With the exception of lawyers (and perhaps scientists), we humans are simply not used to dealing in absolutes, moral or otherwise. When we use words like 'never', we normally mean something more like 'to the minimum degree possible, extremely rarely, or only in very unusual circumstances', rather than 'in no circumstance that is hypothetically conceivable'. For example, I feel quite comfortable in saying that I never eat mushrooms (ugh, so slimy), even though the odd one probably slips in unidentified, and I would certainly eat a plateful at gunpoint. So it is perhaps not such a contradiction for someone to hold the view that it is 'never' morally permissible (in the first sense) to harm an innocent child, but that it would be right to do so in a far-fetched scenario where it would save a far greater number of children. Perhaps the tick-box questionnaire taps into more everyday uses of absolutes like 'never' and 'morally right', while the discursive nature of the second part of the study encourages participants to think of more unusual circumstances that could overrule what we normally think of as moral absolutes.

If there is a lesson here, it is probably that it does not pay to be too dogmatic with regard to questions of morality. No matter how strongly held or (to you) logically coherent your viewpoint, there are probably some equally good arguments for precisely the opposite position – arguments that, given different circumstances, you might end up making yourself.

The Arts Critic

Below, you will see a number of creative works. Your task is to rate each for creativity, using a 7-point scale (1 = not creative; 7 = very creative).

Paintings

Anna Scott

Leah Edevane

David Jones

Elliot Le Feuvre

Haikus

Each is made of dust
The brown Allegheny roars
Wide, flat, dusty road
AIRA CADY

Ghosts of factories
A woman in the branches
Blue feathers, hidden
JANE CLARKE

Instrumental Music

(listen at www.Psy-Qbook.com – click on 'Psy-Q Companion Site')

Piece 1 (© Emma Moore)
Piece 2 (© Jonah Dissanayake)

ANSWERS

If you are like most people, you probably gave the highest ratings to the painting by Leah Edevane, the poem by Aira Cady and the music by Jonah Dissanayake.

How did I know? The answer is that, when evaluating art, we find it almost impossible to separate the art and the artist, and equally difficult to set aside our preconceptions regarding the types of people that are generally regarded as creative. Specifically, we find it hard to shake the stereotypes regarding (a) gender and (b) unusual versus common names.

With regard to music, the common stereotype runs that men are more creative than women, and that people with unusual names are more creative than those with common names, both of which point to the composition of 'Jonah Dissanayake' being rated as more creative than that of 'Emma Moore'. If you haven't guessed by now, the names are fictitious; both pieces were by the same 'composers' (namely, me and my mates). In a study where different people saw different names attached to *the same* piece of music, the piece scored 6/7 for creativity when attributed to a composer with a rare male name, but only 4/7 when attributed to a composer with a common female name.

For poetry, the gender stereotype disappears, but the unusual-name stereotype remains, which is why I predicted that you would prefer the haiku by 'Aira Cady' to the one by 'Jane Clarke'. In fact, both poems were exactly equally creative, having been written by a random online haiku generator.*

With paintings, gender and name seem to interact in a bizarre way that nobody quite understands. Female painters with rarer

---

* Call it a *mere exposure* effect (see It's All Chinese to Me), but, having read through these poems countless times, I actually quite like them. The first seems as though it might be about how everything in the universe (from the natural river to the man-made road) is made from the same atoms and molecules ('each is made of dust'), while the second might be about the decline of clothing factories that used to provide employment for many women, particularly in the north of England.

names (e.g., Leah Edevane) are deemed more creative than those with more common names (e.g., Anna Scott). For men, the pattern is reversed: male painters with common names (e.g., David Jones) are deemed *more* creative than those with rarer names (e.g., Elliot Le Feuvre). The researchers who conducted the study describe this finding as completely unexpected and offer no explanation. But is it just possible that the current vogue for proudly working-class male artists (e.g., the sculptor Damien Hirst, the film director Danny Boyle and the designer Paul Smith) is in the process of turning our prejudices on their head?

Web Links
The haikus were randomly generated using http://poetry.namegenerator fun.com/

Why not try making your own?

Card Trick 1

Look at the four cards below. We know for a fact that each card has a letter on one side and a number on the other.

Truthful Terry says: 'Every card that has a D on one side has a 3 on the other.'

What is the fewest number of cards that you need to turn over to find out whether Truthful Terry is actually telling the truth? And which ones?

ANSWER

D and 7. Very few people get this right. You probably said D and 3, didn't you? Let's go through each card in turn to figure out why D and 7 is the right answer. Remember, the statement that we are testing is: 'Every card that has a D on one side has a 3 on the other.'

D: Obviously we need to turn this card over to check that there is a 3 on the other side (everybody gets this one right).

K: Equally obviously, there's no need to turn this over. Given that the letter on this card is not D, it makes no difference whether the number on the back is 1, 3 or 333 (again, everybody gets this one right).

3: This is a tricky one. Most people think that you need to turn this card over to see whether there is a D on the other side. This would be necessary had Terry claimed that 'Every card that has a D on one side has a 3 on the other, **and vice versa**'. But Terry did not say 'and vice versa'. So suppose we do turn this card over and the letter on the back is Z. Terry said nothing about whether or not a card that has Z on one side has 3 on the other, so this card is consistent with his claim. Now suppose we turn this card over and the letter on the back *is* D. Again, the card is consistent with his claim. These two examples show that *whatever* letter is on the back of this card, it is consistent with Terry's claim; so there is no need to turn it over.

7: This is the other tricky one. It doesn't occur to most people that we need to turn this card over to check that the letter on the back is *not* D. If it *is* D, then Terry's claim that 'Every card that has a D on one side has a 3 on the other' is patently false: this card has D on one side but 7 (not 3) on the other.

Why is this card trick so difficult? There are two answers.

The first answer is that we show what is called a *confirmation bias*. Most people, being fairly charitable sorts, want to turn over the 3, find a D on the back and say, 'Well done, Terry!' (i.e., to confirm that he is right). Ironically, the only way to check the truth of Terry's statement is to try to *disconfirm* it: i.e., to try to find evidence that he is wrong (in the form of a D on the other side of the

7 card). It is only by showing that Terry's claim stands up against all the possible counter-examples we can throw at it that we can find out that he is right.

Confirmation bias isn't just seen in these artificial exercises; there are examples of it absolutely everywhere in our daily lives (we also came across one earlier in Liar, Liar). Why, for example, do many people believe in homeopathic remedies, which countless studies have shown to be ineffective? At least part of the answer is confirmation bias. People who believe that homeopathy works actively seek out opportunities to confirm that belief (e.g., people who have recovered after taking homeopathic remedies) and ignore evidence that might disconfirm it (e.g., comprehensive reviews of placebo-controlled studies).

So that's one reason why this card trick is difficult to solve. To find the second reason, we need to try a slightly different version . . . (please turn to p.139)

Web Link
The author and film-maker Jon Ronson has a particularly interesting and entertaining example of confirmation bias which you can listen to at: http://jonronson.com/Jon_Ronson_Confirmation_Bias.mp3

Morality Play: Agree/Strongly agree (continued from p.126)

You agreed (or strongly agreed) with the statement that 'Even if an action might harm an innocent person, it is sometimes morally permissible to commit it'.

In the space below, you should list up to five example situations where it is sometimes morally permissible to commit an action that might harm an innocent person.

1. ....
....

2. ....
....

3. ....
....

4. ....
....

5. ....
....

Now please turn to page 128 to find out what the rest of your answers say about you.

Card Trick 2
(continued from p.137)

This time the four cards represent four people in a bar. Each has the person's age on one side and what they are drinking on the other. You are working as the barman (a step down from health minister, admittedly, but probably a step up from roulette-machine checker).

Suddenly the manager comes in, looking worried. He's had a tip-off that the police are about to pay a visit, and wants you to double-check that everyone who is drinking alcohol is over eighteen. Of course, you don't want to bother more customers than is absolutely necessary. So how few people can you get away with checking? And which ones?

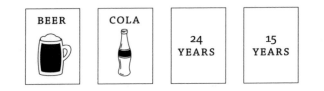

ANSWER

This time, the answer is completely obvious. We need to 'turn over' the beer drinker to check that he is at least eighteen and the fifteen-year-old to check that she is not drinking anything alcoholic. But this puzzle has exactly the same format as the last; the only difference is that I have swapped letters and numbers for drinks and ages. Why is this one so easy while the last one was so difficult?

One reason is that this re-framing of the question avoids the problem of confirmation bias. Where the claim is a rule which we *know* that people sometimes try to break ('You must be over eighteen to drink alcohol'), we know that to check it, we need to try to disconfirm it by looking at any potential rule-breakers: i.e., the fifteen-year-old. It would not occur to us to 'check' that the twenty-four-year-old *is* drinking alcohol, even though most people do the exact equivalent in the original version of the puzzle.

In the previous section I promised to outline a second reason why the original puzzle is hard. The comparison between the two versions should give you a clue. Can you guess? . . .

Think about the difference between the two versions of the puzzle. The second version is easy, because we can use a mental short-cut or heuristic (see Red or Black) that we've built up from our experience of bars and drinking ('Check that anyone who's drinking alcohol is over eighteen'). In contrast, the first version of the puzzle is hard because we don't have any short-cut to hand. The only way to solve the puzzle is to think it through logically.

But when we try to do so, most of us fall flat on our faces. So this task tells us something quite profound about human reasoning: although we like to think of ourselves as logical thinkers, when it comes down to it, most of us are actually incapable of even basic logical reasoning and get through life relying on short-cuts and hunches. We've already met a few examples of how these short-cuts, hunches and reasoning failures can lead us to incorrect conclusions (Anchors Away, Carrot or Stick?, The Patient, The Health Minister, Red or Black?), and there are yet more to come.

'All I Have To Do Is Dream'

So sang the Everly Brothers, and – later – Roy Orbison and Kermit the Frog. And if they had been talking about learning (they weren't), they would have been right.

That's right. You learn in your sleep.

To see this for yourself, try this simple exercise, ideally just before you go to bed. Place the four fingers of your non-dominant hand (your left hand if you are right-handed, and vice versa) on the D, F, G and H keys of the computer keyboard printed below.

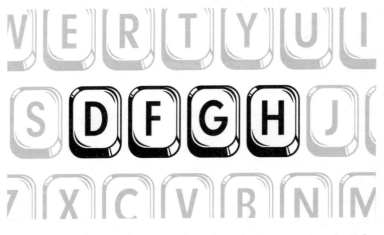

Moving only your fingers and, without lifting your hand off the page, tap out the sequence H D G F H as many times as possible in thirty seconds. Ask a friend to time you, and to count the number of accurate sequences. Alternatively, if you have a real computer keyboard (or tablet or phone) to hand, tap out the sequence on that, using a word processor or note-taking application to record what you type; then count up the number of accurate sequences afterwards.

Now go to bed.

In the morning, do the exercise again. What do you notice?

ANSWER

That's right – you have magically improved at the tapping task.

Participants who completed this experiment under controlled conditions (at 10 p.m. at night and 10 a.m. the following morning) showed a 20 per cent boost in speed, with no loss of accuracy. We know that the crucial thing was the sleep, not simply the twelve-hour gap, as participants who completed the task at 10 a.m. and then 10 p.m. did not show the improvement.

How is it that you are able to learn during your sleep? The brain stores information – whether memories, facts or, as in this case, patterns of muscle movement – by modifying the strength of connections between neurons. When two neurons fire at the same time, the strength of the connection between them increases. So, learning the tapping sequence while awake involves strengthening particular connections. What seems to be going on when you are asleep is that the brain replays patterns of neuron-firing that have occurred during the day. This means that, while asleep, you are – as far as the relevant cells are concerned – practising the task,* just as surely as if you were awake and actually doing it.

This leads to an interesting prediction. If you consciously replay the tapping pattern in your head (i.e., just think about it, rather than actually doing it), then – just like when the brain replays the tapping pattern in your sleep – this should boost performance. A number of studies have shown that this is true, not only for tapping sequences, but also for other motor tasks such as drawing complex figures.

So if you are a musician whose opportunities for practice are

---

* This also works for learning facts. A 2013 review of revision techniques found that one of the most effective was spreading material over several days, rather than cramming, presumably because this allows the brain to continue revising while you are asleep. (Incidentally, the student favourites of highlighting, under-lining and re-reading were among the least useful revision techniques, presumably because they encourage only shallow engagement with the material.)

limited by noise-sensitive neighbours, don't worry: you can actually practice quite effectively just by thinking through the finger movements needed to play the song.

Now, where did I put my air guitar?

The Interpretation of Dreams

... is the title of Sigmund Freud's landmark 1899 book on dream analysis. On the left below are some of the dreams discussed by Freud; on the right are the interpretations that he gave. Your job is to match each dream to its interpretation. I should warn you that this is not the feelgood pap of most modern-day dream dictionaries ('rainbows represent hope and success'): Freud's main preoccupations are sex and death. Readers of a sensitive disposition should look away now.

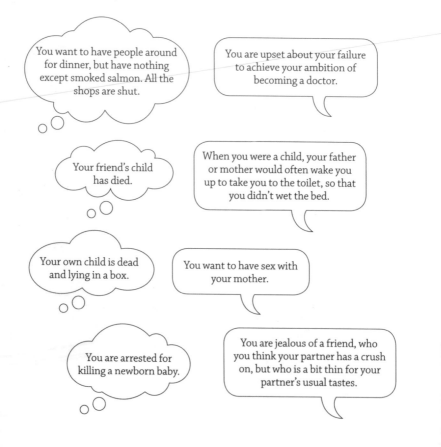

You want to have people around for dinner, but have nothing except smoked salmon. All the shops are shut.

You are upset about your failure to achieve your ambition of becoming a doctor.

Your friend's child has died.

When you were a child, your father or mother would often wake you up to take you to the toilet, so that you didn't wet the bed.

Your own child is dead and lying in a box.

You want to have sex with your mother.

You are arrested for killing a newborn baby.

You are jealous of a friend, who you think your partner has a crush on, but who is a bit thin for your partner's usual tastes.

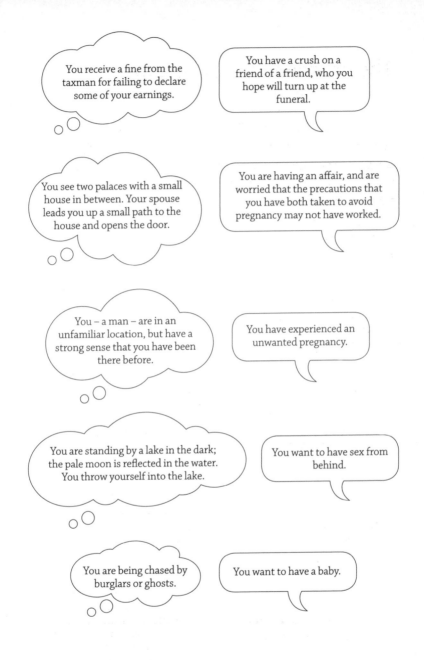

ANSWERS

Freud's interpretations are shown below. Most are fairly self-explanatory, though notes are given for interpretations that require an understanding of Freudian symbolism.

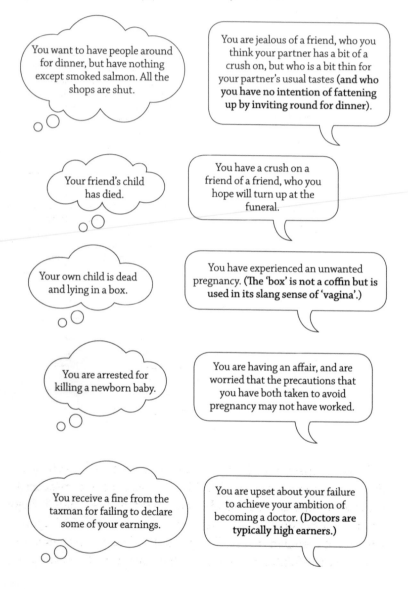

You want to have people around for dinner, but have nothing except smoked salmon. All the shops are shut.

You are jealous of a friend, who you think your partner has a bit of a crush on, but who is a bit thin for your partner's usual tastes (**and who you have no intention of fattening up by inviting round for dinner**).

Your friend's child has died.

You have a crush on a friend of a friend, who you hope will turn up at the funeral.

Your own child is dead and lying in a box.

You have experienced an unwanted pregnancy. (**The 'box' is not a coffin but is used in its slang sense of 'vagina'.**)

You are arrested for killing a newborn baby.

You are having an affair, and are worried that the precautions that you have both taken to avoid pregnancy may not have worked.

You receive a fine from the taxman for failing to declare some of your earnings.

You are upset about your failure to achieve your ambition of becoming a doctor. (**Doctors are typically high earners.**)

You see two palaces with a small house in between. Your spouse leads you up a small path to the house and opens the door.

You want to have sex from behind. (**The symbolism here is fairly obvious.**)

You – a man – are in an unfamiliar location, but have a strong sense that you have been there before.

You want to have sex with your mother. (**Freud's famous 'Oedipus complex'; the familiar location is your mother's vagina.**)

You are standing by a lake in the dark; the pale moon is reflected in the water. You throw yourself into the lake.

You want to have a baby. (**Throwing oneself into the water represents coming out of the water – i.e., being born. The moon represents the mother's bottom.**)

You are being chased by burglars or ghosts.

When you were a child, your father (**burglar**) or mother (**ghost in her white nightgown**) would often wake you up to take you to the toilet, so that you didn't wet the bed.

What do these interpretations have in common? According to Freud, all dreams involve wish-fulfilment. Most people are at least somewhat familiar with this idea, and so feel a little guilty if they dream – for example – that a friend or relative has died. An important part of Freudian theory, though, is that dreams often involve *disguised* wish-fulfilment. So it's not that you want – for example –

your friend's child to die; what you actually want is the person who you hope will turn up at the funeral. Furthermore, dreams often represent not current wishes, but wishes from childhood. Many of these wishes – such as the desire for sex with one's mother – have been *repressed*: eliminated from conscious thought and held in the unconscious.

In Freudian psychoanalysis, the therapist offers patients interpretations of their dreams, fantasies and free associations (e.g., see The Raw Shark Test). The aim is that this will allow the patient to achieve *insight* into his own problems, and therefore arrive at possible solutions. Of course, there is no way for anyone to know whether or not the interpretations offered by the therapist are accurate or insightful – least of all the patient, who is expected not only to have repressed his most important thoughts and desires, but also to actively put up defence mechanisms.

But this is exactly the problem with Freud's approach. Its emphasis on subjective interpretations that are impossible to either confirm or refute makes it untestable; and any scientific theory is useless unless it is testable. For example, the theory that 'smoking causes cancer' is testable. We can test it by investigating one of the predictions that follow from this claim: e.g., that, when holding other factors constant, smokers have higher rates of cancer than non-smokers. The theory that dreams represent the disguised fulfilment of often repressed wishes cannot be tested in this way. To see why, consider the theory that dreaming about a familiar location reflects a repressed childhood desire to have sex with one's mother. We can't test this claim simply by asking people who experience this dream if they have this repressed desire: the desire is repressed, so they wouldn't know.*

Consequently, Freud's theory is – to borrow a quotation from the physicist Wolfgang Pauli – 'not even wrong'. The theory that the sun goes around the earth, while wildly incorrect, at least has the virtue of being a testable theory. Being wrong is not something

---

* This reminds me of the way that airline passengers are forced to claim to 'know' that nobody could have put anything in their bags without their knowledge.

that Freud's theory could even aspire to, as this would require it to make a prediction that could be tested.

Web Link and Further Reading

While writing this section I came across this, the only known recording of Freud's voice: http://www.youtube.com/watch?v=5jJ6Lhk1pNg. I don't speak German, and so didn't understand a word (actually, no, I did hear him say *Psychology*), but found him surprisingly softly spoken, even timid-sounding.

Freud's books are now out of copyright, and so are available free – or very cheap – in ebook editions. A good place to start is Freud's *Dream Psychology: Psychoanalysis for Beginners*.

Morality Play: Disagree/Strongly disagree (continued from p.126)

You disagreed (or strongly disagreed) with the statement that 'Even if an action might harm an innocent person, it is sometimes morally permissible to commit it.'

In the space below, you should list up to five reasons why it is never morally permissible to commit an action that might harm an innocent person.

1. ....

....

2. ....

....

3. ....

....

4. ....

....

5. ....

....

Now please turn to page 128 to find out what your answers say about you.

The March of Time: Part 1

In *A New Refutation of Time* the Argentinian essayist Jorge Luis Borges characterises time as a river, a tiger and an all-consuming fire, all in the space of a single sentence. Perhaps because it is such an abstract concept, when talking about time, we cannot help but use metaphors: time is an ocean, a thief, a miser, a prison, a teacher, a healer; time is money. But could the metaphors we use to *talk* about time be so powerful as to shape the way that we *think* about time?

To find out, use a stopwatch to time yourself completing the series of three-part 'true or false' questions that begin on the next page. An example is shown below.

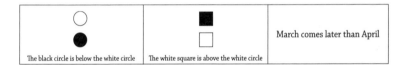

| The black circle is below the white circle | The white square is above the white circle | March comes later than April |

For this example, the answers are, from left to right: True, False, False.

For the date questions, we are talking about months *within a given calendar year*. So, although you might normally think of January as coming after December (i.e., New Year's Day is just after Christmas), for the purposes of these questions January comes *earlier* than December, not later (i.e., January 2015 comes before December 2015).

These questions are obviously very easy, and most people get all of them right. (I won't be telling you the answers at the end!) The important factor is *speed*; move through the questions as quickly as possible, shouting out your answers as you go. If you do make the odd mistake, don't stop to correct yourself; just carry on.

The March of Time: Part 2

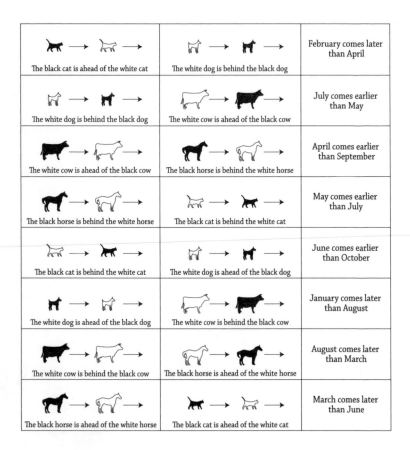

The black cat is ahead of the white cat	The white dog is behind the black dog	February comes later than April
The white dog is behind the black dog	The white cow is ahead of the black cow	July comes earlier than May
The white cow is ahead of the black cow	The black horse is behind the white horse	April comes earlier than September
The black horse is behind the white horse	The black cat is behind the white cat	May comes earlier than July
The black cat is behind the white cat	The white dog is ahead of the black dog	June comes earlier than October
The white dog is ahead of the black dog	The white cow is behind the black cow	January comes later than August
The white cow is behind the black cow	The black horse is ahead of the white horse	August comes later than March
The black horse is ahead of the white horse	The black cat is ahead of the white cat	March comes later than June

STOP THE STOPWATCH!

Now take a short break before timing yourself on the next batch of eight questions.

The March of Time: Part 3

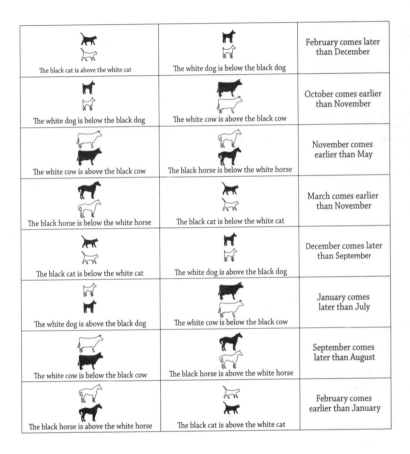

The black cat is above the white cat	The white dog is below the black dog	February comes later than December
The white dog is below the black dog	The white cow is above the black cow	October comes earlier than November
The white cow is above the black cow	The black horse is below the white horse	November comes earlier than May
The black horse is below the white horse	The black cat is below the white cat	March comes earlier than November
The black cat is below the white cat	The white dog is above the black dog	December comes later than September
The white dog is above the black dog	The white cow is below the black cow	January comes later than July
The white cow is below the black cow	The black horse is above the white horse	September comes later than August
The black horse is above the white horse	The black cat is above the white cat	February comes earlier than January

STOP THE STOPWATCH!

Note down your times. Were you quicker for the first batch or the second?

Most people are quicker for the first batch. Or, at least, this was the finding of a more sophisticated computer-based version of this study conducted at Stanford University.

But can you guess why?

ANSWER

The key difference is that the picture questions in the first batch used horizontal spatial relationship terms (*ahead of* and *behind*), while those in the second batch used vertical terms (*above* and *below*).

But why does thinking about horizontal – rather than vertical – spatial relationships help us when we're figuring out the order of months in the year? The answer is that many of the metaphors that English uses for talking about time are based on horizontal spatial relationships. For example, we talk about events in the future as being *ahead of* us and those in the past as being *behind* us. Indeed, terms such as *ahead of* and *behind* are so ingrained in our way of talking and thinking about time that we rarely think of them as metaphors at all. But metaphors they are, nonetheless. Last week is not literally 'behind' us in the sense that, for example, a child might hide behind the sofa, or a commuter behind his newspaper. The metaphor that we march through time 'looking forward' to future events, sometimes 'looking back' on past events, is exactly that: a metaphor.

If the idea that we travel horizontally through time – with the past behind us and the future ahead – is really just a metaphor, as opposed to some literal truth about the space–time continuum, there ought to be other languages that talk about time differently. Could there be a language that uses a vertical metaphor: where, for example, past events are 'up' and future events 'down'? The answer is yes. One such language is Mandarin Chinese. Does this mean that if we asked native Mandarin-speakers to complete the same test that you have completed, they would do better on the second batch (with the vertical picture questions) than the first (horizontal)? Again, the answer is yes. The Stanford study found that – even though the entire study was conducted in English – Mandarin-speakers did better at the time-based questions after the vertical than the horizontal picture questions, presumably because they are used to thinking about time vertically rather than horizontally. In other words, even though they were answering questions in English, the Mandarin-speakers were 'thinking in Mandarin'.

In order to understand what these studies tell us, I would like to take you back (or – if you are a Mandarin-speaker – up) to 1984, or at least to George Orwell's famous novel of the same name. In this fictional dystopia, the authoritarian government has created a new language, 'Newspeak', and erased words such as 'democracy' and 'liberty' from the dictionary. 'The purpose of Newspeak,' writes Orwell, 'was not only to provide a medium of expression for the world-view and mental habits proper to the devotees of Ingsoc [English Socialism, the political creed of the government], *but to make all other modes of thought impossible*' [emphasis added].

Orwell here is adopting a radical position of *linguistic determinism*: that one's language has such a powerful influence over one's way of thinking that if a language has no word for a particular concept (e.g., democracy), then it is literally impossible to conceive of it. While something like this view was taken seriously by a few psychologists in the 1950s, it was quickly undermined by studies which showed that speakers of languages with only two colour terms ('light' and 'dark') – such as the Dani languages spoken in the highlands of New Guinea – can nevertheless distinguish between different colours for which they had no names (e.g., between blue and red, or green and yellow). These studies (see the bonus online section **The Reddest Red** at www.Psy-QBook.com) demonstrated that it *is* possible to conceive of an idea that one's language has no word for (e.g., 'greenness'). Even for non-colour concepts such as 'cat', 'triangle' or, indeed, 'democracy', a moment's thought reveals that the concept must have come first and picked up a name later. The alternative – that the words *cat, triangle* and *democracy* already existed, and then hung around waiting for a meaning – is clearly absurd.

These days, nobody – at least, no psychologist or linguist – believes that language *determines* thought. The Stanford study of which you completed a cut-down version was designed to investigate a much more modest possibility: that language *shapes* thought. This claim seems to be supported by the study. These days, most psychologists and linguists think that language shapes thought in exactly the opposite way to that which Orwell proposed. A particular language does not *prevent* you from thinking about something that you might like to think about (like democracy). Rather, a particular language sometimes *forces* you to think about things that you might otherwise have ignored (or might prefer not to specify).

For example, speakers of Guugu Yimithirr, a language spoken by a remote Aboriginal tribe in Australia, do not use terms like *in front of* and *behind* or even *left* and *right*. Rather, all positions are described in absolute geographical terms. So, a Guugu Yimithirr speaker might warn you about someone behind you by saying 'There's someone to the east/west/north/south of you', or even ask you to raise your 'south' hand. Thus Guugu Yimithirr shapes its speakers' thoughts by forcing them to think about something – the speaker's and listener's positions in absolute geographical space – that would rarely occur to most English-speakers.

Closer to home, while an English-speaker could say, 'I'm meeting a friend later', giving no clue as to the gender of that friend, a French speaker has no such luxury. He must say that he is meeting either *un ami* (male) or *une amie* (female). So French shapes its speakers' thoughts by forcing them to consider questions that need never occur to an English speaker ('Should I lie and say *un ami*, when it is really a female friend?').

But these effects should not be exaggerated; we are mostly talking about tendencies rather than absolutes. For example, although vertical and horizontal time metaphors predominate in Mandarin and English respectively, each language does use a few of the non-preferred type, particularly in certain specific contexts.

Speaking of which, another test of your Psy-Q is coming right *up*.

It Feels So Right

Of all the tests in this book, this is the simplest, consisting of three straightforward questions. So what are you waiting for? . . .

1. A notebook and pencil cost £1.10 in total. The notebook costs £1.00 more than the pencil. How much does the pencil cost?

2. If it takes 5 machines 5 minutes to make 5 hammers, how long does it take 100 machines to make 100 hammers?

3. A forest is being ravaged by a tree-killing disease. Every day the area of dead trees doubles. If it takes 30 days for the disease to kill off the entire forest, how long does it take the disease to kill off half of the forest?

ANSWER

All three questions have an obvious answer: (a) 10 pence; (b) 100 minutes; (c) 15 days.

But, as the saying goes, fools rush in where angels fear to tread. The obvious answers are all wrong. The correct answers are:

(a) 5p (the notebook costs £1.05)
(b) 5 minutes (i.e., the time it takes for X machines to make X hammers)
(c) 29 days (on the 30th day the area of dead trees doubles from covering half of the forest to covering the whole forest).

Each of these answers is pretty obvious when you stop to think about it; but that's just it. Many people don't stop to think about it, given that there is an 'obvious' – though wrong – answer.

The test was a measure of your *cognitive style* (or *thinking style*). People who just can't help but give the answer that 'feels right' have an *intuitive* cognitive style; they are impulsive and let their hearts rule their heads. People who spot the trap have an *analytic* cognitive style; they stop and think before figuring out the solution.

Now, far be it from me to say that one cognitive style is better than another. But people who have an analytic style are:

- less likely to cheat on tests
- more intelligent, and more likely to attend a prestigious university
- more patient (see I Just Can't Wait), which – as we will see later – is itself a predictor of resistance to addiction, gambling and obesity (see Cake Addicts)
- less susceptible to framing effects (see The Health Minister) and sunk-cost effects, which we will meet in a future section (I won't spoil the surprise).
- less likely to be religious
- more likely to be male

Yes, men outperform women on this test (with an average of around 1.5 and 1.0 correct responses respectively), even when controlling for scores on a standardised test of mathematical ability. Indeed, mathematical ability doesn't have that much to do with it, as the calculations are fairly easy. What is difficult is spotting the trap in the first place. While men give a variety of wrong answers, women are more likely to give the intuitive-but-wrong answer (tests of 'pure IQ' find no such differences). Of course, nobody is saying that these differences are genetic. Perhaps society discourages women from thinking analytically as opposed to intuitively, and perhaps intuitive reasoning is actually more useful than analytic reasoning in most everyday scenarios.

A surprising outcome, though, is that the notion of 'female intuition' – which you may have been tempted to dismiss as pop-psychology pap – does seem to contain a kernel of truth. Whether or not it is a good thing, women really are more intuitive thinkers than men.

This leads to a question . . .

Men Are from Mars, Women Are from Venus

When it comes to their psychology, you've probably heard it said that 'Men are from Mars, Women are from Venus'. But are they *really* that different? What's your guess?

On the vast majority of psychological traits, men and women are not dramatically different. When gender differences *are* observed, they are generally tiny, and hugely exaggerated so as to make for a more interesting story. Even when men and women have significantly different *average* scores on a particular measure or test, this often hides a huge overlap between the two groups: between-gender differences are dwarfed by individual within-gender differences.

To see what this means, let's take a measure on which men and women really do differ dramatically: how far they can throw a ball.

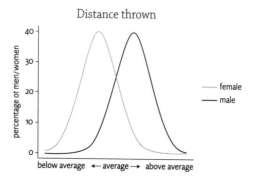

The curves for both men and women follow what is called a *normal distribution* or *bell curve*. Most men can throw a ball averagely far, a few can throw it *really* far, and a few can throw it only a tiny distance; and the same is true for women. For ball-throwing, the averages (represented by the peaks) are quite far apart, and the overlap between the two curves is relatively small. In fact, not only does the average man throw quite a bit further than the *average* women; he also throws further than 98 per cent of *all* women.

Now let's plot some psychology-related gender differences on the same scale.

Every psychologist will tell you that men are better at spatial perception than women.* And it's true. But how much better?

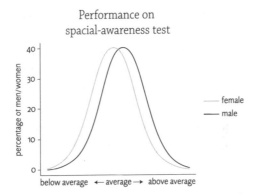

Performance on spacial-awareness test

Well, a bit, but not much. In fact 33 per cent of women have better spatial perception than the average man.

What's more, the reason I chose this example is that spatial perception is perhaps the psychological measure on which men show the *biggest* gender advantage. Let's look at a more typically sized male advantage: mathematical problem-solving.

---

* A related finding is that women's ability on spatial-perception tasks improves when they are menstruating. This finding is interesting because it demonstrates that the (albeit tiny) gender differences observed in spatial-perception tasks are directly related to differing levels of the male and female sex hormones (particularly testosterone and estradiol).

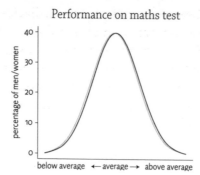

Performance on maths test

below average ← average → above average

Yes, men do better,* but by such an infinitesimally small amount that 47 per cent of women do better than the average man. (Of course, if this number were 50 per cent, men and women would be showing exactly equal performance.)

Now let's look at something where women outperform men: language (in this case, a standardised test that involves detecting grammatical errors – part of something called the *Differential Aptitude Test*). This is like the spatial-perception difference in reverse. On average, women are better than men, but 33 per cent of men are better than the average woman:

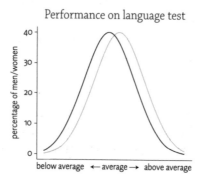

Performance on language test

below average ← average → above average

---

* Even this small difference may be due not to inherent genetic differences but to a self-fulfilling-prophecy effect: girls do worse in maths tests because they expect to do worse in maths tests. When told they are taking a special 'gender-fair' maths test (of course, no such thing actually exists), girls perform just as well as boys.

But, again, the reason I chose this test is that it shows one of the biggest female advantages ever observed in psychology. A more typically sized female advantage is for self-rated happiness. This is like the maths difference in reverse: women report higher average happiness levels, but 47 per cent of men report levels higher than the average woman (again a figure of 50 per cent would represent total gender equality):

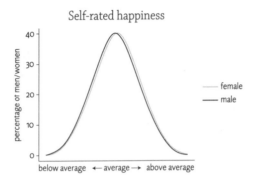

These are not isolated examples. A recent review of 124 gender differences found that 30 per cent were of the *maths/happiness* size, 15 per cent were of the *spatial perception/language* size and 48 per cent were somewhere in between.* Just 8 per cent were bigger, but even the biggest psychological gender difference of all (attitudes towards masturbation and casual sex) was less than *half* the size of the difference in throwing ability.

So all of the following 'genderalisations' (all staples of the 'Men are from Mars, Women are from Venus' gurus) are true. But, in each case, the difference is *much smaller* than the by no means huge *maths/happiness* differences illustrated above:

---

* The researchers behind the test discussed in It Feels So Right did not report their findings in a format that allows the equivalent calculations to be performed. The average scores suggest a relatively large difference, but certainly one much smaller than differences in throwing ability.

- **Men are** ... more likely to put success down to their own efforts ... more likely to interrupt in conversations ... more prone to verbal aggression ... more competitive and more successful in negotiations ... more aroused by pornography ... more assertive ... and more confident at using computers. They also have higher self-esteem and are more confident about their bodies.
- **Women are** ... more likely to put both success and failure down to luck ... better at spelling ... more talkative ... happier to divulge personal information to strangers ... more prone to anxiety, neuroticism and ruminating on their problems ... more gregarious ... more conscientious ... better at processing facial expressions (see the bonus online section The Eyes Have It) ... and better at delaying gratification (see I Just Can't Wait). They also smile more than men, particularly if they are aware of being observed.

But before you start quibbling that this means that men and women really are from different psychological planets, let me stress again that these are tiny, tiny differences: pretty much all psychological gender differences are small enough to be essentially irrelevant in the face of the massive within-gender variation between individual men and individual women.

In summary, if men are from Mars, then women are from Snickers, one might be slightly nuttier than the other, but underneath they're basically the same.

Focus on Your Knitting

So we now know that, contrary to popular belief, men and women show almost identical performance on most measures of brainpower. But what about multitasking? As a recent TV advert put it, 'If there's one thing a woman does well, it's many things', right?

We'll find out soon.

First, let's measure your own multitasking ability. You'll need a friend to help you.

The test is made up of five blocks. Each block contains somewhere between three and seven true-or-false maths problems. Your friend will read the problem to you, and you should answer 'true' or 'false', out loud, as quickly as possible. Your friend will then give you a letter to remember. After you have solved all the problems in the block, you should try to remember all of the letters in the correct order.

Here's a practice:

Practice Block

Friend reads	You answer	Friend reads
$2 \times 3 \times 1 = 6$	**True**	G
$4 - 1 - 2 = 0$	**False**	P
$1 + 4 + 7 = 11$	**False**	D
Now tell me the letters in order. (Friend fills in response here.)	*G, P, D.*	

Now turn over to begin the test.

Focus on Your Knitting: Test

Block A

Friend reads	You answer	Friend reads
17 + 2 + 8 = 28	True/False	T
7 × 2 × 2 = 28	True/False	N
3 × 11 × 0 = 33	True/False	P
29 − 8 − 7 = 17	True/False	H
Now tell me the letters in order.(Friend fills in response here.)		

Block B

Friend reads	You answer	Friend reads
7 × 6 × 2 = 84	True/False	S
2 + 1 + 7 = 11	True/False	N
54 + 4 + 14 = 72	True/False	K
5 − 4 − 1 = 0	True/False	T
4 × 3 × 4 = 48	True/False	H
2 + 4 + 8 = 10	True/False	L
67 − 8 − 7 = 50	True/False	Y
Now tell me the letters in order.		

Block C

Friend reads	You answer	Friend reads
2 × 3 × 3 = 18	True/False	Q
2 × 5 × 5 = 50	True/False	N
23 − 7 − 2 = 14	True/False	L
3 − 0 − 3 = 3	True/False	Y
26 + 6 + 6 = 38	True/False	J
Now tell me the letters in order.		

Block D

Friend reads	You answer	Friend reads
1 × 3 × 2 = 5	True/False	F
8 − 1 − 2 = 5	True/False	Q
3 + 11 + 7 = 20	True/False	Y
Now tell me the letters in order.		

Block E

Friend reads	You answer	Friend reads
1 × 6 × 6 = 36	True/False	J
3 + 73 + 7 = 103	True/False	F
54 − 6 − 8 = 40	True/False	P
12 × 2 × 3 = 72	True/False	N
0 − 1 − 1 = −2	True/False	S
2 + 8 + 13 = 23	True/False	Y
Now tell me the letters in order.		

ANSWERS

To find your score, first count the total number of letters in the correct position within each block. For example, the correct answer for Block A is T, N, P, H, so if you said 'T, N, P, H', you would score 4 points. If you said, for example, 'T, N, **B**, H', you would score 3 points.

Write your scores for each block in the table below, then add them up to find your total score (out of a maximum of 25).

Block	Score	Maximum
A		4
B		7
C		5
D		3
E		6
Total		**25**

The average score is about 19/25, with most people scoring somewhere in between 15 and 23. If you scored 24 or 25, congratulations: you are an excellent multitasker! If you scored less than 15 then – sorry – you are a poor multitasker.

Interestingly, the findings of a recent study suggested that people who were poor multitaskers (as measured by a version of this test) were actually *more* likely to attempt multitasking in real life. Why? Well, it turns out that people who attempt a lot of multitasking do so because they are impulsive and sensation-seeking (see **Your Personality Profile**): exactly the characteristics you don't want in a multitasker. As this test shows, effective multitasking requires lots of mental effort and concentration; things that tend to be in short supply among impulsive sensation-seekers.

So, are women really better at multitasking than men? Until recently, psychologists seemed to have been surprisingly reluctant to investigate this question. For example, the study mentioned above didn't even report separate scores for men and women, although it would have been trivially easy to do so.

The authors of three recent multitasking studies, however, were brave enough to take on this question directly. The first, which involved simultaneously monitoring three separate clocks and a list of names, found that men actually did better than women, but only by about 10 per cent.* A second study, which involved completing word-search and Sudoku puzzles, found no gender difference, with both men and women showing worse performance when asked to switch back and forth between the puzzles, rather than completing one after the other. A third, which found a female advantage, is probably the most persuasive, as it used some of the types of task involved in everyday multitasking: finding restaurants on a map, dealing with a phone call and searching for a lost key. That said, the female advantage was relatively small, about the same size as for the language test discussed in the previous section (Men Are from Mars . . .).

So, are women really better multitaskers than men? The fairest conclusion is, 'yes, a little bit; but not for all types of task'.

One thing, however, is clear. If you're the sort of person who loves to multitask . . .

. . . then you're exactly the sort of person who probably shouldn't try to multitask.

Web Link and Further Reading
The title of this section comes from a piece of advice that Steve Jobs, then CEO of Apple, is said to have offered to Mark Zuckerberg, the young CEO of Facebook, 'Focus on your knitting. Don't try to do everything. Do one thing well': http://allthingsd.com/20111107/zuckerberg-says-amazon-and-apple-are-allies-while-google-building-their-own-little-version-of-facebook/

---

* Interestingly, the authors found some evidence that this difference was due to men's (slightly) superior spatial abilities (see Men Are from Mars . . .), which give an advantage on the clock-watching task, because of our tendency to use space to represent time (see The March of Time).

The pSHEchologist

What do you call a female psychologist?

ANSWER

A psychologist, you sexist.

Quoth the Raven's 'What's My Score?'

IQ (Intelligence Quotient) tests have had a bad press. It is often argued that we have no idea what 'intelligence' is, and that if these tests measure anything meaningful at all, it is just the quality of the test-taker's education.In one sense this is true. 'Intelligence' isn't something with an objective definition on which we can all agree (like, say, height): even experts disagree as to how we should define the concept. And, yes, many IQ tests measure things that can be improved with schooling, such as vocabulary, general knowledge and the ability to see similarities between different objects (e.g., a table is like a chair, because both are items of furniture).

But in a more important sense, these criticisms miss the point. Although we will never all agree on exactly what we mean by 'intelligence', people's IQ-test scores are a good predictor of both their academic achievement and their earnings. So whatever it is that IQ tests are measuring, it is something that we care about. And while many IQ tests measure things that are taught more or less explicitly in school, many do not.

Enter *Raven's Progressive Matrices*, a test first developed in the 1930s by a psychologist named John C. Raven. Many experts consider this test to be the best single measure of intelligence because it is a non-verbal test, a test that is not based on language.* This

---

* More comprehensive measures such as the Weschler Adult Intelligence Scale and the Weschler Intelligence Scale for Children are made up of ten to fifteen individual tests, the results from which are combined to give the final IQ score. Interestingly, though, scores on different types of test (vocabulary, short-term memory, processing speed and visual processing) are highly correlated, meaning that if you score high (or low) on one type of test, you generally score high (or low) on all of them. For this reason, most psychologists don't have much truck with the objection that particular individual tests are unfair. If, say, a Raven's-style test is such a bad measure of intelligence, how come it is an excellent predictor of your vocabulary, your verbal reasoning skills, your short-term memory and so on?

means that – unlike vocabulary, general knowledge or 'similarities', all of which can be taught in school – it is a *relatively* pure measure of intelligence, as opposed to simply the quality of the test-taker's education. This also means that the test is *relatively* fair to test-takers from different ethnic and socio-economic groups. At least, it is fairer than – say – a vocabulary test, which might include words that are not commonly used by the relevant group.

Notice that I have twice stressed the word 'relatively'. No test will ever be completely immune to the effects of schooling, if only because school provides practice in essential test-taking skills such as sitting down, shutting up and concentrating on doing what you are told. Similarly, no test will ever be completely 'culture-fair', as parents from different ethnic and socio-economic groups differ in the extent to which they value – and encourage their children to value – abstract reasoning and logical thinking. In short, no test is perfect, but a progressive-matrices-style test is the best in town.

So let's take one. The test begins below. It has twenty-five questions, and there is no time-limit. Each question takes the form of a 3 × 3 grid (or 'matrix') from which one item is missing. Your job is to choose, from eight possible items on the right, A–H, the one that completes the grid best. (I'm not going to give you any more instructions than that; you must figure out for yourself what 'completes the grid best' means in each case.)

1.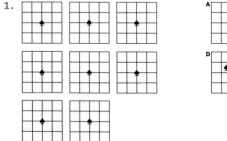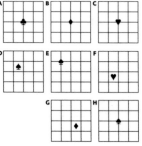

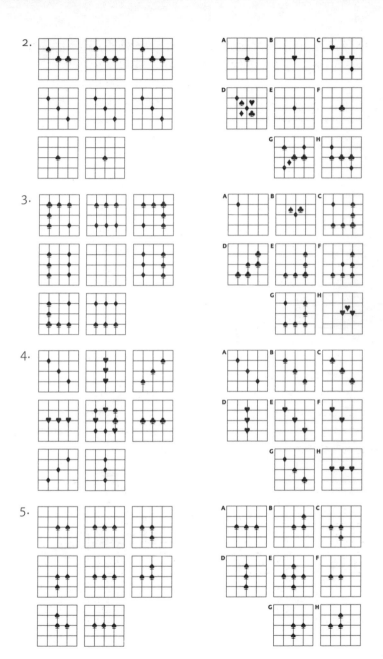

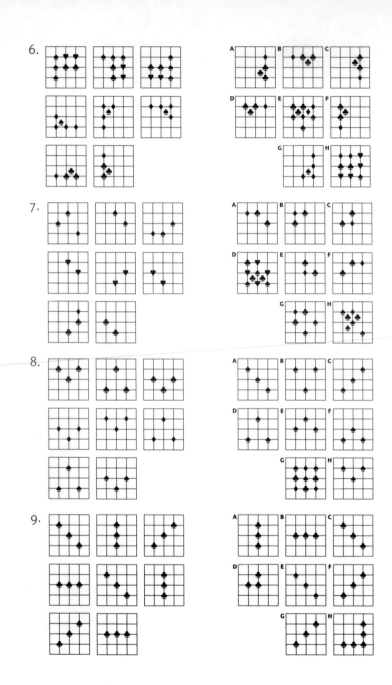

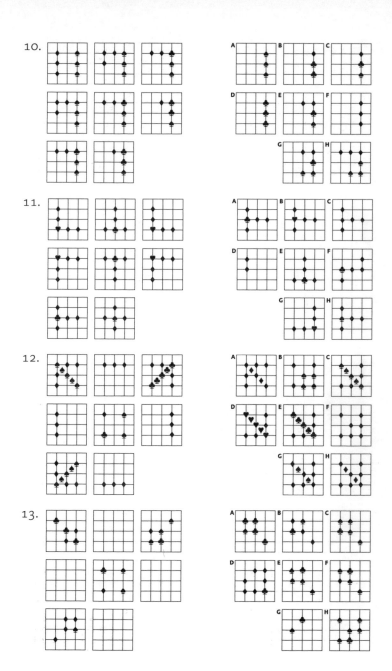

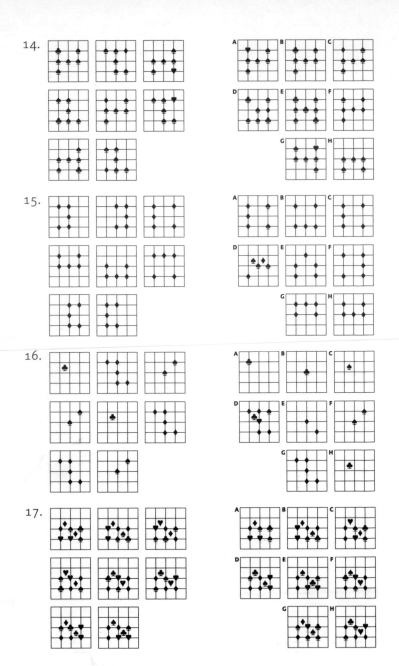

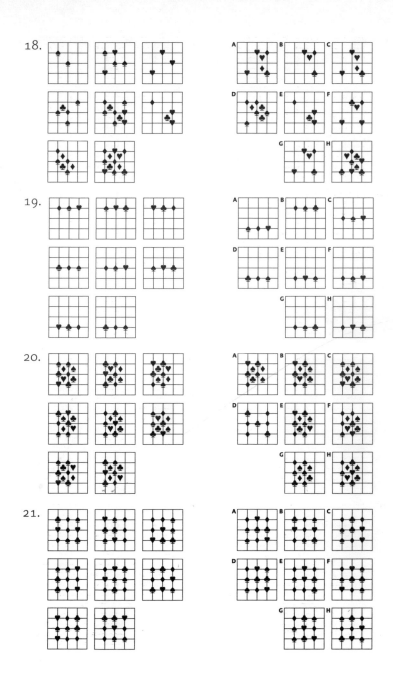

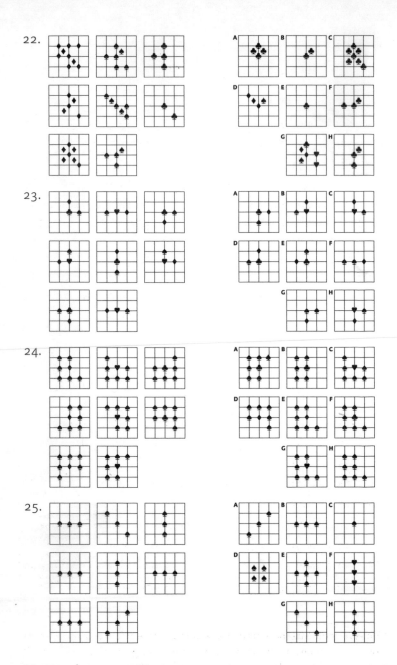

Now work out your IQ score.

ANSWERS

Score one point for each correct answer:

1:H, 2:A, 3:C, 4:B, 5:F, 6:D, 7:B, 8:H, 9:C, 10:D, 11:A, 12:H, 13:E, 14:A, 15:F, 16:H, 17:A, 18:G, 19:F, 20:D, 21:F, 22:B, 23:D, 24:F, 25:H.

Before working out your IQ, it's important for you to know that the only way to get a proper measure is to take a full test, administered by a qualified clinical or educational psychologist. That said, the test that you have just taken is of higher quality than most of those that you will find for free on the web, and while you should not take your result as gospel, it is probably in the right ballpark.*

With that caveat in mind, consult the table below to convert your raw score (number correct) to an IQ.

Score	IQ	Percentile	Classification	Score	IQ	Percentile	Classification
≤5	≤73	3.59	Borderline (70–79)	14	104	60.51	Average (90–109)
6	77	6.26	Borderline (70–79)	15	108	70.31	Average (90–109)
7	79	8.08	Borderline (70–79)	16	111	76.83	High Average (110–119)
8	84	14.31	Low average (80–89)	17	114	82.47	High Average (110–119)
9	88	21.19	Low average (80–89)	18	119	89.74	High Average (110–119)
10	92	29.69	Average (90–109)	19	123	93.74	Superior (120–129)
11	94	34.46	Average (90–109)	20	125	95.85	Superior (120–129)
12	98	44.69	Average (90–109)	21	132	98.36	Very Superior (≥ 130)
13	101	52.66	Average (90–109)	≥22	≥139	99.53	Very Superior (≥ 130)

---

* However, note that these norms come from a sample of (400) participants who took the test online. People who take online IQ tests generally have higher IQs than the population at large, so this test probably underestimates your actual IQ a bit, but not too much (probably by no more than 10 points).

IQ scores are designed so that the mean (or average) is 100. So, average performance corresponds to 12/25 (an IQ of 98) or 13/25 (an IQ of 101). Look across to the *Percentile* column to see the percentage of people that you are smarter than. For example, if you got 19/25, you are smarter than almost 94 per cent of people; but if you got 10/25, you a smarter than only about 30 per cent of people (i.e., 70 per cent of people are smarter than you).

This is all very well, but what does it mean for you? A lot! As well as some other things that we will meet later in the book (which I'll keep under wraps for now) – IQ scores are correlated with . . .

- **academic performance**; though one recent study found that IQ seems to be less important than self-discipline.
- **income**; though this is influenced by many other things too, of course, including parental income, social class and . . .
- **occupation**. Unsurprisingly, certain occupations tend to have higher or lower average IQs than the average for the general population. For example, doctors (121), college professors (115), high-school teachers (110), elementary/primary school teachers (107), NFL quarterbacks (105) and – just about – police offers (101) are above the average (100), while farmworkers (96), plumbers (96), carpenters (94) and cleaners (90) are below. Of course, these are just *averages*. For example, in the survey in question, the brightest farmworker (121) was a lot brighter than the thickest college professor (110). Incidentally, some celebrities rumoured to have particularly impressive IQs are Stephen Hawing (160), Quentin Tarantino (160), Sharon Stone (154) and Shakira (140). The highest IQ in the world (210) belongs to a civil engineer from South Korea, Kim Ung-Young (not to be confused with the North Korean dictators Kim Jong-Il and Kim Jong-Un).
- **mortality**. Yes, stupider people die younger. A recent review found that the effect seems to be real and not a 'confound'* caused – for

---

* A confound is a third factor that obscures the relationship between two things we're interested in, by being related to both of them. For example, say we want to investigate the link between drinking (the first thing we're interested in) and

example – by some people getting diseases that lower their IQ before eventually killing them. Instead, cleverer people are likely to be better at avoiding illnesses and injuries, better able to deal with them when they arise (thanks in part to their increased earning power) and more likely to eat healthily and exercise (though the effects of social class are difficult to pick apart here). Another possibility is that there is no causal link at all, and that a well-put-together brain is just an indicator of an overall well-put-together body.

- **birth order.** First-born children tend to have higher IQs than their later-born siblings (even when tested at the same age). This seems to be caused by two factors. The first is that only first-borns have a period of undivided parental attention. The second is a paradoxical 'tutoring effect': the older child 'tutors' the younger, but this boosts the IQ of the tutor more than the tutee, presumably because explaining something first requires you to get it straight in your own head.

- **parental IQ.** The claim that cleverer parents (who, as we have seen, also tend to be wealthier parents) have cleverer children is perhaps a rather controversial one in the wider world. But among researchers, *some* genetic basis for IQ is basically accepted as fact. Many studies have shown, for example, that identical twins (who share 100 per cent of their genes) have more similar IQs than mere siblings (who share 50 per cent of their genes), even if separated at birth. However, figuring out the relative contributions of genes and the environment is not straightforward, partly because genetically smarter children may seek out more intellectually stimulating environments and partly because the mother's womb is a particularly important part of 'the environment', but one that is very difficult to disentangle from genetics (identical twins share not only their genes but also a womb).

---

heart disease (the second thing we're interested in). A confound – a third factor that muddies the waters – would be diet: heavy drinkers are also likely to eat unhealthily, which is another risk factor for heart disease. Another example, and a more detailed explanation, is given in the next section.

To sum up, how you get on in life is determined partially by your genetically endowed intelligence, yes, but also by your environment and your own actions; so it's up to you to make the most of what you've got by working hard, developing self-discipline and seeking out intellectual stimulation at every opportunity.

Web Link

The test included in this section was reproduced by kind permission of Eric Jorgenson, who runs an online IQ-testing site. Why not contribute to this project, by taking the tests at: http://en.iniq.org/?

The Fool Hath Said in His Heart, 'There Is No God'

According to the Bible (specifically, Psalm 14:1) atheists are 'fools'. But many modern-day atheists, such as Richard Dawkins, have claimed precisely the opposite: that religious people are *less* intelligent than atheists. Who's right?

Now I don't want any squabbling over what we mean by 'religion' or 'intelligence'. In the studies in question, religion was measured simply by giving people questionnaires about their beliefs. Intelligence was measured by IQ tests such as the one you completed in the previous section, which do not seem to confer any particular advantages on either believers or non-believers (remember too that one IQ test tends to give pretty much the same score as another). So . . .

TRUE or FALSE? Religious people are less intelligent than atheists.

ANSWER

True. A 2013 review that pooled the results of no fewer than sixty-three previous studies found a negative correlation between religious belief and intelligence.* The correlation was small but highly statistically significant. Let's take a minute to quantify each of those terms.

Statisticians express the relationship between two measures using a number called a *correlation coefficient* (sometimes abbreviated to *r*). This number ranges between 0 (i.e., no relationship between religion and IQ) and 1 (i.e., you can predict someone's IQ score perfectly by asking them about their religion). On this scale, the relationship between religion and IQ was around 0.25†: small – reflecting the fact that lots of other things (including genetics) have a larger influence on IQ – but by no means negligible, and comfortably statistically significant.

The concept of statistical significance was explained in more detail in **The Tea Test**, but the take-home message is this: the chances of researchers finding an apparent relationship between IQ and intelligence of this size (i.e., 0.25 on the 0–1 scale) by chance alone – if none actually existed – is less than 1 in 1,000 (i.e., $p<0.001$).

Admittedly, nearly all of the studies included were American, meaning that 'religion' essentially equates to 'mainly Protestant

---

* Eagle-eyed readers will have noticed that this is not *exactly* the same as saying that religious people are less intelligent than atheists, as the researchers did not split participants into these two groups. What the correlation actually shows is that the more religious you are, the less intelligent you are. To see why these two generalisations aren't quite the same, imagine two religious people, one very religious and very unintelligent, the other only slightly religious and slightly unintelligent. These people fit the generalisation 'the more religious you are, the less intelligent you are' but not the generalisation 'religious people are less intelligent than atheists' (neither person is an atheist). Although the authors of the review paper discussed failed to make the distinction between these two generalisations, they are probably close enough for most practical purposes.

† Actually -0.25 (*minus* 0.25) as the relationship is negative: the *more* religious you are, the *less* intelligent you are.

Christianity', but a separate investigation found a similar relationship between belief and average IQ when looking across different countries (137 of them) rather than across individuals.

So, the statistical relationship between religious belief and intelligence is clear. The more important and controversial question is what drives this relationship. A mantra in statistics that has almost crossed over into general parlance is that *correlation does not (necessarily) equal causation*. What does this mean? In general, whenever we see a correlation between two measures – in this case, intelligence and religiosity – there are three basic possibilities (note that, in principle, both the first and the second could be true):

(a) low intelligence *causes* high religiosity (i.e., the less intelligent you are, the more likely you are to accept religious claims);

(b) high religiosity *causes* low intelligence (i.e., the more religious you are, the less you are able to exercise your 'intelligence muscles' via abstract scientific reasoning and exposure to ideas such as evolution);

(c) there is *no causal link* between intelligence and religiosity at all. Both low intelligence and high religiosity are caused by some third factor or 'confound', such as age (i.e., older people are more religious and – as we will see in the next section – tend to score lower on IQ tests, as scores improve with each generation).

The third possibility is probably the least likely, as the authors of this review study controlled for age, as well as gender and education. The maths behind this is complicated but, in effect, just involves taking groups of people matched on these measures and seeing if the relationship between religiosity and IQ still holds for them. If the relationship between religiosity and IQ holds for (a) highly educated old women, (b) poorly educated young men, (c) moderately educated middle-aged women and so on, then it can't be caused by age, gender or education.

The second possibility (that high religiosity causes low intelligence) has not really been tested but seems plausible, though perhaps only for those with more extreme beliefs. Many moderately religious people are comfortable with scientific thinking (including evolution by natural selection), and so probably get plenty of opportunity to engage in abstract reasoning.

The first possibility (that low intelligence causes high religiosity) is directly supported by a number of prospective studies which have shown that IQ tests given in childhood predict levels of religious belief later in life (in some cases, as much as twenty-five years later): the more intelligent you are as a child, the less likely you are to be religious as an adult.

But why? The authors of the review discuss three possibilities. First, intelligent people tend to be less conformist, and so are more resistant to religious dogma. Second, intelligent people tend to have a more analytical than intuitive thinking style; they let their heads rule their hearts, as opposed to vice versa (see It Feels So Right). Finally, intelligent people may have less *need* for religion. Religion helps with self-control (see I Just Can't Wait), self-worth ('I am a valuable person') and resilience to life's trials and tribulations ('It's the will of God'): all things that intelligent people tend to have quite a lot of anyway.

But if you're an atheist, don't feel too smug; I'm saving up an unsettling challenge especially for you (see Hitler's Sweater).

And if you're religious, don't despair. This review found that while religiosity is a reasonably good predictor of IQ, it is not a predictor of success at school, which may turn out to be much more important in the long run. More importantly, these findings do not – indeed cannot – prove or disprove any particular system of beliefs. Perhaps an analytic thinking style is a curse that prevents 'clever' atheists from seeing truths that can only be 'felt' and not 'figured out'. Maybe 'intelligent' people are right about most stuff, but wrong about the only thing that ultimately matters.

Idiocracy?

The year is 2505. The number one movie in America is *Ass*: a ninety-minute close-up of someone's backside that won eight Oscars, including 'best screenplay'. The slogan of the leading fast-food restaurant is 'F--- you, I'm eating'. A typical question in an IQ test runs as follows: 'If you have one bucket that holds two gallons and another bucket that holds five gallons, how many buckets do you have?'

Of course, this is just a movie (Mike Judge's *Idiocracy*), but in real life are we getting stupider or smarter? In the very long term, the answer is surely 'smarter'; it would be hard to find anybody who would seriously argue that modern-day humans are less intelligent than cavemen.

But what about the recent past, say around a hundred years?

What do you think: are we stupider or smarter than the Victorians?

ANSWER

Crazy as it sounds, there is actually pretty good evidence for both possibilities.

Let's take the happier possibility first. When people are given IQ tests (e.g., of the kind you completed in Quoth the Raven's 'What's My Score?'), we find that scores have, on average, increased by about three points per decade since at least the Second World War. This effect is so famous within psychology that it has its own name: the *Flynn Effect*, named after its discoverer, Professor James Flynn. These gains are not restricted to the developed West; IQ scores have increased by pretty much the same rate across the globe. Many different explanations for this increase have been proposed, including better nutrition, the spread of formal schooling, increased familiarity with test-taking and a more intellectually stimulating environment in the form of books, films, TV, computers and so on.* Furthermore, the decline of farming and manufacturing and the rise of service industries mean that, for an increasing number of people, a day's work involves manipulating not tools and machinery but abstract categories and concepts: exactly the sorts of things that crop up in IQ tests.

But, in a sense, this is exactly the problem with using IQ tests to investigate whether or not people are getting smarter. Maybe IQ tests are measuring not 'intelligence' in a pure sense but simply people's familiarity with abstract reasoning, test-taking and so on. Some researchers have therefore argued that a better measure of intelligence is reaction time: how long it takes people to – for example – press a button when a light comes on. A link to a website that allows you to measure your own reaction time (for comparison with the averages set out below) is given in Web Links (though actual studies use a more sophisticated method which allows researchers to separate the time taken to react and the time taken to physically press the button).

Using reaction time as a measurement of intelligence isn't as crazy as it sounds. For one thing, it correlates very well with traditional measures. That is, people who are very quick at the button-press task generally score highly on paper-and-pencil IQ tests. For another, some researchers argue that the most appropriate definition of 'intelligence' is the rate at which electrical potentials in the brain oscillate: in other words, that people who are more intelligent have, quite literally, quicker brains. Because faster oscillations allow for speedier reactions, reaction-time measurements tap into this notion of intelligence pretty directly.

When intelligence is measured in this way, we find that we are becoming not brighter but stupider. The average reaction time in

---

* Some commentators have argued that 'Google is making us stupid' by encouraging us to skim-read a wide range of material, rather than to read and study more deeply. However, there is little direct evidence for this claim, and the Flynn Effect has continued into the twenty-first century, particularly among developing countries, for whom the internet is a relatively recent phenomenon.

the post-war period is approximately 250 milliseconds* (i.e., 0.25 seconds), as opposed to around 190ms in the Victorian era, which translates roughly into a decrease of 1.2 IQ points per decade on traditional scales. Again, various explanations have been proposed, including the build-up of neurotoxins in the environment and the increasing average age of the population (older people have slower reaction times).

But perhaps the best-supported theory is the one that is outlined by the narrator at the start of *Idiocracy*: since less intelligent people tend to have both (a) more children and (b) less intelligent children,† a gradual decline in average intelligence is inevitable.

So, IQ-test studies suggest that we are getting more intelligent, while reaction-time studies suggest that we are getting stupider. Is there any way to reconcile the two, apparently contradictory, findings? One possibility is that our raw, inbuilt intelligence, our brain-speed – as measured by reaction-time tests – is indeed declining, but that this is more than offset by improvements in health, education and the intellectual environment, resulting in higher IQ-test scores. Speculative, perhaps, but if this possibility is true, then we have no reason to fear an *Idiocracy* any time soon. Phew!

Web Link
Measure your own (approximate) reaction time at: http://getyourwebsite here.com/jswb/rttest01.html

---

* Mine, as measured by the website in the Web Links section is 267ms. Clearly I'm no genius.

† Some evidence for the partial heritability of IQ (i.e., that, on average, less intelligent people have less intelligent children) was discussed in the section Quoth the Raven's 'What's My Score?'.

Stereo Types

STOMP is the name of a musical percussion show that has enjoyed huge success worldwide. It is also the name of a questionnaire that is used to assess people's tastes in music: the *Short Test Of Musical Preferences*. A number of psychological studies have found that it is possible to discover a remarkable amount of information about a person simply by asking about his or her musical tastes. To find out what yours say about you, fill in the questionnaire below.

For the following items, please indicate your basic preference level for the genres listed, using the scale provided.

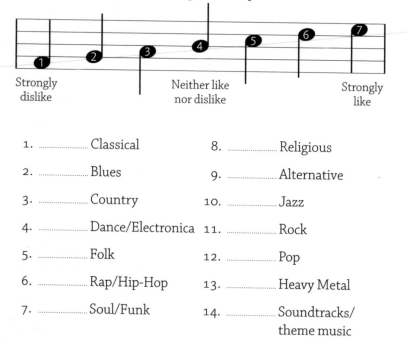

Strongly dislike   Neither like nor dislike   Strongly like

1. .... Classical
2. .... Blues
3. .... Country
4. .... Dance/Electronica
5. .... Folk
6. .... Rap/Hip-Hop
7. .... Soul/Funk

8. .... Religious
9. .... Alternative
10. .... Jazz
11. .... Rock
12. .... Pop
13. .... Heavy Metal
14. .... Soundtracks/theme music

ANSWERS

Studies conducted using the STOMP have found that people's musical preferences tend to be rather systematic. For example, people who like blues music also tend to like jazz and classical, while those who enjoy soundtracks also like religious music and pop. What this means is that, although the test lists fourteen genres (and there are, of course, many more), we can collapse all of these into four 'super genres':

- To find out how much you like music that is **Reflective and Complex**, take the average of your scores for Blues, Classical, Folk and Jazz (i.e., add these scores together, then divide by 4).
- To find out how much you like music that is **Intense and Rebellious**, take the average of your scores for Alternative, Heavy Metal and Rock (i.e., add up, then divide by 3).
- To find out how much you like music that is **Upbeat and Conventional**, take the average of your scores for Country, Pop, Religious and Soundtracks (i.e., add up, then divide by 4).
- To find out how much you like music that is **Energetic and Rhythmic**, take the average of your scores for Electronic, Hip-Hop/Rap and Soul (i.e., add up, then divide by 3).

This is where the fun begins. The first thing we can do is find out how typical your tastes are of your gender and ethnicity (yes, I'm afraid the stereotype is true: white people like Rock and Metal, while black people prefer Hip-Hop and Soul). The table overleaf shows the average score for different ethnic groups on each of the four super-genres (though note that this study was conducted in the United States, and the results many well be different for other countries). The style that is most preferred by members of each category is shown in **bold**. How do you compare?

	Male				Female			
	Reflective & Complex	Intense & Rebellious	Upbeat & Conventional	Energetic & Rhythmic	Reflective & Complex	Intense & Rebellious	Upbeat & Conventional	Energetic & Rhythmic
White	4.08	**5.10**	3.40	3.65	3.71	**5.07**	3.90	3.99
Hispanic	4.23	**5.16**	3.60	4.22	3.66	**5.03**	4.04	4.57
Asian	4.22	**4.75**	4.03	4.44	3.96	4.59	4.21	**4.75**
Black	3.82	3.28	3.66	**5.03**	3.55	3.39	4.18	**5.30**
Other	4.26	**4.94**	3.43	3.97	3.69	**4.99**	3.75	4.25

More interestingly, we can use your musical preferences to make certain predictions about your personality, and even your intelligence. If you haven't already done so, you should complete the sections Your Personality Profile and Quoth the Raven's 'What's My Score?', in order to find out whether or not these predictions are accurate. These predictions are based on studies in which researchers asked participants to complete the STOMP, as well as a personality test (and various other tests of their self-opinion and IQ), and looked for relationships between the scores.*

---

* A health warning: as is very often the case in psychology, we are talking about *statistical generalisations*, not hard and fast rules. For example, pretty much everyone accepts the statistical generalisation that 'men are taller than women' because, overall, it is true of men as a group and women as a group. At the same time, this does not mean that every man is taller than every woman, and it would not make sense to argue that the existence of some very short men and some very tall women disproves the generalisation. The statements below about – for example – 'people who prefer Reflective and Complex music' should be understood in the same way: as generalisations about tendencies of that group as a whole, rather than as descriptions that apply to each and every individual member. It is also important to bear in mind that the studies in question were conducted in the United States, so these generalisations may not hold elsewhere (particularly in countries with very different musical traditions).

- People who prefer **Reflective and Complex** music (Blues, Classical, Folk and Jazz) score highly on openness to experience, and see themselves as unathletic, politically liberal and intelligent (and, indeed, perform well on objective IQ tests).
- People who prefer **Intense and Rebellious** music (Alternative, Heavy Metal and Rock) show almost exactly the same profile, except that they are more likely to see themselves as athletic.
- People who prefer **Upbeat and Conventional** music (Country, Pop, Religious and Soundtracks) are the polar opposite. They have low scores for openness to experience and intelligence (again, according to both self-report questionnaires and objective IQ tests) but tend to be agreeable, extroverted and conscientious, and see themselves as attractive, wealthy and athletic, as well as politically conservative. This group is the least prone to depression.
- People who prefer **Energetic and Rhythmic** music (Electronic, Rap/Hip-Hop and Soul) are also extroverted, agreeable, attractive and athletic. However, they do not share the political conservatism, wealth or lower intelligence scores of the Upbeat and Conventional group.

It is important to bear in mind that most of the relationships uncovered by the researchers (e.g., between a preference for Upbeat/Conventional music and lower IQ scores) were, although statistically significant, rather small. In The Fool Hath Said in His Heart..., we met the *correlation coefficient*, a number that expresses the size of a relationship between two measures, ranging from 0 (no relationship) to 1 (perfect relationship). On this scale, most of the relationships between measures (including between love of Upbeat/Conventional music and lower IQ) were around 0.2 or smaller.

That said, a follow-up study by the same researchers found that most of the stereotypes that were expressed about certain groups in a questionnaire study (e.g., that fans of Classical, Rock and Religious music are intelligent, liberal and conservative respectively) did contain a kernel of truth. Another follow-up study by these authors found that, when students were given the task of getting to know each other in an online-dating-type set-up, they not only chose to discuss musical preferences more than any other topic but also used them to successfully predict many of their partner's personality traits and personal values.

So the next time you meet a stranger and are curious to know her political views, you can get a very good idea simply by asking whether she prefers jazz or soundtracks.

Horoscope Horror Show?

Aries, Taureans and Geminis are generally taller than Librans and Scorpios.   TRUE □/FALSE □

Pisceans are more likely to have schizophrenia than are people with other star signs.   TRUE □/FALSE □

Librans and Scorpios have the best chance of living to 100, Pisceans the least.   TRUE □/FALSE □

Librans and Scorpios tend to do better in school than Cancers and Leos, and are also more likely to become professional footballers.
                                                      TRUE □/FALSE □

A Sagittarius is more likely to become a teenage mother than an Aquarius (at least, in Sweden).   TRUE □/FALSE □

ANSWER

All of these statements are true.

Does this mean that we should believe everything that's written in our horoscope? Of *course* not; horoscopes are clearly a load of nonsense. So how can it be that all of the statements are true? The answer is that your star sign is determined by the month of your birth, which has important effects on both your physical and psychological development.

In terms of height, babies born in April get the most sunlight at what seems to be a particularly crucial point in their physical development, three months after their birth (July); babies born in October, the least (January). Nobody is quite sure why winter-born babies have a (very slightly) elevated risk of developing schizophrenia (with the peak in February–March), although it may again be related to a lack of sunlight (and therefore vitamin D) at a particularly crucial stage in development. Similarly, there are a number of different explanations of why autumn-born babies are more likely to live to a hundred than winter-borns. It may be to do with avoiding particularly high or low temperatures at the point of birth or conception, or that it is best to avoid being a young and vulnerable infant at the peak season for particular diseases (whose effects can last into adulthood and old age).

Differences in performance at school – in both sports and the more academic subjects – have a different type of explanation. In the UK (where these studies were conducted), the cut-off date for starting school is 1 September. So Librans and Scorpios (and some Virgos) will always be the oldest children in a given year group, Cancers and Leos (and the unluckier Virgos) the youngest. Since the oldest children are almost a full year older than the youngest in the same year group, this gives them a huge advantage in both sports (where they will be bigger and stronger) and academic subjects: young children develop so quickly that, for example, a five-year-old is much more intellectually advanced than a four-year-old. In Sweden the school starting cut-off is 1 January. This means that although a girl who is born in, say December 1992, is slightly older than a girl born in January 1993, in terms of her year group she is the youngest and consequently 'acts younger' (i.e., she's more likely to do reckless things, including getting pregnant).

So could there actually be something in horoscopes? Perhaps, for example, Aries are perceived as aggressive because they tend to be tall? In a word, 'no'. Remember that, in all of these cases, what matters is the *season* of the birth, not the month. So in the southern hemisphere, where spring starts in September, it will be Libras, Scorpios and Sagittarians who are tall, rather than Aries, Taureans and Librans.

Why, then, do so many people swear by the truth-telling power of a horoscope? Confirmation bias (see **Card Trick**) means that, if you throw out enough general statements, some will stick. If you have a friend who believes in horoscopes, try reading the following passage, telling your victim that it is specific to his or her sign:

You have a need for other people to like and admire you, and yet you tend to be critical of yourself. While you have some personality weaknesses, you are generally able to compensate for them. You have considerable unused capacity that you have not turned to your advantage. Disciplined and self-controlled on the outside, you tend to be worrisome and insecure on the inside. At times you have serious doubts as to whether you have made the right decision or done the right thing. You prefer a certain amount of change and variety and become dissatisfied when hemmed in by restrictions and limitations. You also pride yourself as an independent thinker, and do not accept others' statements without satisfactory proof. But you have found it unwise to be too frank in revealing yourself to others. At times you are extroverted, affable and sociable, while at other times you are introverted, wary and reserved. Some of your aspirations tend to be rather unrealistic.

Did they fall for it? This is a standard text that has been doing the rounds since 1949, and that people rate as – on average – 85 per cent accurate, regardless of star sign. So while season-of-birth effects are real, horoscopes are – as far as scientific validity is concerned – a horror show.

Are You a Conspiracy Theorist?

Please rate each of the following claims as

(a) very unlikely, (b) unlikely, (c) likely or (d) very likely:

	Very Unlikely	Unlikely	Likely	Very Likely
'New Coke' – launched in 1985 – was deliberately inferior and was part of a marketing ploy designed to boost sales when Coca-Cola Classic was reintroduced.*				
AIDS is caused by the HIV virus.				
Man-made climate change is a hoax.				
Martin Luther King Jr was killed by the FBI and/or CIA.				
Princess Diana was killed in a plot organised by members of the British royal family.				
Smoking increases your risk of lung cancer.				
The moon landings were faked.				
The US government and/or military has evidence of aliens that it has covered up (e.g., at Roswell or Area 51).				
The US government organised 9/11, or at least allowed it to happen, in order to have an excuse to invade Afghanistan and/or to restrict civil liberties at home.				
The US government deliberately allowed the attack on Pearl Harbor, as it wanted a reason to enter the Second World War.				

* Non-US readers might not be familiar with the New-Coke saga. The fact that the company launched New Coke, only to reintroduce Coca-Cola Classic shortly afterwards is undisputed. The claim that you are being asked to judge is that New Coke was deliberately designed to be inferior to the previous recipe.

ANSWERS

There's no point in me giving you the right answers. The very *raison d'être* of a conspiracy theory is to claim that the agreed-upon 'right' answers are actually wrong.

What is interesting is what happened when this survey was given to 1,377 visitors to climate-change blogs.* The findings revealed that conspiracy theorists don't pick and choose their conspiracies: if you believe one conspiracy, you believe them all.

For some things this makes sense. For example, if you believe the US government is inherently power-crazed, untrustworthy and violent, regardless of whoever happens to be in power at the time, then it makes sense to see Pearl Harbor, 9/11 and the assassination of MLK simply as different manifestations of this same underlying dastardliness.

But for other conspiracies, this makes no sense at all. Why should someone who believes that New Coke was a deliberately inferior product also think that climate change is a hoax, that there is no link between smoking and lung cancer and that the British royal family killed Princess Diana? Although, there were – as always – some individual exceptions, overall, this is exactly what happened. Most people either believed in absolutely every conspiracy mentioned in the questionnaire or none at all.

This makes conspiracy theorists look rather silly. If you ask a conspiracy theorist why he (it is almost always a he) does not believe the official version of, for example, 9/11, he will say that he is a free-thinker who has taken a dispassionate and scientific look at all the available evidence and come to an independent conclusion. Indeed, he will probably genuinely believe this to be the case.

But isn't it a bit of a coincidence that he has come to an exactly parallel conclusion about lots of completely unrelated phenomena, such as the moon landings and climate change? The findings

---

* The study's authors characterised these blogs as broadly 'pro-science, but with a diverse audience'. A number of climate-change sceptic blogs were approached but declined to take part.

of this study suggest that – actually – he has just bought an off-the-shelf all-purpose conspiracy theory that he applies to every debate in town.

In other words – and here comes the psychology bit – the findings suggest that 'conspiracy thinking' is less a rational response to an individual phenomenon than a personality trait or pattern of thinking. Conspiracy theorists seem to have a particular susceptibility to confirmation bias (see Card Trick), gleefully seizing on any evidence that supports their largely predetermined conspiracy view, while failing to look for evidence that might undermine their view or support the official account.

I'm not a conspiracy theorist. But if I were, I'd be tempted to suggest that the 'survey' referred to above never happened, and that the journal article was planted by the US government in order to smear as 'conspiracy theorists' the brave free-thinkers who had uncovered some major conspiracies.

But I'm not a conspiracy theorist. So I won't.

What a Shape Sounds Like

One of these shapes is a *kiki*. The other is a *bouba*. Which do you think is which? Why?

ANSWER

The first is the *bouba*, the second the *kiki*, right?

While there is, of course, no 'right' answer, this is the answer generally given by around 95 per cent of participants. Somehow, the *bou* sound just feels rounded, while the *ki* sound feels sharp and jagged.

Where do these feelings come from? Perhaps we are making associations with familiar English words. *Bouba* sounds a little like 'balloon' (or even – Ooh, Matron! - 'booby'), while *kiki* sounds almost exactly like 'key, key', and keys do tend to be rather angular (at least, at the business end). Or maybe the associations come from writing? The *ou* sound of *bouba* is written with rounded letters, while the *k* of *kiki* is angular.

While these associations are probably playing some small role in this specific example, they don't tell the whole story. For one thing, we still get the effect if we replace them with other words that don't sound particularly like any real English words (e.g., which is the *takete* and which is the *maluma*?). For another, we still get the effect if we test speakers of other languages with very different vocabulary and written scripts to English (e.g, Swahili, Bantu and Tamil), or even two-year-old children, who have not yet learned to read at all.

So why do so many languages share these same sound–shape correspondences? Think about the shape of your mouth when you produce these sounds: a big, open, round mouth for *bouba* versus a small opening with your lips stretched thinly for *kiki*. One popular theory, then, is that the *bouba/kiki effect* is caused by connections in the brain between areas that process visual input – including both shapes on the printed page and shapes formed by speakers' lips – and areas that are responsible for perceiving and producing speech sounds. Words like *bouba* literally 'feel' round, because you can feel your lips forming a round shape when you say them.

We see these types of effect with some real English words too. For example, words such as *large*, *huge* and *enormous* involve opening wide our lips or entire mouths, whereas *little, tiny, mini, petite, itsy-bitsy, teenie-weenie* (yellow polka-dot bikini) involve stretching our lips to make a tiny gap. This may be one reason why retailers prefer prices that end in 99. When you say, for example, 'one *ninety-nine*', you are not only making these tiny sounds, but even saying the word 'teenie' (well, almost), as opposed to producing a big, booming *TWO* pounds.

Could there be links between other sensory modalities? If shapes have sounds, can they have tastes too? . . .

What a Shape Tastes Like

Below are listed some pairs of foods. For each pair, one food is generally rated as going best with more rounded, organic shapes (a) while the other is generally rated as going best with more angular shapes (b). Your job is to say which is which. To make this section even more fun, why not arrange a dinner party (admittedly, it won't be a particularly classy one) and try it out on your friends?

(a) rounded, organic shape   (b) angular shape

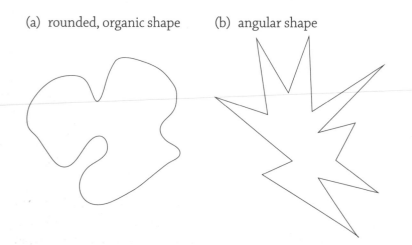

- Cranberry jam / Blueberry jam
- Mint chocolate / Brie cheese
- Ready-salted crisps / Salt and vinegar crisps
- Milk chocolate / Dark chocolate
- Sparkling water / Still water
- Rolos / Maltesers
- Brie cheese / Cranberry juice
- Goat's cheese / Mature cheddar cheese
- Sweet tastes (e.g., sugar) / Bitter tastes (e.g., lemon)

ANSWERS

(a) rounded, organic shape: Blueberry jam, Brie cheese, Ready Salted Crisps, Milk chocolate, Still water, Rolos, Brie cheese, Goat's cheese, Sweet tastes (e.g., sugar)

(b) angular shape: Cranberry jam, Mint chocolate, Salt and vinegar crisps, Dark chocolate, Sparkling water, Maltesers, Cranberry juice, Mature cheddar cheese, Bitter tastes (e.g., lemon)

You should be noticing a pattern here: sweet-tasting foods tend to be matched to more rounded, organic (*bouba*) shapes, while bitter, sour or tangy foods – and fizzy drinks – tend to be matched to angular (*kiki*) shapes. A similar effect is found for smells: raspberry and vanilla are associated with *bouba* shapes, while lemon and pepper, as well as particularly intense and/or unpleasant smells, are associated with *kiki* shapes.

Unlike the sound+shape effects discussed in the previous section, these associations do not seem to be shared by all cultures, and are therefore probably not caused by hard-wired connections between different brain areas; more likely they are learned. One possibility, then, is that these links are simply a historical accident and that there is, in fact, nothing particularly 'sharp' about 'sharp cheese' or 'round' about 'well-rounded wines'.

But just because particular links are learned or culturally specific, it doesn't follow that they are entirely arbitrary. It is possible, for example, that people view angular shapes as somehow more 'lively' than rounded shapes, and therefore a better match for more 'lively' products, such as drinks that sparkle or foods that make a loud, crunching noise. Another possibility is that people consider rounder shapes to be 'nicer' than angular shapes, which tend to look like painful weapons, and so associate the latter with bitter foods that are more unpleasant or, at least, more of an acquired taste.

Whatever the source of these links, there is some evidence to suggest that they are exploited – consciously or otherwise – by manufacturers. For example, quite a few beers and at least one brand of carbonated water use an angular star as part of their branding (though the symbolism of the star as a badge of excellence is presumably also at play here), while fruit juices and smoothies tend to favour more rounded, freely flowing logos. And I'm no cheese expert, but is there a manufacturing reason why smooth-tasting brie is always round, while sharp-tasting cheddar is always rectangular?

So if you are hoping to make your millions by coming up with a product that will take the world by storm, the symbolism of both sounds and shapes should certainly give you – sorry – food for thought.

What's in a Face? #1

We saw in Your Perfect Partner that facial attractiveness is an important criterion for choosing a partner, particularly for men. But what makes one face more attractive than another? To find out, look at the faces below and choose the pair (row a, b, c or d) that you find most attractive. Turn the page to find out the subconscious reason for your choice, and how your own face rates.

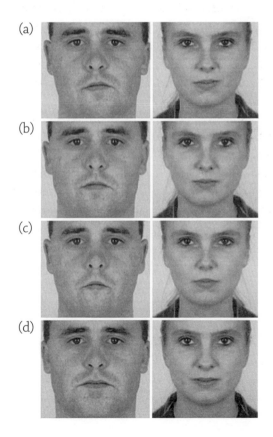

ANSWER

Most people consider the second row of faces (b) to be the most attractive. The first row (a) shows raw, untransformed photographs. In the second row these photos have been digitally manipulated to make them more symmetrical, which most people find more attractive. Notice, for example, how the wonky mouths in the first pair have been straightened out in the second. The third and fourth pairs show symmetrical faces that have been created in an old-fashioned way, simply by mirroring either the left side (row c) or the right side (row d). This, of course, makes the faces symmetrical, but in an artificial way: their noses seem either too narrow or too wide and their eyes either too close together or too far apart. Studies done back in the day when mirroring was the only way to create symmetrical faces incorrectly led researchers to the conclusion that symmetrical faces were *less* attractive. Actually, raters were just turned off by the artificial look of the mirrored faces. Now we are able to create more natural-looking symmetrical faces (as in row b), we know that symmetrical faces are rated as *more* attractive.

Our preference for symmetry is largely unconscious. When participants who rated the faces above as part of an experiment were asked about symmetry, three-quarters reported being unaware of the symmetry manipulation and – even when told – insisted that it had not influenced their judgements. Nevertheless, the majority still rated the second pair as the most attractive.

Why do we find symmetrical faces more attractive? The preference seems to be genetic, shaped by evolution. Many facial asymmetries are caused by disease, stress and vitamin deficiencies, both before birth and during childhood. We have therefore evolved a preference for symmetrical faces because it gives us a better chance of being attracted to partners who are genetically well equipped to deal with these adverse events. Indeed, people who have symmetrical faces and bodies seem to be fitter and healthier all round. Highly symmetrical men are more intelligent, more athletic, less prone to depression and better at singing and dancing than other men; they also have more satisfied partners.

Do attractive faces share any characteristics other than symmetry? Yes, they do. Perhaps surprisingly, one is *averageness*. That's right: average-looking equals good-looking. If you create an average face by digitally combining photographs of many different people, the result is a face that is rated as better-looking than almost all of the original faces (we will meet some more 'averagely attractive' faces in two further What's in a Face? sections, Brown-Eyed Girl and Face-Off).

Why do we consider average faces good-looking? One reason is that faces that deviate too far from the average – just like those that are too asymmetrical – may be indicators of genetic mutations or susceptibility to disease. A less obvious reason is that average faces, which – by definition – look like many other faces, feel more familiar, with the consequence that we like them more. As we saw in It's All Chinese to Me, familiarity breeds not *contempt* but *content*. This is why average-looking monkeys, dogs, horses and even watches are rated as 'better-looking' than more unusual members of each category.

But there is a twist to this tale. Although most good-looking people have 'average' faces, the rare people who are rated as *exceptionally* good-looking do not: they have a little something extra.

For women, this little something extra is femininity. To put it bluntly, the less a woman looks like a man (i.e., the smaller her jaw, brow, nose and overall head, the bigger her eyes, and the thicker her lips), the more attractive she is rated (by both men and women, and across many different cultures). Again, the reasons are evolutionary: a more feminine-looking face equals higher oestrogen levels equals greater fertility. This means that, by taking a good-looking 'average' female face (left), and then feminising it some more (right), we can artificially create just about the best-looking woman possible. Psychologist Lisa DeBruine and her colleagues have done just that. Would you like to meet her?

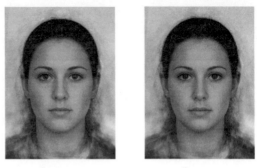

Average   Better

For men, this little something extra is ... complicated. For most people, an average masculine face is made better-looking if it is feminised, and worse-looking if it is masculinised. Feminised male faces look warm, soft, kind and gentle, while masculinised male faces – as we will see in **Face-Off** – look cold, hard, mean and aggressive. But women with a self-confessed preference for 'bad boys' are the exception: they rate highly masculine-looking men as more attractive.

But if your face doesn't tick the boxes of symmetry, averageness and femininity, don't despair. For one thing, faces that don't meet these criteria are, by definition, distinctive-looking, which many people find attractive in its own right. For another, physical attractiveness is not all that people look for in a partner (see **Your Perfect Partner**).

And if all else fails, you could always manipulate your face digitally. For fun online tools that let you do this, see ...

Web Link and Further Reading
Manipulate your face digitally at: http://www.perceptionlab.com/morph/fof/index.html

David Perret's *In Your Face* is a fascinating and very readable popular introduction to – as the book's subtitle puts it – *the new science of human attraction*.

Tips for Dancers?

TRUE or FALSE? Lap-dancers earn more money per shift when they are at the most fertile point of their menstrual cycle.

ANSWER

True. The relevant study was conducted in lap-dancing clubs in Albuquerque, New Mexico (home to the TV series *Breaking Bad*). Dancers were asked to keep a diary of their tips each night, and the results divided into three phases: menstrual (days 1–5), fertile (9–15) and luteal (18–28); days 6–8 and 16–17 were dropped because estimating fertility is an inexact science, and the researchers wanted to give themselves a little leeway.

The results were startling: dancers earned an average of around $335 per five-hour shift in the most fertile phase, compared with $260 during the luteal phase and just $185 during the menstrual phase. Were the dancers somehow making more effort during their most fertile phase? It seems unlikely. Most lap-dancers report sticking to the same costume, dance routine and conversation night in, night out, for – in most cases – literally thousands of dances. From the dancer's point of view, the aim is to make as much money as possible from every single dance. It simply does not make sense to keep any moves or chat-up lines in reserve for special occasions; if something works, keep it in the routine.

Rather, women who are at the most fertile point of their cycle give off physical and even chemical signals of this fact: signals that men not only pick up but also respond to with their wallets. At their most fertile phase women's soft-tissue features – including the ears, fingers and breasts – actually become more symmetrical (see **What's in a Face?**), with the result that they are rated as more physically attractive by men. What is more, in blind smelling tests, body odour samples from women in this fertile 'oestrous' stage are rated as more intense, pleasant and attractive than samples taken from the same women at other times.*

---

* We saw in the previous section that most women prefer more feminine-looking, 'nice' men to more masculine-looking 'bad boys'. But when they are at the most fertile point of their cycle, most women show increased liking of highly masculine faces. Again the reasons are evolutionary: a more masculine-looking face equals greater fertility.

The idea that the females of other species have fertile periods that they signal to males by means of physical and chemical signals is uncontroversial (think of female baboons and their red bottoms). Prior to these studies, most researchers thought that evolution had abandoned this strategy in humans, perhaps in favour of monogamous-pair strategies, which offer more protection for children. This theory may contain more than a hint of wishful thinking. We love to think of ourselves as somehow superior to other animals, and find it a little unsavoury to be reminded of just how much biology we all share. (Certainly, a man who referred to a woman as being 'on heat' would make himself pretty unpopular pretty quickly.) These studies suggest that we humans are not actually so special after all. When it comes to sexual signalling, we really are – in many respects – nothing but mammals.

What's in a Name?

More than you'd think.

The popular book *Freakonomics* introduced to a wider public the finding that your name is a good indicator of your parents' income, educational level and social class. For example, children named Alexandra, Lauren, Madison, Benjamin, Samuel or Jonathon tend to have higher-earning parents that those named Amber, Kayla, Alyssa, Cody, Brandon or Justin. For some names, even the particular spelling can be revealing. For example, mothers who name their daughter *Jasmine, Jasmin* or *Jasmyn* have, on average, about one year's more formal education than those who name their daughter *Jazmine, Jazmyne* or *Jazzmin*.

A recent study took this idea further, by showing that your name can also predict something about your parents' politics. Yes, Democrats and Republicans actually favour different names. Have a look at the list below, and see if you can guess which is which.*

Frank
Joseph
Kate
Kurt
Liam
Ryan
Sam
Thea
William

---

*For the benefit of non-US readers who might be unfamiliar with American politics, the Democrats are the more left-leaning party – roughly equivalent to the UK Labour Party – while the Republicans are the more right-leaning party – roughly equivalent to the UK Conservative Party.

ANSWER

Names more commonly given by Democrat parents: Liam, Ryan, Sam, Thea. Names more commonly given by Republican parents: Frank, Joseph, Kate, Kurt, William.

You might think that parents name their children after particular Democrat or Republican heroes or celebrities, and try to think up examples of each among the names listed. But this doesn't work very well, as most parents don't name their kids after other people (and certainly not after politicians), but just go for names that they like the *sound* of.

Here lies the clue. Republicans and Democrats like different sounds.

A 2013 study found that Republican parents are more likely to choose names that contain the sounds **F, OH, K** and **W** (e.g., Frank, Joseph, Kate, Kurt and William), while Democrat parents are more likely to choose names that contain the sounds **L, AYE, S** and **TH** (e.g,. Liam, Ryan, Sam and Thea).

Why? The 'Republican' sounds are harsher, more rugged and – in a completely objective sense – more masculine. That is, the sounds **F, OH, K** and **W** are much more common in boys' than girls' names (the authors of the study got hold of a list of all the common names in the United States and counted up instances of the sounds in each). The 'Democrat' sounds **L, AYE, S** and **TH** are softer and more feminine, again in the objective sense that they are more common in girls' than boys' names. (Sounds that are not mentioned here turn up roughly equally often in boys' and girls' names, and so are not predictive of parental politics.)

Once you know this, it's fun to speculate about all kinds of celebrities. For example, did **Kurt** Cobain have Republican parents (his father *did* force him to join the wrestling team)? Did **Katy** Perry (her parents *were* preachers)? Is a William who – like Oasis singer **Liam** Gallagher – chooses to be a Liam (a Democrat name) rather than a Will or a Bill (both Republican names) making a statement (and, if so, is Bill Clinton the exception)? And what about actors?

Ryan Gosling did play a Democrat in *The Ides of March*, while Rock Hudson is as Republican as they come.

Let's not get carried away, though. As the authors of this study point out, there are many other factors that have a much bigger influence on naming decisions, particularly ethnic, religious and family traditions. Then again, this only makes it all the more remarkable that a correlation with political leanings shines through regardless.

A final factor to consider is that some names double up as words with particular meanings in their own right. So, for example, if your child is *Kurt* or *Frank* by name because you are hoping that he will be *curt* or *frank* by nature, it's pretty clear that you're a Republican (*House of Cards* Democrat 'Frank' Underwood is actually called Francis, a feminine Democrat name.). And as for Johnny Cash's *Boy Named Sue* (a Democrat name so feminine that it's actually more commonly a girl's name), the story goes that it was inspired by Sue K. Hicks. No prizes for guessing his occupation: lawyer.

Hitler's Sweater

Are you an atheist? If so, then presumably you will have no problem reading aloud the following statements:

I dare God to paralyse my mother.
I dare God to make me die of cancer.
I dare God to make me be in a car crash.

Can you do it?

ANSWER

It's pretty uncomfortable, isn't it?

A study conducted at the University of Helsinki found that reading these statements out loud caused atheists to sweat just as much as religious people (both groups were self-described), as assessed by a machine that measures skin-conductance levels. (The more you sweat, the better your skin conducts electricity.)

Were the atheists stressed out simply because they were thinking and talking about these horrible events? Or did they think that merely talking about an unpleasant event somehow makes it more likely? Probably not. When asked to read similar statements that did not mention God ('I wish my parents were paralysed/I would die of cancer/I would be in a car crash'), the atheists did not sweat nearly so much.

So did the atheists *really* believe in God, even just a little bit? Not necessarily. The fact is, we all seem to find it hard to entirely escape certain 'superstitious' beliefs, even if – logically speaking – we know them to be entirely irrational.

Try this one: take an empty water bottle and, using a marker pen, write 'POISON XXX' on it, and draw a skull and crossbones. Then fill it with tap water and drink it. You can do it, of course, but – admit it – you had to force yourself just a little bit, didn't you?

What if I were to dip into the water a cockroach that had been completely sterilised to kill every last germ? Not so thirsty now, eh?

Here's another one: how would you feel about trying on a sweater that had briefly been worn by someone who you consider to be the personification of evil: perhaps a mass murderer or fanatical leader (Hitler, for example). A study conducted in the United States found that people considered this to be more unpleasant than if the sweater had been worn by a personal enemy or a hepatitis patient, or had been briefly dropped on to 'a small pile of dog faeces'.

One more: make yourself some scrambled or fried eggs, adding a few drops of a completely odourless and tasteless blue food colouring. Now eat it. Difficult, isn't it?

What is going on here? Why do we have these superstitious beliefs that we know full well to be completely illogical? Why do we think that something is poisonous when we know that it is not? Why do we think that evil can be transmitted like germs when we know that this is impossible?

What we need to bear in mind here is that it is only extremely recently that we have discovered exactly why some foods are good to eat while others are poisonous, and why diseases can be spread by physical contact while 'evil' cannot (the germ theory of disease is less than 200 years old). For the rest of human history, we have had to make do with much more general rules of thumb such as 'don't eat blue things' and 'don't touch things that you find unpleasant'. And because people who did eat blue things and handled rotting corpses were swiftly weeded out by natural selection, these rules of thumb have become part of our genetic make-up. So the reason that it is so hard to eat a blue fried egg is that you are forcing yourself to overcome feelings of disgust that have been hard-wired into you by thousands of years of evolution.

The claim that we have evolved to have religious belief – endorsed by atheist biologists such as Richard Dawkins and Stephen J. Gould – is obviously a controversial one. But if it is true, this could explain why an atheist has just as much difficulty daring God to paralyse his mother as he does eating a blue fried egg or trying on Hitler's sweater.

Getting All EmotIQnal

Have you noticed how the people who get promoted at your place of work (or the students that do best at your school, college or university) aren't always the hardest-working, the best-performing or the cleverest? What do they have that others – perhaps you – lack?

The answer, according to the psychologist Daniel Goleman, is a high level of *emotional intelligence*. The idea is that, just as we all vary in conventional abstract intelligence (IQ), so we all vary in our emotional intelligence (E-IQ): our ability to read, control and use emotions (both other people's and our own). In an article in the prestigious *Harvard Business Review*, Goleman claimed to have found evidence that emotional intelligence is twice as important for 'excellent performance' as technical skills and conventional IQ.

Twice as important, wow! I bet you are itching to find out your E-IQ, right? Go ahead: take the test overleaf. (Notice that statements where agreement represents a *lack* of emotional intelligence – e.g., 'I find it hard to understand the non-verbal messages of other people' – are reverse-scored: i.e., Strongly disagree = 5, Strongly agree = 1.)

	Strongly disagree				Strongly agree
1. I know when to speak about my personal problems to others.	1	2	3	4	5
2. When I am faced with obstacles, I remember times I faced similar obstacles and overcame them.	1	2	3	4	5
3. I expect that I will do well on most things I try.	1	2	3	4	5
4. Other people find it easy to confide in me.	1	2	3	4	5
5. I find it hard to understand the non-verbal messages of other people.	5	4	3	2	1
6. Some of the major events of my life have led me to re-evaluate what is important and not important.	1	2	3	4	5
7. When my mood changes, I see new possibilities.	1	2	3	4	5
8. Emotions are one of the things that make my life worth living.	1	2	3	4	5
9. I am aware of my emotions as I experience them.	1	2	3	4	5
10. I expect good things to happen.	1	2	3	4	5
11. I like to share my emotions with others.	1	2	3	4	5
12. When I experience a positive emotion, I know how to make it last.	1	2	3	4	5
13. I arrange events others enjoy.	1	2	3	4	5
14. I seek out activities that make me happy.	1	2	3	4	5
15. I am aware of the non-verbal messages I send to others.	1	2	3	4	5
16. I present myself in a way that makes a good impression on others.	1	2	3	4	5
17. When I am in a positive mood, solving problems is easy for me.	1	2	3	4	5

	Strongly disagree				Strongly agree
18. By looking at their facial expressions, I recognise the emotions people are experiencing.	1	2	3	4	5
19. I know why my emotions change.	1	2	3	4	5
20. When I am in a positive mood, I am able to come up with new ideas.	1	2	3	4	5
21. I have control over my emotions.	1	2	3	4	5
22. I easily recognise my emotions as I experience them.	1	2	3	4	5
23. I motivate myself by imagining a good outcome to tasks I take on.	1	2	3	4	5
24. I compliment others when they have done something well.	1	2	3	4	5
25. I am aware of the non-verbal messages other people send.	1	2	3	4	5
26. When another person tells me about an important event in his or her life, I almost feel as though I have experienced this event myself.	1	2	3	4	5
27. When I feel a change in emotions, I tend to come up with new ideas.	1	2	3	4	5
28. When I am faced with a challenge, I give up because I believe I will fail.	5	4	3	2	1
29. I know what other people are feeling just by looking at them.	1	2	3	4	5
30. I help other people feel better when they are down.	1	2	3	4	5
31. I use good moods to help myself keep trying in the face of obstacles.	1	2	3	4	5
32. I can tell how people are feeling by listening to the tone of their voice.	1	2	3	4	5
33. It is difficult for me to understand why people feel the way they do.	5	4	3	2	1

ANSWER

To find your emotional intelligence score, simply add up all the numbers that you circled. The average score is somewhere around 128, out of a possible maximum of 165. Women generally score slightly higher than men, with averages of around 131 and 125 respectively. Therapists (135) score a bit higher than the average, and prisoners (120) and drug-abuse patients (122) a bit lower.

Although emotional intelligence has proved to be a huge commercial success, with companies spending large amounts of money to measure and boost their employees' E-IQ, many academic psychologists are more sceptical.

One problem is that it's not clear whether tests of emotional intelligence measure anything that can't be captured by combining a conventional IQ test (see The Raw Shark Test) and a conventional personality test (see Your Personality Profile). If, as most academic studies suggest, they don't, then someone who is 'emotionally intelligent' is basically just someone who's clever, and also a nice guy (i.e., agreeable and outgoing).

A second problem is that it would seem to be pretty easy to fake the test, in order to portray oneself in a positive light to an employer. Although there are more sophisticated versions available, the test I gave you is ludicrously easy to fake. 'Strongly agreeing' with every statement *without even reading it* would give you an extremely high score (150), while being a little more careful with the reverse-scored items would result in a perfect 165. Conventional IQ tests, on the other hand, are impossible to fake (unless you want to seem *less* clever than you are). And while it is, of course, possible to lie in personality tests, it's not always clear exactly how you should fake your answers. (For example, does the employer want a quiet perfectionist or an office joker?) So it would seem that, if anything, you can learn much more about an employee from traditional tests than fancy, and often expensive, E-IQ tests.

But the biggest problem is that we have no way of knowing whether or not the claims made for E-IQ (e.g., that it is twice as important as IQ and technical skills) are true. The reason is that the vast majority of studies, including those referred to in Goleman's books and articles, have been conducted by private companies who market E-IQ tests and training courses, and who do not make their data available for scrutiny by academics or journalists.

So, while we can all agree that the ability to get on with others is important both in business and in life in general, shelling out for training in emotional intelligence is not necessarily a particularly intelligent thing to do.

Be on Your Guard

So far in this book, you've played a doctor, a radiologist, a health minister, a roulette-machine checker and a barman. This time, though, I think I've found your true calling: prison guard. There's just the small matter of an interview, but it's a formality. I have only one simple question.

A group of prisoners have become uncooperative, and are failing to follow your orders. Do you:

(a) reason with them, bearing in mind at all times the need to treat the prisoners with respect and dignity

or

(b) force them to walk around naked, to complete punishing physical exercises, to use a bucket instead of a toilet and to undergo sleep deprivation?

ANSWER

Of course, you answered (a), and would never resort to the tactics described in (b).

Would you?

While very few people would ever *plan* to use these demeaning and inhumane forms of discipline, this is exactly what happened, not only in real prisons such as Abu Ghraib and Guantánamo Bay but also in a mock prison set up at Stanford University in the 1970s, where the prisoners – like the guards – were mere volunteers in a psychology experiment, and so completely innocent of any crime.

Along with Milgram's Shocking Experiment, Philip Zimbardo's Prison Study is perhaps the most famous psychology experiment ever conducted, having been the subject of a feature film (*The Experiment*), a novel (*Black Box*) and numerous re-creations, including one by the BBC. Like Milgram, Zimbardo wanted to investigate why perfectly normal people are capable of doing truly terrible things, as in the real-life prisons mentioned above, as well as the concentration camps of the Second World War.

The usual conclusion drawn from the study is that absolute power corrupts absolutely: that the very act of placing people in a position of unchecked power causes them to naturally resort to violence and cruelty, and that – given the wrong circumstances – any of us could do such unspeakable things (which is why you must always 'be on your guard' against this possibility).

Professor Alex Haslam – who we met earlier in the section on Milgram's Shocking Experiment – disagrees. Haslam was in charge of the re-creation of the experiment run by the BBC. In this version of the experiment the guards did not behave nearly so badly. Why? Because they were not encouraged to do so. Haslam points out that, although it is often reported that Zimbardo did not give the guards any particular instructions, he certainly gave them a general sense of how they should behave:

You can create in the prisoners feelings of boredom, a sense of fear to some degree, you can create a notion of arbitrariness that their life is totally controlled by us, by the system, you, me . . . We're going to take away their individuality in various ways. In general what all this leads to is a sense of powerlessness.

Remember that the guards knew that this was just an experiment, for which both they and the prisoners were being paid, and that they were therefore under an obligation to follow the experimenter's instructions. Having heard these instructions, the guards would naturally assume that Zimbardo's goal was to see what happens when prisoners are subjected to 'boredom, fear and powerlessness', and that treating them with respect and dignity would undermine the whole purpose of the experiment. So, exactly as with Milgram's experiment, at least some of the guards may have played along because they 'assumed that the discomfort caused to the victim is momentary, while the scientific gains resulting from the experiment are enduring'. In other words, they may have played along out of a desire to be 'good people' – people who, having been paid to do an experiment, do it right.

This explanation doesn't apply to all the guards. For one thing, not all guards behaved sadistically, either in Zimbardo's original study or in Haslam's re-creation. For another, the guards who did were not simply following the instructions they had been given, but instead went above and beyond, by inventing their own controlling tactics, rules and punishments.

Is it therefore possible that at least some of the guards were not 'good people turned bad' – either by their position of power or by Zimbardo's instructions – but had somewhat sadistic tendencies all along? Was there something about the recruitment process that encouraged such people to apply?

To find out, two researchers at Western Kentucky University placed two recruitment adverts in the University newspaper; one virtually identical to that for Zimbardo's original study, the other omitting the crucial phrase 'of prison life':

Male college students needed for a psychological study ~~of prison life~~. $70 per day for 1–2 weeks beginning May 17th. For further information and applications, e-mail@address.com.

Actually, the 'study' was simply a questionnaire booklet, containing measures of aggression, authoritarianism, Machiavellianism, narcissism, social dominance, empathy and altruism. Guess what. The participants who responded to the advert that included the words 'of prison life' scored higher on every single one of the negative traits, and lower on both of the positive traits.

The implication is that at least some of Zimbardo's prison guards, and – indeed – guards who committed atrocities in real-life prisons, may not have been sweet and innocent people corrupted by unfortunate circumstances but people who had found an outlet for some darker personality traits that they had had all along.

Web Links and Further Reading

Philip Zimbardo gives his own account of what happened in his famous study in *The Lucifer Effect: Understanding How Good People Turn Evil*.

Pictures and further details of the Stanford Prison Experiment and the BBC re-creation can be found at

http://www.prisonexp.org/
http://www.bbcprisonstudy.org/

What's in a Face? #2: The Talking Dog

By now you may be wondering what I do when I'm not teaching or writing popular science books. The answer is that I'm an academic psychologist (see **Spot the Deference**) and spend most of my research time asking adults and children to rate sentences using a smiley-face scale. What on earth for? Before I tell you, let's see if I can predict the ratings that you will give on one of these tasks.

Billy the dog is learning to speak English, but because he's only a dog, he doesn't always get things right. (Remember, this study is designed for children aged four and upwards!) Your job is to help him by telling him when he says it right (happiest face), when he says it wrong and it sounds a bit silly (saddest face) and when it's somewhere in between (one of the middle three faces).

Here are a few practice sentences to get you started:

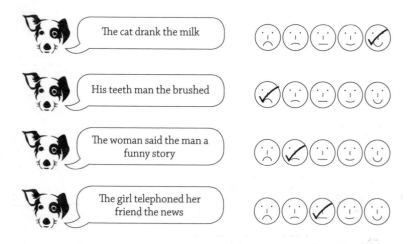

The test proper begins on the opposite page.

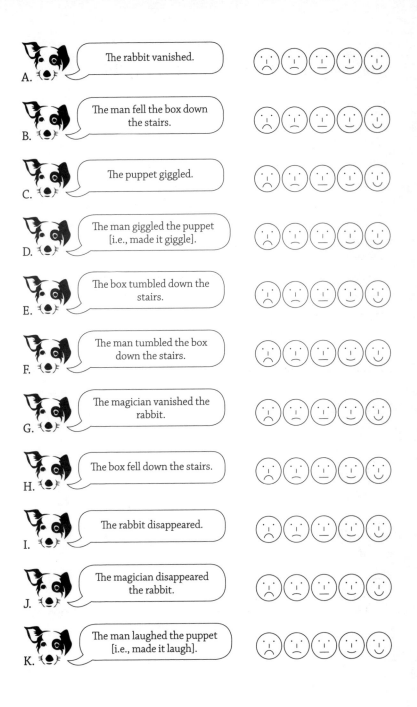

L.

The puppet laughed.

ANSWER

Add up your scores for sentences **A, C, E, H, I and L** (where the saddest face =1, the not quite so sad face =2 and so on). These sentences are all perfectly grammatical, so I'd be a little surprised (and, frankly, a little worried) if your total is much under 30 (if it's more than 30, you can't add up).

Next, add up your scores for sentences **B, J and K**.

Finally add up your scores for sentences **D, F and G**.

If you are like the adults who completed my study, the total for B+J+K will be two or three points smaller than the total for D+F+G; probably in the region of 6 and 9 respectively.

What is all this about?

Well, the unique thing about human language is that it lets us say things that we haven't heard before. Let's stop to think how a child might learn to do that.

Suppose a child hears someone say both of the following sentences:

The plate broke. [THING] [ACTION]
The man broke the plate. [CAUSER] [ACTION] [THING]

After hearing lots of pairs of this type, the child can set up a rule: if you hear a [THING] [ACTION] sentence, it's also possible to produce a [CAUSER] [ACTION] [THING] sentence with the same words.

This rule is very useful. Imagine that a child now hears someone say

The ball rolled. [THING] [ACTION]

She can use this [THING] [ACTION] ➡ [CAUSER] [ACTION] [THING] rule to produce a brand-new sentence; one that she has never heard before:

The man rolled the ball.   [CAUSER] [ACTION] [THING]

So far, so good. But there is a problem. Although this rule produces lots of grammatical sentences, it also produces ungrammatical sentences.

The rabbit disappeared.   [THING] [ACTION]
The magician disappeared the   [CAUSER] [ACTION] [THING]
rabbit.

If you have children of your own, you have probably heard them making exactly these kinds of mistakes. So how do they learn to stop? (We know that they must do at some point, as adults don't go around saying this sort of thing.) One possibility is that parents correct children's grammatical errors, but this doesn't seem to be right. Imagine, for example, a child saying 'We goed to the park', when actually it was the zoo. Most parents are far more likely to correct the factual error ('No, the zoo!') than the grammatical error ('No, went!'). And in any case, many errors happen when children are talking to each other at school or nursery, with no eavesdropping adults to correct them.

So how *do* children learn to stop making these mistakes? One suggestion is that the child goes through the following reasoning (not consciously, of course): 'I've heard *disappear* hundreds of times, but never in one of these [CAUSER] [ACTION] [THING] sentences. Surely if this were allowed, I would have heard it by now.'

The idea that children are capable of this type of reasoning may seem a bit far-fetched, but actually they do it all the time. How do children learn, for example, that dogs don't drive cars, read books or go to school? Simple: children have seen dogs hundreds of times, but have never seen one driving, reading or sitting in a classroom. This 'if it were possible, I would have seen it by now' reasoning happens completely automatically, without any conscious thinking or adult assistance. In fact, the alternative – that children have to figure out consciously whether or not dogs can drive, or have it explained to them by adults – is clearly absurd.

The study you have just completed tests the idea that children learn which sentences are ungrammatical in exactly the same way:

- I've seen dogs hundreds of times, but never seen one driving a car.
  - Surely if this were possible, I would have seen it by now.
    - So I'm going to assume it's not possible.

- I've heard *disappear* hundreds of times, but never in a [CAUSER] [ACTION] [THING] sentence.
  - Surely if this were possible, I would have heard it by now.
    - So I'm going to assume it's not possible.

That is, the more you hear a particular word, the more you assume it can't appear in sentence types you haven't heard it in. So, because you have heard *fall, laugh* and *disappear* (relatively common words) much more often than *tumble, giggle* and *vanish* (relatively rare words), your belief that they are barred from [CAUSER] [ACTION] [THING] sentence types is stronger for the former than the latter.

At least, that's the prediction; and having tested it in many different studies, I can confidently say that it's one that is well supported, for both adults and children as young as four years of age.

So, that's the day job. But before I get back to that, there's the small matter of this book to finish. So let's move on from testing your grammar to testing your literacy . . .

Web Links and Further Reading
Journal articles reporting this research – and all of my academic writing – can be found at: www.benambridge.com.

A very readable introduction to this topic is Steven Pinker's popular book *The Stuff of Thought*, which also introduces another possible solution to this problem.

Literacy Test

So, you've measured your IQ (Quoth the Raven's 'What's My Score?'), your reasoning ability (Card Trick), your thinking style (It Feels So Right), your intuitions regarding grammatical acceptability (What's in a Face? #2: The Talking Dog) and your ability to spot typos (Reading and Righting). But none of these intelligence, grammar or reading tests is quite like the following literacy test. You have three-and-a-half minutes to complete the test, which is assessed on a simple pass/fail basis: If you get one wrong, you automatically fail.

1. Draw a line through the two letters below that come last in the alphabet:

   Z V B D N K I P H S T Y C

2. In the first circle below write the last letter of the first word beginning with 'L':

3. Cross out the number not necessary when making the number below one million:

   1,000,0000

4. In the line below, cross out each number that is more than 20 but less than 30:

   25 21 16 48 23 53 47 22 37 98 26 20

5. In the space below write the word 'noise' backwards and place a **d** over what would be the second letter should it have been written forward:

....

6. Look at the line of numbers below and place on the blank the number that should come next:

2 4 8 16 ....

7. Print the word 'vote' upside down but in correct order:

....

8. Print a word that looks the same whether it is printed forwards or backwards:

....

9. Write down on the line provided what you read in the triangle:

Paris in
the
the springtime ....

10. Write right from the left to the right as you see it spelled here:

....

ANSWERS

You have just completed a cut-down version of a real 'literacy test' administered to would-be voters in the US state of Louisiana in the 1960s. For what it's worth, my own 'correct' answers are given below. I say 'for what it's worth' because the whole point of this test is that – for black test-takers – there *were* no correct answers. The questions were designed to be sufficiently confusing and ambiguous to allow the marker, the voter registrar, whatever wiggle-room he needed to fail black test-takers (although this wasn't much, as the registrar was judge and jury, and applicants had no right of appeal). So, along with my own 'correct' answers, I've put a possible reason that the registrar might give for marking this answer as incorrect if it were given by a black applicant. (I know that these reasons don't often make much sense, but that's just the point: they don't have to.)

1. Draw a line through the two letters below that come last in the alphabet:

   Z̶ V B D N K I P H S T Ɏ C

   Registrar: 'Ah, but there *aren't* two letters that come last in the alphabet. Only z comes last in the alphabet.'

2. In the first circle below write the last letter of the first word beginning with 'L':

   Registrar: 'The first word in the alphabet that begins with 'L' is 'L', as 'L' is itself a word: the name for the letter 'L'. 'L' is the last (and first) letter of 'L', so you should have written 'L'.

3. Cross out the number not necessary when making the number below one million:

   1,000,000̶0̶

Registrar: 'You should have crossed out the *first* zero after the final comma. This is the first unnecessary number, and therefore *the* unnecessary number.'

4. In the line below, cross out each number that is more than 20 but less than 30:

   ~~25 21~~ 16 48 ~~23~~ 53 47 ~~22~~ 37 98 26 20

   Registrar: 'You missed 20. (I'm judge and jury remember!)'

5. In the space below write the word 'noise' backwards and place a d over what would be the second letter should it have been written forward:

esidn

   Registrar: 'Noise *was* written backwards, so you should have placed a 'd' over the second letter of *esion*. In any case, you were asked to place a 'd' *over* (i.e., above) the letter, not on top of the letter.'

6. Look at the line of numbers below and place on the blank the number that should come next:

   2 4 8 16 32 ....

   Registrar: 'No, to get each number (e.g., 16), you have to multiply the previous number (8), by the number two before that one (2). So to get the blank number, you have to multiply the previous number (16) by the number two numbers earlier (4) to get 64' or even 'These are the house numbers of registered voters on Main Street. The next registered voter lives at number 17.'

7. Print the word 'vote' upside down but in the correct order:

   ΛO⅃E

   Registrar: 'This isn't in the correct order. Look, if I turn it right way around, it says 'ETOV' not VOTE'.

8. Print a word that looks the same whether it is printed forwards or backwards:

RADAR

Registrar: 'No, if this is printed backwards, it looks like ЯАDАЯ. The only correct answer is the word "A".'

9. Write down on the line provided what you read in the triangle.

Registrar: 'No, you were clearly told to write down on the line the phrase "provided what you read in the triangle"' (though this would rarely be necessary, as most people incorrectly miss out the second 'the').

10. Write right from the left to the right as you see it spelled here:

right

Registrar: 'This is like the last one. You should have written the phrase "right from the left to the right", just as you saw it spelled in the test.'

OK, so you're not going to learn much by reading the answers. But we can learn quite a lot by examining the test: specifically, the lengths to which some white people were prepared to go to enforce racial discrimination. This raises the question of just *why* certain people are racist. In trying to answer this question, psychologists have unearthed some uncomfortable home truths about our species.

The first is that most people are at least a little bit racist, as revealed by something called the *implicit association test* (which you can take for yourself: see Web Links). After a few preliminary stages comes the main two-part test. In Part A, a face or word appears in the centre of the screen and participants must press (say) the left-hand key if the face is white or the word is positive (e.g., *happy*) and the right-hand key if the face is black or the word is negative (e.g., *mean*). In Part B, participants must press the left-hand key if the face is white or the word is negative, and the right-hand key if the face is black or the word is positive.

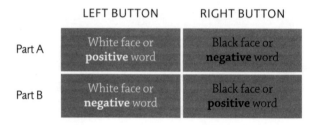

	LEFT BUTTON	RIGHT BUTTON
Part A	White face or **positive** word	Black face or **negative** word
Part B	White face or **negative** word	Black face or **positive** word

In all cases, participants must press the button as quickly as possible. If a participant is able to respond more quickly when – in terms of the required key-press – white is paired with positive and black with negative (Part A) than vice versa (Part B), then this is taken as evidence of implicit racism.

So here is the first unpleasant truth: in the first study of this type, all but one of the twenty-six white participants made speedier responses in the white+positive and black+negative part of the study (Part A), even though, when asked about their racial preferences directly, the vast majority (nineteen out of twenty-six) expressed either no preference or a preference for black people.

Here is the second: this discrimination starts young. A 2006 study found that white six-year-olds displayed a white-preference not only in this implicit test but also when asked to select their preferred face from a black–white pair, choosing the latter on 84 per cent of occasions. Even more dramatically, when offered the opportunity to look at faces of their own race or a different race, babies just *three months old* look for longer at the former (it's well established that looking time constitutes a measure of preference, as babies also look longer at their own mother than strangers, and longer at attractive than unattractive faces, as rated by adults).

These studies tell us that racial biases are widespread and start young, but not why we have them. Sadly, the findings of other studies suggest that these biases are part and parcel of a universal human tendency to divide each other up into groups, and discriminate against members of groups other than one's own.

In a classic study from the 1970s, Henri Tajfel divided schoolchildren into two groups, on the basis of something deliberately trivial: whether they preferred the paintings of Paul Klee or Wassily Kandinsky (they were shown examples of each). Each child was then asked to determine how a reward would be shared between a pair of anonymous children: one from the child's own group, one from the other group. Most children chose not to maximise the joint amount received by the pair, or even the amount received by the child's group mate. Instead, children chose to maximise the *difference* between their group mate and the member of the other group (in favour of the former, naturally). Discriminating against a different group seems to be almost second nature, even when the groups themselves are completely meaningless.

Again, this discrimination starts young. In a related study researchers asked nine-month-olds to choose a snack – a Graham cracker or a green bean – and then introduced them to two puppets: one who preferred the same snack as the child and one who preferred the other snack. A series of puppet shows demonstrated that children preferred scenes where a third character was nice to the puppet that was 'like them' (helping him find his ball) and mean to the puppet that was 'not like them' (stealing his ball).

But *why* do we have this tendency to divide each other up and discriminate against members of other groups? The answer is probably evolutionary. For most of our history as a species, food and other resources have been scarce, and we have had to band into groups and tribes in order to compete for them. Against this backdrop, fear and suspicion of outsiders – members of rival tribes – was presumably necessary for survival.

In the modern world, of course, there is no need – indeed, no justification – for fear of outsiders. We would all be better off if we could put a stop to discrimination for good; the question is, how to achieve it. Fortunately, psychology has begun to suggest some answers. In one recent study, for example, white participants were given training in telling black faces apart from one another. The reasoning was that helping people to overcome their tendency to lump all members of a particular race together – visually as well as in terms of character and behaviour – might help them to overcome their prejudices. And do you know what? It seems to work. Participants who received this training showed reduced discrimination (as measured by the implicit association test), while a no-training control group did not.

Some pessimists say that we have made almost no progress in combating racial discrimination. A quick look at the literacy test at the start of this section should quickly disabuse us of that notion; what was government policy in the 1960s is unthinkable today, not only in the United States but in most of the world. On the other hand, while official state-sanctioned racism has been largely eradicated, the implicit association test reminds us that personal prejudices remain hidden within many – perhaps most – of us. The training study discussed above suggests an obvious solution: if you're worried that you might, deep down, harbour some unconscious prejudices, try to meet as many members of the relevant group as possible, in order to learn to view them as individuals rather than a homogeneous 'them'.

In short, if you want to 'pass' not only this ridiculous literacy test but also the implicit association test, you need to learn to discriminate *between* people of other races rather than *against* them.

Web Link
Take the implicit association test at:

https://implicit.harvard.edu/implicit/demo/takeatest.html

Roll Play

How do you prefer to hang your toilet roll? Do you like the loose end to be far away from the wall (known as the *over* style) or next to the wall (the *under* style)?

over

under

I must admit, it had never even occurred to me that there were two possible ways to hang the roll, until somebody – I forget who – admonished me for hanging it the 'wrong' way. (I have also forgotten which way that was.) Nevertheless, there is some evidence to suggest that your preferred style is a predictor of your earning power.

So, over or under?

ANSWER

Well, obviously there is no 'correct' answer as such, but the most comprehensive survey to date (conducted in the United States) found that 68 per cent of respondents surveyed chose *over*. Counter to the claims of various smaller polls and informal hunches, there was no evidence to suggest a difference between men and women or between older and younger people.

One interesting difference was observed, though: of respondents earning £20,000 or less, 73 per cent bucked the trend by preferring the *under* style. Opining on another survey, conducted by a toilet-roll manufacturer, Dr Gilde Carle ('Relationship Expert to the Stars') offered the following insightful analysis:

- If you roll over, you like taking charge, crave organisation and are likely to over-achieve.
- If you roll under, you're laid-back, dependable and seek relationships with strong foundations.
- If you don't care, as long as it's there, you aim to minimise conflict, value flexibility and like putting yourself in new situations.

These surveys – to put it mildly – do not quite meet the standards required for a scientific study, and their conclusions should obviously be taken with more than just a pinch of salt. What is surprising, though, is how many people have an opinion on the issue. The comedian Jay Leno famously confessed to changing the hanging of the roll at other people's houses, and both Martha Stewart and Ann Landers are passionate advocates of the *over* style. We leave the final word, however, to Paul Burrell, butler to Diana, Princess of Wales:

Of course it should be over. If it were down, it would unravel all over the floor. Royals don't have that problem, because they have sheets of tissue which are fanned out into an attractive display and sit in a box.

A Trivial Pursuit: Part 1

Now, I'm afraid this one is going to require a little bit of home-work. But stick with it as, without giving too much away, the few minutes of time that you will need to invest here could really pay dividends in the future.

I would like you to spend five minutes (time yourself – it's longer than you think) imagining a typical university professor – perhaps one at Oxford, Cambridge, Harvard or MIT – and listing on a blank sheet of paper the **behaviours**, **lifestyle** and **appearance** attributes of this typical professor.

Please don't turn the page until you have spent a full five minutes on this task.

A Trivial Pursuit: Part 2

As soon as you have completed Part 1 from the previous page, please answer the following multiple-choice questions (either by circling your chosen answers in this book or by noting them down on a separate sheet of paper):

1. What name is given to atoms of the same element that have different atomic weights?

   (a) Isotopes
   (b) Isobars
   (c) Doppelgängers
   (d) Protons

2. Who won the (soccer) World Cup in 1930?

   (a) Italy
   (b) Uruguay
   (c) Hungary
   (d) Argentina

3. In which country is the most western point of Europe?

   (a) Portugal
   (b) Ireland
   (c) Spain
   (d) France

4. Who wrote the classic book of military tactics *The Art of War*?

   (a) Alexander the Great
   (b) George Washington
   (c) Napoleon Bonaparte
   (d) Sun Tzu

5. What historical event was investigated by the Warren Commission?

   (a) The Challenger disaster
   (b) The assassination of President Kennedy
   (c) The assassination of Martin Luther King, Jr.
   (d) Apollo 13

6. Which is the largest of the Galápagos Islands?

   (a) Fernandina
   (b) Isabela
   (c) Santa Cruz
   (d) Santiago

7. What is the highest power of the variable (such as x) in a quadratic equation?

   (a) Four
   (b) Two
   (c) Three
   (d) One

8. Which of the Apollo missions resulted in the first moon landing?

   (a) Apollo 9
   (b) Apollo 11
   (c) Apollo 13
   (d) Apollo 8

9. Whose life was the basis for the film *Shadowlands*?

   (a) C. S. Lewis
   (b) W. H. Auden
   (c) Richard Attenborough
   (d) John Betjeman

10. Who played Atticus Finch in the 1962 film of *To Kill a Mockingbird*?

   (a) Gregory Peck
   (b) Cary Grant
   (c) Rock Hudson
   (d) James Garner

A Trivial Pursuit: Part 3

Before I tell you the answers, I would now like you to spend a
further five minutes imagining a particular type of person – this
time, a football hooligan. Again, please take a blank sheet of paper
and list the **behaviours**, **lifestyle** and **appearance** attributes of
this typical hooligan.

Again, please read no further until you have done this.

A Trivial Pursuit: Part 4

Surprise: another quiz! I promise this is the last one. Again, don't forget to make a note of your answers.

1. Which is the biggest of the Mediterranean's islands?

   (a) Sicily
   (b) Sardinia
   (c) Corsica
   (d) Cyprus

2. Who starred as surveillance expert Harry Caul in Francis Ford Coppola's *The Conversation*?

   (a) Gene Hackman
   (b) Clint Eastwood
   (c) Elliott Gould
   (d) Burt Lancaster

3. Which was the third Harry Potter book to be published?

   (a) *Harry Potter and the Chamber of Secrets*
   (b) *Harry Potter and the Prisoner of Azkaban*
   (c) *Harry Potter and the Order of the Phoenix*
   (d) *Harry Potter and the Half-Blood Prince*

4. From which two metals is bronze usually made?

   (a) Copper and zinc
   (b) Iron and magnesium
   (c) Copper and tin
   (d) Iron and lead

5. The first *Godfather* movie, *Columbo*, *Hacky Sacks* and *The Joy of Sex* were all first seen in which year of the 1970s?

   (a) 1970
   (b) 1972
   (c) 1971
   (d) 1973

6. In photography, what does the R in SLR stand for?

   (a) Rangefinder
   (b) Randolph
   (c) Reflector
   (d) Reflex

7. Which country is alternatively known as the Union of Myanmar?

   (a) Thailand
   (b) Tibet
   (c) Burma
   (d) Vietnam

8. In Greek mythology, which creature has the head of a bull and the body of a man?

   (a) Griffon
   (b) Minotaur
   (c) Centaur
   (d) Cyclops

9. What disease is caused by the parasite Plasmodium falciparum?

   (a) Leishmaniasis
   (b) Malaria
   (c) Schistosomiasis
   (d) Creutzfeldt-Jakob Disease

10. In which year did Mexico City stage the Olympic Games?

   (a) 1962
   (b) 1968
   (c) 1972
   (d) 1976

ANSWERS

Let's see how you got on. Here are the answers to the first quiz:

(1) Isotopes; (2) Uruguay; (3) Portugal; (4) Sun Tzu; (5) The assassination of President Kennedy; (6) Isabela; (7) Two; (8) Apollo 11; (9) C. S Lewis; (10) Gregory Peck.

And the second:

(1) Sicily; (2) Gene Hackman; (3) *Harry Potter and the Prisoner of Azkaban*; (4) Copper and tin; (5) 1972; (6) Reflex; (7) Burma; (8) Minotaur; (9) Malaria; (10) 1968.

So, did you do better in the first quiz or the second? Amazingly, a group of Dutch psychologists found that people given the 'professor' task performed slightly better on a subsequent general knowledge quiz (on average, equivalent to around 6 out of 10) than those given the 'football hooligan' task (on average, equivalent to somewhere between 4 and 5 out of 10).*

Whether or not this worked for you, it's pretty incredible that the Dutch group found a difference between the 'professors' and 'football hooligans' (in reality, students at the University of Nijmegen†). What is going on here? These researchers explain this

---

* Notice that the way that they set up the study was a bit cleaner than the way I had you do it. They asked one group of people to think about a professor and a *different* group to think about a hooligan, and then gave them *exactly the same* quiz. Because I asked the same person (i.e., you) to think first about a professor and then about a hooligan, I had to give you two different quizzes, which might not have been perfectly matched for difficulty. Now you know how the study is supposed to work, why not try running the cleaner version on some friends? Simply give one group the 'professor' task, the other group the 'hooligan' task, and then ask each person all twenty questions.

† The city of Nijmegen is itself the subject of one of my favourite general knowledge quiz questions. If asked what country Nijmegen is in, most British people who have heard of the city at all will say 'Holland'. This isn't quite right. Nijmegen is in the Netherlands, but it is not in Holland. North and South Holland are just two provinces of the twelve that make up the Netherlands.

finding in terms of what they call the *perception-behaviour link* (or what we might call 'monkey see, monkey do'). When we see people acting in a particular way, we often start to unconsciously imitate their behaviour and mannerisms. Why do we do this? Essentially because we want others to like us, and people like people who are like themselves (as we just saw in Literacy Test). Taking this a step further, the idea is that, even if we can't see them, just *thinking about* people who have certain characteristics (like smart professors and dumb hooligans) is enough to make us start to behave like them, in terms of both their thought processes and their physical actions. Another study which tested this claim found that participants who were given lists of characteristics of elderly people walked more slowly down the hallway when leaving the experiment.

This is where everything starts to get messy. Another group of researchers re-ran this slow-walking study, with tweaks designed to tighten up the method, such as timing the participants' walking speed using an infra-red beam rather than a stopwatch, and ensuring that the experimenters carrying out the study did not know which participants had seen the elderly-related words, and hence avoiding any *expectancy effect* (see YOU Are the Psychologist). The slow-walking effect disappeared. The author of the original study (Professor John Bargh, of Yale University) countered that this new study had some other differences that could have eliminated the effect, and pointed to two successful replications, as well as one conducted for a BBC television programme (see Web Links).

What about the 'Trivial Pursuit' study? Two research teams have re-run this experiment and found no difference between the 'professors' and the 'football hooligans'. However, unlike the original, these studies were published not in peer-reviewed journals (where they are subject to scrutiny from fellow researchers) but on a website dedicated to failed replications of famous psychology studies (see Web Links). However, one could argue that this is hardly the fault of the authors. Academic journals – much like newspapers – are generally quick to publish the original headline-grabbing story but reluctant to publish a boring follow-up story saying, 'Um, you know that thing we said before? Well, maybe it wasn't true.'

So where does that leave us? Personally, I'm sceptical of this particular study. My problem is that a general knowledge quiz isn't the right test here. For most questions, you either know the answer or you don't, and even if it were possible to boost your brainpower to Einstein level, there is no way that this could leave you with knowledge that wasn't there in the first place. Perhaps, for example, we could compare the 'professors' and the 'football hooligans' on the time taken to complete a test that, while challenging, is still solvable by most people (like, for example, the tests you completed in Prelude or Requiem? or The March of Time). If you're a psychology student, this could make an interesting and relatively easy-to-run research project.

In the meantime, next time you play Trivial Pursuit, it can't hurt – and may even help – to spend a few minutes thinking about that knowledgeable professor. On the other hand, if you're ever unlucky enough to find yourself in a fight, try to think like a football hooligan.

Web Links

The BBC replication of the slow-walking study can be seen at: http://www.youtube.com/watch?v=5g4_v4JStOU

The site dedicated to failed replications of psychology studies is: www.psychfiledrawer.org

What's in a Face? #3: Brown-Eyed Girl

A UK judge recently ruled that a defendant should not be allowed to give evidence in court wearing a full-face veil, on the basis that 'The ability of the jury to see the defendant for the purposes of evaluating her evidence is crucial.' This ruling reflects the widespread belief that we are able to tell when a person is lying by closely watching his or her mannerisms.

In fact, this belief is probably untrue (look back to Liar, Liar). But do some people just *look* more trustworthy than others, regardless of what they are saying or doing?

Look at the pairs of faces below. Your job is to choose which face in each pair looks more trustworthy:

Man A   Man B

Woman A   Woman B

By the way, if you are wondering why these people are all so good-looking, the answer is that they are not real people at all, but composites created by averaging across many different photos (see What's in a Face? #1). They are also Czech, which probably helps.

ANSWER

Most people think that Man A looks more trustworthy than Man B. For the women, people are split roughly 50/50.

A study conducted in the Czech Republic found that men with brown eyes (A) were rated as more trustworthy than men with blue eyes (B; the photos were presented in colour). But why should men with brown eyes be thought of as more trustworthy? The mystery deepens further when we find out that the 'brown-eyed' men were still rated as more trustworthy, even if the faces were digitally edited to have blue eyes instead (which why I was happy to have you complete the study in black-and-white).

So it must be something other than their brown eyes that makes brown-eyed men *look* more trustworthy (there's no evidence that they actually *are*). But what? The answer seems to be face shape, which is correlated with eye colour. Brown-eyed male faces tend to have a round chin, a broad mouth with upward-pointing corners, big eyes and eyebrows closer to each other – all characteristics of faces that are rated as more trustworthy. Blue-eyed male faces tend to have a longer and more pointed chin, a narrower mouth, smaller eyes and further-apart eyebrows – all characteristics of faces that are rated as less trustworthy. Interestingly, face shape does not predict perceived trustworthiness for women, partly because women's faces are more similar to one another's than men's, and partly because females are rated as more trustworthy across the board.

But *why* are men with rounder chins, broader mouths and bigger eyes perceived as more trustworthy? There seem to be at least three reasons. First, rounder chins and bigger features make people seem more 'baby-faced', and hence 'innocent-looking'. Second, narrower mouths and eyes make people look angry (think about how you purse your lips and narrow your eyes when you are angry). Conversely, broader mouths and bigger eyes make people look happy, and – all other things being equal – you're better off trusting someone who is happy than someone who is angry. Third, men with larger facial features (which, remember, tend to go along with brown eyes) are perceived of as more masculine (think of the tall, *dark*, handsome stranger), and hence as more dependable and trustworthy.

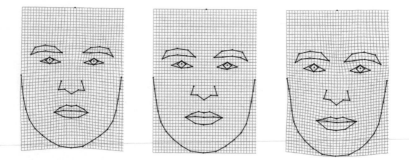

Visualisations of (from left to right) the least trustworthy, average and most trustworthy male faces. The visualisations were created (by the authors of the original paper) by mapping the rated faces to a standardised grid and aggregating the characteristics of faces judged as particularly trustworthy and untrustworthy respectively.

So, rather than ruling that nobody should wear a veil when giving evidence, perhaps the judge should have ruled that everybody in court should wear a veil throughout the proceedings; otherwise, we risk the jury being swayed by such irrelevant factors as face shape and – indirectly – eye colour.

At My Wick's End

You have a small candle, a box of drawing pins and a book of matches. Your task is to attach the candle to the wall so that it does not drip on to the floor below it.

What do you do?

Under Pressure

Knowing what you now know, how many solutions can you find to the following problem (a genuine exam question)?

How it is possible to determine the height of a tall building with the aid of a barometer?

By the way, if you don't know what a barometer is, it's a device that measures atmospheric pressure (as used by many amateur weather forecasters).

ANSWER

The boring solution is to use the barometer to measure the atmospheric pressure at the top and bottom of the building, and use the difference in pressure – which decreases with altitude – to work out the height.

But what I was *really* getting at was functional-fixedness. How many other ways to 'determine the height of a tall building with the aid of a barometer' did you think of?

Here are some possibilities:

- Tie the barometer to a rope to make an improvised plumb line. Throw the line off the top of the building, mark the height of the building on the rope, then measure it when you get home.
- Throw the barometer off the top of the building, time how long it takes to hit the floor and use the relevant equation to calculate the distance that it travelled.
- Take the barometer out on a sunny day and work out the ratio of the barometer to its shadow. Then measure the shadow of the building, and use the ratio to calculate the height of the building.
- Take the stairs up the building, marking off barometer-lengths vertically on the wall. Count the number of marks to discover the height of the building . . . in barometer units . . .
- . . . or convert to standard measurement units by finding out the height of the barometer (perhaps from the manufacturer, if you don't have a tape measure).
- Find someone who knows the height of the building (perhaps the porter, janitor or caretaker) and promise to give them your fancy barometer if they will tell you how tall the building is.

How many did you get? Did you come up with any more? Here's my own. It's a bit pedantic but, like many of the others, plays on the fact that the question says '*with the aid of* a barometer' and not '*using only* a barometer':

- Sell the barometer and use the money to buy a bus ticket to the offices of a surveyor, who you then pay to measure the building.

Incidentally, the story goes that this was a question asked in a real physics exam, and the professor agonised over whether or not to give the student marks for one of the smart-alec answers above. I'm afraid I don't have much sympathy for the student, as I think it's fair to say that all exam questions include an implicit 'using the material from the relevant part of the course you have just taken'.

Still, fair play to the student – if he, in fact, existed – for avoiding functional-fixedness.

In that spirit, I will offer a prize to whoever comes up with the most imaginative use for this very book. Email your photos to uses@Psy-Qbook.com.

Good luck!

Spare the Rod and Spoil the Child?

TRUE = I believe that children need physical discipline.

FALSE = I believe that spanking has lasting damaging effects, including making children more aggressive.

So, what's your answer: TRUE or FALSE?

ANSWER

Our attitude towards spanking is deeply ambivalent. On the one hand, the practice carries quite a social stigma, is counselled against by experts (including the American Academy of Pediatrics) and is illegal in thirty-two countries. On the other hand, in both the UK and the United States, surveys have found that over a third of parents reported spanking their children at least once a month.

This is a debate where passions run high, so, before we go any further, let's clarify what we mean by 'spanking'. We're talking here about a mild, open-handed slap – usually to the hand or bottom – that causes no lasting damage. These days almost everyone agrees that anything more, including the caning that was routine in schools only a couple of generations ago, is beyond the pale.

There is no shortage of studies showing that children who are spanked are more aggressive. But, as we saw with religion and IQ (The Fool Hath Said in His Heart, 'There Is No God'), this tells us nothing about the direction of causality. Does spanking *cause* children to be more aggressive, or are parents simply more likely to spank children who are more aggressive to begin with?

To find out, we need to restrict our analysis to *longitudinal* studies that control for children's initial aggression levels. That is, we identify children who are (a) spanked and (b) not spanked at Time 1, ensuring that the two groups are matched on a baseline measure of aggression (and anything else that we're interested in), and then compare them at Time 2, months or years down the line. When this is done, we find that children who are spanked are indeed more prone to aggression (though, actually, the study in question lumped in aggression with rule-breaking and anti-social and oppositional behaviours), and also to depression, anxiety and stress.

But – and this is a huge 'but' – the difference between the spanked and non-spanked groups, though statistically significant, is absolutely tiny. Remember in the section Men Are from Mars . . . we saw what a tiny difference, such as men's advantage for mathematical problem-solving, looks like when represented graphically? That's right – the two lines overlap so much that you can barely separate them without the aid of a magnifying glass. This is exactly what the difference between spanked and non-spanked children looks like. Non-spanked children are less aggressive, but by such an infinitesimally small amount that 47 per cent of the non-spanked children are more aggressive than the average spanked child. (Remember that, if this number were 50 per cent, the two groups would be identically aggressive.)

Two popular alternative punishments – shouting and making threats that aren't carried through – fared little better, with both also leading to infinitesimally higher levels of aggression in children. Positive discipline, such as explaining why a particular action was wrong, or praising good behaviour rather than punishing bad, seemed to have no effect either way. I guess this makes it the winner by default, though winning by having no effect at all looks to me like a pretty hollow victory. You might as well discipline your child using homeopathy.

So what should you do? In practice, most parents probably take the decision to spank or not to spank on the basis of their own personal feelings on the matter. What this study tells us is that this approach is basically fine. Although passions on the subject run high, in reality, whether or not you spank your child probably has very little effect on how he or she turns out.

Video Gains?

OK, so spanking causes – at most – a very tiny increase in aggression among children. What about that other often discussed culprit: video games (or, as we Brits rather quaintly call them, computer games)? The question is certainly an important one, as games are big business: in many countries, including the United States, the games industry is bigger – in purely financial terms – than either the music or film industry.

This issue has provoked a huge debate in the scientific literature, and I won't bore you with the details.* Probably a fair conclusion is that – again – the effect is real, but pretty tiny. If we look at real-world aggressive behaviour, controlling for the fact that people with aggressive tendencies are more likely to be drawn towards violent games in the first place, we are left with an effect of about the same size as for spanked versus non-spanked children (see the previous section).†

Perhaps more interesting – though usually deemed less mediaworthy – are the possible *beneficial* effects of video games (or *video gains*). Several studies have found that games improve visuo-

---

* Though, for any readers who are interested in this type of thing, the back-and-forth between Craig Anderson (Iowa State University) and Christopher Ferguson (Texas A&M) is a textbook example of the debate over inclusion criteria and effect sizes in meta analysis.

† We see a slightly bigger effect if we look at experimental studies, in which participants who are randomly assigned to play a violent game (e.g., *Call of Duty*) show more aggressive behaviour afterwards than participants given a non-violent game (e.g., *Portal 2*). However, since we can't allow participants to beat each other up in the lab, this 'aggressive behaviour' normally involves nothing more than blasting a fictitious partner with white noise or forcing him to drink an unpleasant hot sauce. Sure, this counts as aggression, but it's hardly evidence that violent games can lead – taking an extreme example – to high-school shootings.

spatial processing, memory and hand–eye coordination. One even found that surgeons who played video games in their spare time made 32 per cent fewer errors and performed 24 per cent faster than non-players. Some games also promote social interaction: in the survey discussed in Digital Love, 2 per cent of couples who met online did so in virtual game worlds (e.g., *World of Warcraft*). Perhaps most impressively of all, one study found that having dyslexic children play the Nintendo Wii game *Rayman Raving Rabbids* for a total of twelve hours increased their reading ability, apparently by improving their concentration. And on a personal note, everything I know about persistence, patience and problem-solving I learned by playing *Lemmings* on the Amiga.

So my advice to parents is this: you're probably never going to be able to stop your children playing violent games, but you could always try to persuade them to mix in some more cerebral games too. And even if you can't, at least they'll be boosting their hand–eye coordination.

Of course, we adults wouldn't waste our time with games. We spend our 'screen time' on more important things, like … using social media. That can't do any harm … can it?

Shut Your Face(book)?

TRUE or FALSE? People with higher levels of Facebook use are more likely to cheat on their partner and eventually split up.

ANSWER

TRUE, at least on the basis of one recent study. Now, before I get sued by Mark Zuckerberg & Co., I should point out that this was a correlational study, and – as we've already seen – correlation does not necessarily equal causation: just because people who use Facebook more are more likely to cheat on their partner, this does not mean that a high level of Facebook usage *causes* cheating. In fact, it would seem much more likely that some third factor is at play. For example, one possibility is that at least some people had already decided to cheat on their partner and started scouring Facebook for opportunities to do so. Another, slightly more charitable, possibility is that people who check their Facebook page every few minutes are emotionally needy, and hence exactly the sort of people who might find it difficult to resist if someone shows an interest in them.

Does this mean that, if your other half is a Facebook addict, you should suspect the worst? Happily, the answer is 'not necessarily'. The relationship between high Facebook use and what the survey called 'negative interpersonal relationship outcomes' (break-up, emotional cheating and physical cheating) is a subtle and complex one. For a start, high Facebook use does not predict cheating and break-ups directly. It's actually a two-stage process: high Facebook use predicts conflict over Facebook use, and it is this conflict that predicts cheating and break-ups. In other words, it's not your partner's constant Facebook use that is the problem, but the fact that you can't stop nagging him or her about it. And even this is only true for couples that have been together for less than three years; any longer than that, and there is no relationship at all between Facebook use and cheating or break-ups (perhaps because these relationships are stronger, perhaps because one partner is resigned to the other's Facebook addiction and has got bored of nagging).

So, if you've just updated your status to 'In a relationship', perhaps you should both think about toning down your Facebook use just a little, or – if not – at least agreeing not to fight about it.

Cake Addicts?

Ever wondered why you can't stop snacking?

Actually, you probably *can* stop. But I'm sure you've seen the TV documentaries about people who can't, even when they've grown to such a size that they are unable to leave the house. They know they need to stop, they want to stop, but they can't. Why not? Is it possible that these people are literally *addicted* to food? Or are so called 'food addicts' just people with no willpower?

What do you think?

ANSWER

Most experts agree that food addiction* works in pretty much the same was as addiction to cigarettes, alcohol†, cocaine, heroin, caffeine or any other drug. This may seem surprising, but if we run through a checklist of the characteristics of drug addiction, food addiction ticks all of the boxes: addicts . . .

- experience powerful cravings that often result in them taking more than they intended. They want to cut down their use, but have been unable to do so, even though it causes problems for their health, and their personal and professional lives (i.e., they show **loss of control**).

---

*Officially 'addiction' no longer exists as a diagnosis. The 2013 edition of the American Psychological Association's *Diagnostic and Statistical Manual of Mental Disorders* (*DSM-V*) dropped the term, apparently because it was felt to imply moral weakness. In practice, although the manual now lists only 'disorders' (e.g., *alcohol use disorder; stimulant use disorder; gambling disorder*), most researchers are still quite happy to use the term 'addiction'.

† The satirical newspaper *The Onion* published an article that perfectly sums up our contradictory attitude to various forms of addiction, *I'm like a chocoholic, but for booze*: www.theonion.com/articles/im-like-a-chocoholic-but-for-booze,10739/

- show **tolerance**: since a particular amount has an ever-decreasing effect, it is necessary to take more to achieve the desired effect.
- show **withdrawal**: the substance is taken just to stave off withdrawal symptoms.

Few would deny that food addicts meet the first – and probably most central – criterion, loss of control. This description seems particularly apt for those who continue overeating even past the point of becoming prisoners in their own homes. It is also clear that food addicts show tolerance: nobody wakes up one morning and decides to eat ten Yorkies. It's just that eating one bar no longer gives you the buzz that it used to, so you eat another. But, soon, eating two bars doesn't give you the buzz that it used to . . . and so on.

Withdrawal is more controversial. Nevertheless, although food addicts don't experience the classic 'cold turkey' symptoms of anxiety, shaking and a drop in body temperature (associated with heroin withdrawal), they certainly report milder symptoms, such as headaches and irritability (if you're a caffeine addict, you probably experience these symptoms when you miss your breakfast coffee). In any case, although tolerance and withdrawal are indicators of *physical dependence*, it is the behavioural aspect, the loss of control, that is generally regarded as most central to *addiction*.

Not convinced? Perhaps you insist on similarities at a biological or genetic level. Well, both drugs and food stimulate the brain's reward system, as – for that matter – does pretty much anything that people enjoy (music, sex, shopping or caring for your children). And not only are both food and drug addiction heritable, but the two often run in the same families.

So, the simple answer, is yes, food addiction is essentially just like drug addiction.

But what is addiction anyway? The prevailing view (e.g., the view expressed on the website of the American Psychiatric Association) is that addiction is a disease, just like asthma, diabetes or cancer. The addict can no more will away his addiction than a cancer patient can will away his tumour.

But this doesn't seem to be quite right. Many addicts – even those who insist that addiction is a disease, such as the comedian Russell Brand – have been able to quit using nothing more than their own willpower. Motivation may just be key: those who manage to quit are generally those who want to the most, and a few studies have even got drug addicts to quit simply by paying them to do so. This is obviously a problem for the idea that addiction is a disease: you can't cure cancer patients by offering them money to get better.

On this view, an addict is simply someone who places a much higher weighting on short-term gains (e.g., getting his next cake or coke hit) than longer-term gains (e.g., being healthy, employed and able to fit through the front door). This explains why people who do poorly on tests of delayed gratification (see I Just Can't Wait) are more likely to become addicts, whether of food, drugs or gambling. This is not to say that addicts have only themselves to blame. This tendency for delay discounting – like addiction itself – also seems to be heritable. To at least some extent, people who prefer one marshmallow now to two later – or drugs now to good health later – were born that way.

This theory is obviously controversial, but if it is right, then both of the seemingly contradictory views set out at the start of this section are right. On the one hand, food addiction is a 'proper' addiction, like drug addiction. On the other, all addicts are 'just' people with – and perhaps *born* with – insufficient willpower to forgo short-term gains for long-term benefits.

Let's end with a study that suggests one small way in which we might be able to help reduce overeating, though it is unlikely to work for serious addicts. As you may have experienced yourself, when given a large pack of something tasty – say Pringles* – many

---

* Here are three fun facts about Pringles: (1) In most cases, what Americans call 'potato chips' (or just 'chips'), we Brits call 'crisps' (British 'chips' are American 'fries'). However, due to their unusual shape and sub-50-per-cent potato content, Pringles are not crisps. At least, this was the ruling of a high court judge, Mr Justice Warren. This was good news for Pringles' maker, Proctor & Gamble, who

people will polish off the whole lot, often on a kind of autopilot. A recent study (using Lays Stackables, an American chip similar to Pringles) found that simply colouring every seventh chip red (they were either dyed or tomato flavour) *halved* the average number of chips that people ate, effectively by breaking the tube down into a number of more realistic portions (though most people still ate around three of these portions).

So if you find that 'once you pop, you can't stop', but think that measuring out a miserly portion size beforehand takes all the fun out of snacking, why not take a leaf out of Professor Andrew Geier's book (or should that be a chip out of his tube?) and distribute some different-coloured chips at regular intervals. You can still eat as much as you like, but the different-coloured chips should at least let you keep track of your eating and remind you that, once you've popped, actually you *can* stop.

---

successfully argued that the snack should not be subject to Value Added Tax, because it is not a crisp (one of the few food types on which the tax is levied). (2) The inventor had his cremated remains buried in a Pringles tube. (3) The original slogan, 'Once you pop, you can't stop' was replaced by 'Once you pop, the fun don't stop', possibly because the former has an unsavoury whiff of food addiction about it.

The Vanishing Ghost

On the next page you will see a ghost and a dot.

Hold the book horizontally, with the ghost on the right and the dot on the left, a few inches in front of your face. Close your left eye and, with your right eye, stare at the dot. Move the book away from you slowly. At some point – perhaps around a foot, but you will have to experiment – the ghost will vanish. The effect is quite dramatic: it doesn't just fade out of view but disappears in an instant. When you find the sweet spot, move the book back and forth. Here . . . gone . . . here . . . gone.

What's going on? As you probably remember from school science lessons, the back of the eye is covered in a layer of special cells (called photoreceptors), onto which an image of the world is focused. These cells send this image to the brain, via the optic nerve. At the point where the optic nerve enters the eye, there is no room for any photoreceptors. This causes a blind spot: anything projected on to this spot is invisible.

Where's the psychology part? Well, your brain is very clever at covering up the blind spot. Notice how you don't see a 'blank'. Rather, the patterned background continues uninterrupted. Just like some clever photo-editing software, your brain hasn't just cut out the ghost but has automatically copied and pasted the background, so that you are entirely unaware of the gap.

Now that's spooky. Woooooooooh!

That Sinking Feeling

Suppose that you have bought a £300 ticket for a weekend trip to Italy. A few weeks later you buy a £150 ticket for a weekend trip to Spain. You think that you will enjoy the Spain trip more than the Italy trip. Later, when looking at your calendar, you realise that you have made a terrible mistake: the two tickets are for the same weekend. The tickets are non-refundable and non-transferable: you will have to go on one trip and not the other. Which one do you choose?

A couple, Adam and Agnes, spend £150 on a season ticket for the local theatre (the season consists of ten plays). Another couple, Bill and Betty, buy the same ticket, but the theatre is running a special surprise promotion, and the ticket costs only £130. A third couple, Colin and Caroline, also buy the same ticket, but this time the theatre is running an even better surprise promotion, and the ticket costs just £80. Which couple will go to the most plays?

ANSWER

When presented with the first scenario, more than half of the people asked choose to go on the more expensive Italy trip, even though they think they would enjoy the Spain trip more.

The second scenario was tested out for real at the Ohio University Theatre. The couples who had bought the full-price tickets went to more plays (an average of around six out of a possible ten) than the couples who had bought either of the tickets with the surprise discount (an average of around five out of ten).

From a purely rational economic perspective, these decisions make no sense at all. If you think you will enjoy the Spain trip more than the Italy trip, go to Spain. If you want to see a particular play that you already have a ticket for, then go. If you don't want to see it, don't go. People's tendency to make irrational decisions in these situations is known as the *sunk cost* fallacy. The more you have already invested in something – whether in money, time or effort – the more reluctant you are to 'waste' that investment, even if doing so would ensure you a better outcome, such as going on the trip that you would prefer, or not having to sit through a play that you don't really want to see.*

Could there be another explanation? Perhaps, for example, people think, 'Well, on reflection, the Spain trip can't be that great if it costs half as much as the Italy trip' or 'These plays must be really bad if they're knocking almost 40 per cent off the tickets'.

Probably not. Researchers have used a number of clever scenarios to demonstrate that it really seems to be the sunk cost that's important here. Try this one:

You are the CEO of an airline company. An employee suggests that you spend the last £10 million of your research budget on developing a plane that cannot be seen by conventional radar. The only problem is that a rival company is just about to launch another radar-invisible plane that is also faster and cheaper than yours. Should you go ahead and develop your own plane?

When given this scenario, people overwhelmingly (by a ratio of five to one) answer, 'Of course not'. However, if the scenario is changed so that you have already spent £90 million on developing your plane, people equally overwhelmingly vote in favour of spending the extra £10 million needed to bring the plane to market. This makes no sense. Either it is worth spending £10 million on bringing out an uncompetitive plane or it isn't. Whether or not you have already spent £90 million makes no difference.

Maybe you're still not convinced. Maybe you think that abandoning a plane that you've already started working on risks sending a sign of weakness to your competitors. So try this one:

---

* We saw in It Feels So Right that people vary in the extent to which they are subject to sunk cost effects. People with a highly analytical thinking style are most able to avoid them.

A friend is coming round for dinner, and you buy two identical ready meals. One costs £5, while the other is reduced to £3. Otherwise, they are identical in every way (including the use-by dates). You have just cooked both meals when your friend calls to say that he is ill and can't make it. This isn't the sort of meal you can reheat later or freeze; you must eat one now and throw the other away. Which of the two *absolutely identical* meals do you eat?

Come on, admit it: although you know there is absolutely no reason to choose one over the other, you're almost certain to eat the more expensive one. I once found myself in a similar situation when I'd accidentally bought two differently priced train tickets for exactly the same trip. (This may sound odd to overseas readers, but in the UK there are often many different prices for exactly the same train seat.) Of course, when the ticket collector came, I handed over the more expensive ticket, even though I knew there was nothing to be gained by doing so (and, indeed, was already familiar with the sunk cost fallacy).

While these studies provide good evidence that we fall for the sunk cost fallacy every time, they don't tell us *why* we do so. The answer seems to be that we have a general rule or heuristic that 'waste is a bad thing, and should always be minimised'. In general, this is a good rule to have. In the vast majority of scenarios, the course of action that minimises waste is the best one, or, at least – as with my train tickets – one that does you no harm. The problem is that we over-generalise this rule to scenarios where it *does* do us harm: taking the trip to Italy when we would prefer Spain, sitting though a boring play when we'd rather be at home, or spending our last £10 million on developing a useless aircraft.

The evidence that the sunk cost fallacy is caused by the over-generalisation of a 'waste not, want not' rule comes from comparative studies with young children and animals. Young children and animals aren't capable of creating these types of abstract rule and so don't fall for the fallacy. When given similar, though suitably childlike scenarios (involving tickets for fairground rides, rather than weekends away), children ignore sunk costs and simply choose the option they think they'd prefer. The animal studies are more debatable, but suggest that, when fighting to protect their young, animals weigh future benefits over sunk costs: for example, by fighting harder to defend a large litter than a smaller litter, even if they had previously invested more care in the latter.

There are many examples of sunk cost thinking in the real world. Football managers lose matches by failing to drop players who are expensive failures; entrepreneurs lose their houses by pumping more and more money into their failing businesses; and stock-market traders lose billions on risky investments made only in the hope of clawing back their previous losses. And something very like the fictional aeroplane scenario above happened in real life with the British–French plane Concorde. Costs spiralled even as airline ticket prices were collapsing, virtually ensuring a costly white elephant, but nobody could quite bring themselves to pull the plug.

These scenarios show us that the best way to avoid the sunk cost fallacy is to bring in someone to look at the situation with a fresh pair of eyes. A new football manager will often drop an expensive failure or sell him on, because the sunk cost is not his own. So if you're worried that you might be throwing good money after bad, ask someone if your current plan makes sense, without telling them how much money you have already put in. If you don't, you could well find yourself – like the airline executives when Concorde was finally retired in 2003 – experiencing that sinking feeling.

Can't Stand Losing You

Let's assume that you currently have a job that you enjoy, or at least think is OK. What would you do in each of the following scenarios?

Scenario A

The opportunity arises for you to move to a rival company. Your commute will double from thirty minutes to an hour, but they will increase your salary by £1,000 per year. Do you move to the rival company?

☐ Yes   ☐ No

Scenario B

Your company is going through hard times. The owner calls a meeting and says that, with great regret (and you believe that he is sincere), the only way he can keep the company going is if everyone agrees to a £1,000 reduction in their annual salary. The opportunity then arises for you to move to a rival company. Your commute will double from thirty minutes to an hour, but they will match your current wage. Do you move to the rival company?

☐ Yes   ☐ No

ANSWER

When presented with these types of dilemma, people are much more likely to choose to move to the rival company in the second. To an economist this doesn't make much sense: either a longer commute is worth £1,000 a year to you or it isn't.

But this isn't how real people think. For most people, losing something that they already have is much worse than failing to gain something that they don't yet have, even if the two things are exactly equivalent (e.g., £1,000 of salary).

Psychologists call this phenomenon *loss aversion* (many sunk-cost effects are cases of loss aversion; e.g., it's worse to lose the expensive holiday to Italy than to fail to gain the more enjoyable holiday to Spain).

In the scenarios above, there are all kinds of other factors that may complicate the picture. Perhaps you feel a certain loyalty to your existing employer, or perhaps a one-hour commute is impossible because you have to take the kids to school. So, in order to study loss aversion in its purest form, psychologists strip out all of these complications by studying something very simple (and usually trivial).

In one classic loss-aversion study participants were given a mug, which they could either keep or sell. On average, these participants wouldn't sell the mug for less than about $7. A different group of participants were not given the mug to start out with, but were told that they could have either the mug or a sum of money. These participants were prepared to forgo the mug for an average of $3.50. In other words, losing a mug that you already have seems to be *twice as bad* (i.e., requires twice as much compensation) as failing to gain the same mug.

Another way to study loss aversion in its purest form is to offer people gambles, either real or hypothetical. How about a one-off coin toss: heads, I give you £150; tails, you give me £100. Would you take the gamble? Most people would not, which – when you think about it – is a bit odd. Your chances of winning are exactly 50/50, and you stand to gain more than you lose. A mathematician would tell you to take the gamble. So why don't you like it? The only explanation can be that you are loss-averse (and hence risk-averse, see **The Health Minister**): the pain of losing £100 is greater than the pleasure of winning £150. Most people refuse the gamble unless the potential pay-off is around £250; again, a loss is considered to be more than *twice as bad* as the equivalent gain.

Loss-aversion effects are seen in the real world too. One study found that sellers whose houses have decreased in value due to a market slump set asking prices around 25 per cent higher than the going rate for that area. Inevitably, this often means that the house doesn't sell, but the would-be seller decides to stay put rather take a big financial hit. In most cases this hit is illusory, because the seller will be moving to a new house whose price has also dropped recently. But people don't see it that way, and become trapped in their own houses by loss aversion.

And remember I mentioned that, in the UK, train tickets are often vastly cheaper if bought in advance? Of course, this discrepancy is advertised as 'huge savings for pre-booking' rather than 'massive surcharges for turning up on the day', perhaps because the train companies know that the latter framing would encourage more people to pre-book, and so hurt their profit margins.

So, if you want to get someone to do something, such as filling in a form or paying taxes or fines on time, it is much better to threaten them with – say – a £100 penalty for not doing so than a £100 reduction for doing so.

Because, when it's a matter of weighing up potential losses and potential gains, most of us – as in the famous song by The Police – just can't stand losing.

Stick or Switch?

You are crawling along in slow-moving traffic, and constantly being overtaken by drivers in other lanes. You could try to move across, but the traffic is heavy, and it looks a little risky. So, should you stay where you are or move across? Stick or switch?

ANSWER

Since this section follows on from the one about *loss aversion*, you may well have decided to stick, on the basis that the pain of switching into a worse lane is greater than the pleasure of switching into a better one. On the other hand, perhaps the previous section convinced you that loss aversion is irrational, and you resolved to conquer it by switching?

The answer is: it's almost always better to stay where you are.

Why? Well loss aversion is certainly part of the reason. Logical or not, you certainly *will* feel more annoyed if you switch into a slower lane than fail to switch into a faster one.

But the real reason that you should stay where you are – particularly if switching looks dangerous – is that, usually, the other lane isn't moving faster at all; that's just an illusion caused by a misleading *heuristic* or mental short cut (see **Red or Black?** and **Carrot or Stick**).

Because it is very difficult to accurately estimate the average speed of each lane, particularly over a long distance, drivers instead use a stand-in measure that is very easy to estimate: the amount of time spent overtaking versus the amount of time spent being overtaken by others. Common sense would seem to suggest that if you are spending less time overtaking than being overtaken, you should switch lanes. But – as is so often the case with mental heuristics – common sense is wrong.

What this line of reasoning fails to take into account is that your speed is higher when you are overtaking than being over-taken. This means that, say, a 100-yard stretch during which you are overtaking others is over in a few seconds, while a 100-yard stretch during which you are being overtaken may drag on for a minute or more. The illusion that the other lane is quicker arises because your brain focuses on the relative *time* spent overtaking versus being overtaken, forgetting to factor in the *distance* covered in each period.

In fact, a mathematical modelling paper published in the prestigious journal *Nature* demonstrated that, in a typical scenario, if two lanes of traffic are moving at exactly the same speed, a driver in *either* lane will spend almost half as long again being overtaken as overtaking others. The researchers also suggested a number of other cognitive biases that might contribute to this 'grass is always greener' illusion.

First, we have our old friend *loss aversion*, which, in this particular case, is exacerbated by the fact that cars that have been over-taken are 'out of sight, out of mind', while cars that have passed the poor driver sit smugly ahead.

Second, when drivers are overtaking – and hence moving quick-ly – they are less likely to look across at the other lanes for comparison, and so fail to appreciate the gains that they are making. On the other hand, when drivers are being overtaken – and hence moving very slowly or sitting still – they have plenty of time to watch, and agonise over, the gains being made by their rivals.

Third, as we saw in **Red or Black?**, people are generally poor at appreciating that entirely random patterns often look 'streaky'. Consequently a sequence of consecutive bursts of speed in the next lane blinds drivers to the fact that all lanes go through faster and slower periods, which are essentially distributed at random.

Although the idea that *all* drivers spend longer being overtaken than overtaking others is rather counter-intuitive, deep down, most drivers know that it is true. After all, how often have you switched lanes, only to find that you are *still* spending far more time being overtaken than overtaking? The same is true for every driver on the road.

Mind over Matter*

Meet Hamish the hamster.

    Imagine that we put Hamish into a fabulous new machine that can reproduce every single cell in his body to create a duplicate that is perfect in every way. Will the new hamster have Hamish's memories?

    And if you put this question to a five-year-old, what do you think she'd say?

---

* 'What is mind? No matter. What is matter? Never mind.' – George Berkeley

ANSWER

Will the new hamster have Hamish's memories?

Of *course* it will. Hamish's little hamster memories are stored in the cells and connections of his little hamster brain, all of which will be duplicated perfectly. So the new hamster will have all of Hamish's memories, which will seem no less real than if he had been there himself.

But, although you probably knew that, I bet your first instinct was to say 'no'. Mind–body dualism, an idea popularised by the seventeenth-century French philosopher René Descartes, holds that the mind exists separately from the body. Although virtually nobody – and certainly no scientist – is a mind–body dualist these days, we find this idea of a 'ghost in the machine' surprisingly hard to shake off.

This is particularly true for children. In a study that must have been great fun to run, a group of five- to six-year-olds tickled and whispered their name to a real hamster, which the researchers then 'duplicated' using a fancy-looking machine. When asked whether this new hamster knew the child's name, or thought that the child had tickled him, more than half said no.

Of course, as grown ups, we know better to believe than that things have some magical 'essence' that can't be copied, don't we?

What if, instead of Hamish, we used our machine to create a perfect duplicate of an original Van Gogh? If you switched the two paintings around, nobody in the world, nor any machine, could tell them apart. They are literally identical, atom for atom.

So the two paintings are equally valuable. Right?

Your Memory Is Limitless

It's true. Although you probably think of yourself as a fairly average kind of person – and certainly not some kind of memory genius – you remember everything that you have ever seen.

Don't believe me? Opposite are fifty pictures. All you need to do is look at each one for two to three seconds. Don't try to come up with some kind of strategy for memorising them: just look at each picture and try to take it in. I promise that, by the end, you will be able to remember virtually every one.

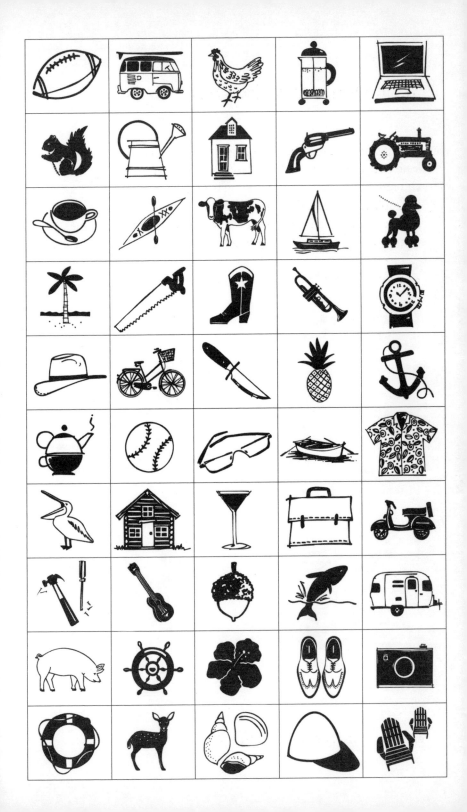

Your Memory Is Limitless: Test

Done? OK, right now list all the pictures in order.

Only kidding.

Of course, you can't remember them all off the top of your head just like that. But try this: below are ten pairs of pictures. In each pair, one picture was in the set that you studied, while the other is new. Your job is simply to pick out the previously seen picture in each pair.

ANSWER

The pictures repeated from the previous set were the anchor, cafetière, canoe, trumpet, caravan, bicycle, tractor, yacht, poodle and the chicken. How many did you get right? All of them? Well congratulations!

It gets better.

Although there were just ten pictures in the test, there was nothing special about those ten: they were not chosen to be particularly memorable. So there is every reason to believe that you would have done just as well with another set of ten. Or another. Or yet another. And so on up to the full set of fifty. So to get an idea of the total number of pictures that you remembered, you can multiply your score by 5. So if you scored 10/10, congratulations, most likely you successfully memorised all fifty. Pretty good, eh?

A much larger version of this study conducted in the 1960s found that, even when the original set comprised 612 pictures, people scored an average of 98 per cent in the recognition test.

A *much* larger version of this study conducted in the 1970s found that even with 10,000 pictures, people scored an average of 83 per cent. And there is no reason to doubt that if they had come back to do a new version of the study, these participants would have been able to learn another 10,000. And another. And another. And so on *ad infinitum*. So your memory really is limitless.

You may feel that the testing method we used here was a bit of a cheat. Surely if you had *really* remembered all of the pictures, you would have been able to list them rather than just picking them out from a choice of two. This objection misunderstands the nature of memory. Certainly, in everyday conversation, what we normally mean by 'memory' is the ability to recall information at will, without any external prompts (in what psychologists would call a 'free recall' test). But a recognition test is a test of memory too.

After all, if the pictures were not stored in your memory in some form, how could you possibly have known which ones you had previously seen?

Do Humans Dream of Electric Sheep?

Like most people whose job description has 'psychology' in it, I am often asked if I can tell what other people are thinking. Of course, I can't actually read your mind (particularly since we've never met). Nevertheless, although it sounds like something from a Philip K. Dick novel, these days it really is possible to put people in a machine that can tell you what they're thinking about.

The method, in very simple terms, is this. First you put the participant in an fMRI scanner, a machine that measures the level of activity taking place in each of several hundred tiny areas of the brain, each just a few millimetres across (though containing several million cells). Next, you show the participant a large number of photographs (usually a couple of thousand) and record the particular pattern of brain activity associated with each. This means that if you then – without looking – randomly select one of these pictures and reshow it to your participant, you can tell which picture it was by looking for its signature pattern of brain activity.

That is impressive enough, but one notable study went a step further. By identifying the signature patterns not only of particular *pictures* but of particular *parts* and *characteristics* of pictures, researchers were able to predict which of 1,000 *new* pictures the participant was looking at, with about 82 per cent accuracy. Other researchers have used similar methods to predict which of a number of possible images a participant is merely *thinking* or even *dreaming* about (and, presumably, whether or not this happens to be an electric sheep).

Not that the technique is restricted to identifying images: one study along similar lines used patterns of brain activity to predict participants' emotional states. Perhaps most incredibly of all, in another study, researchers were able to predict which of two buttons a participant was going to press, not only before she did so but even before she experienced the conscious feeling of making a decision. In other words – if we can permit ourselves a spot of Mind over Matter mind–body dualism – your brain decides the outcome of the election, before setting up a sham polling station where you get to cast your predetermined vote.

This raises the prospect of a true Philip K. Dick scenario. In Dick's short story 'The Minority Report' (later made into a Tom Cruise film), people are arrested not only for crimes that they *have* committed but also for crimes that they *will* commit in the future. In Dick's story, this information is provided by psychics. But suppose researchers found a way to use the brain-scanning technique to predict not which of two buttons a participant would press, but whether or not an armed criminal would pull the trigger. If every citizen were connected to a remote database that could transmit crippling electric shocks, the criminal could be incapacitated and detained before even realising that he had decided to pull the trigger.

Can Psychology Save the World?

To find out, we need to start by playing a quick game.

Golden Balls is a game show on British TV.* The show proceeds like this: After a couple of preliminary rounds in which players build up a jackpot and eliminate rival contestants, the show culminates in a head-to-head between two finalists.

Each finalist is a given a pair of golden balls. The balls are hollow and contain a label: 'split' for one ball in each pair, 'steal' for the other. Each contestant must choose either the 'split' or 'steal' ball and place it in the middle of the table. Although the contestants can see, and talk to, each other, they cannot see inside each others' balls (stop sniggering at the back) and therefore have no way of knowing for certain which the other will select. Contestants can – and, indeed, are encouraged to – make verbal agreements with one another, but, crucially, these agreements are not enforceable.

If both contestants choose the 'split' ball, the jackpot is split evenly between them. If both choose the 'steal' ball, both win nothing. But – and here is the crucial bit – if one contestant chooses the 'steal' ball and the other the 'split' ball, the contestant who chooses the 'steal' ball steals the money, taking home the entire jackpot, while the other contestant leaves with nothing.

So, let's play now. I will be the other contestant.

I promise you that I will choose 'split'.

If you choose 'split', turn to page 296.

If you choose 'steal', turn to page 314.

---

* One thing I love about the show is how its name in different countries reflects national sensibilities. *Golden Balls* is a typical British seaside-postcard innuendo; the sort of thing that doesn't go down well in America, where they prefer the Hollywood melodrama of *Friend or Foe*. And in Australia? 'Sorry mate, you've been *Shafted*.'

ANSWER

The *Golden Balls* finalist faces a tricky dilemma. Most people's thinking probably runs something like this:

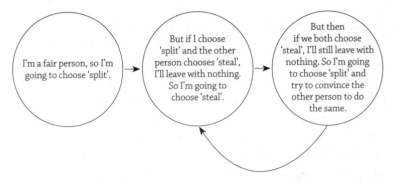

I'm a fair person, so I'm going to choose 'split'.

But if I choose 'split' and the other person chooses 'steal', I'll leave with nothing. So I'm going to choose 'steal'.

But then if we both choose 'steal', I'll still leave with nothing. So I'm going to choose 'split' and try to convince the other person to do the same.

And so on, *ad infinitum*. Notice that even people who decide from the outset that they are going to 'steal' face exactly the same problem of trying to convince the other person to choose 'split'.

The paradox is that while, taking a bird's-eye view of the game, the only rational decision is for both players to 'split', from the perspective of either individual player the only rational decision is to 'steal'. Of course, this problem could be bypassed if there were some way to enforce an agreement to share. And, boy, do people try: they shake hands, the make solemn promises, they swear on their lives. But it's all just hot air. The show pays out according purely to the rules of the game as described above, ignoring any agreements made by the contestants.

Unusually for a TV game show, *Golden Balls* is based on a famous thought experiment from psychology: *The Prisoner's Dilemma*, formulated by Merrill Flood, Melvin Dresher and Albert Tucker in the 1950s.* Two prisoners are held in separate cells and cannot communicate with one another. The police offer a deal: if both confess (like choosing 'split'), they get one year in prison each. If they both testify against each other (like choosing 'steal'), they

---

* The underlying idea dates back to Aristotle and Hobbes, and was also famously characterised by Garrett Hardin as the *tragedy of the commons*.

get two years each. But if one testifies against the other (= 'steals') while the other confesses (= 'splits'), the confessor gets three years while the testifier walks free. The dilemma is similar to the one in the *Golden Balls* final. From a bird's-eye view the best thing is for both prisoners to confess, and so get only one year each. But from the point of view of each individual prisoner, the best strategy is to testify against the other in order to be guaranteed a maximum of two years instead of three, as well as an outside chance of walking free.

Which strategy should you choose? It is impossible to say. The whole point of the paradox is that there is no way for the individual player to make a choice that is rational in the context of the game as a whole. What, then, is the point of the thought experiment? Are psychologists in the habit of dreaming up hypothetically possible – though hardly likely – dilemmas for the sheer hell of it?

Actually, the paradox is a very useful tool not only for understanding human behaviour but also for helping us to come up with ideas for how we might change it for the better.

Consider the case of global warming. As long as every other country continues to release greenhouse gases, it makes no sense for any individual country to limit its own emissions: it will lose out economically by doing so, and the cuts will have virtually no impact on the global scale. Again, the interests of the individual are at odds with those of the players as a whole.

The lesson is that tragedies of the commons, such as global warming, can be averted only by binding agreements that are enforced by an all-powerful outside entity (such as Hobbes's *Leviathan*). *Golden Balls* also teaches us two powerful lessons about what will almost certainly *not* work.

First, if one country sacrifices its own economic performance by cutting emissions, there is no reason to expect others to follow suit. It is virtually certain that at least some, like the predatory *Golden Balls* finalist, will just grab a bigger piece of the world economic pie for themselves. Indeed, it would be irrational not to. If – say – India doesn't, then China will. Second, there is no point in a country making unenforceable pledges, because there is no reason for the other countries to believe that they will stick to them. Emissions targets are worth nothing more than the 'hand on my heart' pleadings heard in every episode of the game show. Indeed, they don't seem to be working. Since 1990, the start of the period covered by an international agreement to reduce greenhouse gas emissions (the Koyoto Protocol), such emissions have actually *increased*. How come? Well, exactly as a *Prisoner's Dilemma* expert would have predicted, the modest reductions made by some countries and regions (including most of Europe) have been wiped out – and then some – by massive increases in other countries (mainly the United States and China).

So is mankind doomed? Or can the *Prisoner's Dilemma* – or its *Golden Balls* incarnation – suggest another solution?

In one particularly memorable episode (see Web Link), one contestant followed an extremely unorthodox strategy. Rather than promising to 'split', the contestant – known only as Nick – promptly announced his intention to choose the 'steal' ball, promising to share the money with the other contestant after the show. His opponent, who – of course – had no reason to believe this pledge, tried to talk Nick into agreeing to both choose 'split'.

But Nick had already gained the upper hand. Whenever his opponent talked of choosing 'split', Nick simply replied, 'I'm not going to pick split, I'm going to steal.'

His opponent was livid: 'We're walking away with no money because you're an idiot.' But in the dying seconds of the game, he relented: 'You know what? I'm going to go with you'.

He did. Nick's opponent chose 'split.'

So did Nick keep his word and share the money after the show? He didn't need to. *He chose 'split' too.*

It was a piece of brinkmanship worthy of a Cold War general. And how about that piece of showboating at the end? Nick knew he had won. He could have chosen 'steal' and then split the money at his leisure (or even decided not to). Instead, he went for the risky option of choosing 'split', for no other reason than to demonstrate his confidence in his scheme.

Could this strategy work for global warming? What if a large and powerful country, instead of making promises of minor reductions, vowed to *increase* its emissions rapidly to such an extent that the world would fry within a couple of years unless other countries reduced theirs?

It's a long shot. But if it works, then psychology – with a little help from an early-evening game show – will have saved the world.

Web Link
Watch Nick's amazing *Golden Balls* triumph at: http://www.youtube.com/watch?v=SoqjK3TWZE8

Prescient Palmistry?

Now I don't have a brain scanner, and so can't read your mind. But if you were here, I could nevertheless make some pretty good predictions regarding your personality (specifically, your agreeableness and neuroticism), your aggression and how easily you can be manipulated by attractive members of the opposite sex. There is just one thing I'd need . . .

A ruler.

Can you guess what I'd do?

ANSWER

That's right, I'd measure your . . .

. . . fingers, of course (what were *you* thinking?)

Palmistry is the practice of reading people's palms to uncover facts about their personalities, or even what life holds in store for them. Of course, palmistry is nonsense, but it really is possible to predict all these things simply by measuring your fingers. Let me show you how.

First, measure the length of your index finger (the second 'digit', if you count your thumb as the first digit) from crease to tip. Then do the same for your ring finger (fourth digit). Finally divide the first number by the second to calculate your '2:4 digit ratio'. For example, my index finger is 7.8cm and my ring finger is 8.2cm, so my ratio is 7.8/8.2 = 0.95, which is precisely the average for a male.

But why does this seemingly arbitrary number hold secrets about your personality? The answer is that the length of these fingers is determined in part by the degree to which you were exposed to androgens as an unborn baby. Androgens are the male sex hormones (the most well known of which is testosterone), whose job it is to 'masculinise' foetuses that are genetically male. The smaller the ratio, the higher the degree of androgen exposure, which is why this number is smaller for men (average = 0.95) than women (average = 0.97).

Perhaps the most striking finding is that male-to-female trans-sexuals have digit ratios that are higher than normal for men but typical for women. This suggests that the experience of being 'born in the wrong body', as reported by many transsexual people, has a genuine biological basis: in terms of 2:4 digit ratios, male-to-female transsexuals really are females.

But androgens don't just determine whether we are male or female; they affect plenty of other things too. Take personality. For women, the higher your level of androgen exposure (i.e., the lower the 2:4 number) the greater your score for 'agreeableness' and the lower your score for 'neuroticism' (look back to Your Personality Profile for more on what these terms mean, and – if you haven't already – to calculate your own agreeableness and neuroticism scores). Presumably this reflects the fact that androgens make people more outgoing and confident, and we tend to find these types of people more agreeable than introverted neurotics.

With regard to aggression, it will not surprise you to learn that greater androgen exposure (lower 2:4 number) is associated with greater levels of aggressive behaviour among men. Such men are also rated as more masculine by females, and are better at very physical sports such as rugby. These high levels of testosterone also mean that such men are more susceptible to being manipulated by attractive women. Men with a low 2:4 number were more likely to accept unfair offers in an ultimatum game (see Take It or Leave It) after viewing sexy photos or handling women's underwear.

So, for all you macho men out there, if you want to prove how masculine you are, there's no need to start a fight: just take out your ruler.

That said, if you do ever end up in a fight, let's hope you're built like one of these guys on the next section . . .

Can Psychology Save the World?:
You Chose 'Split'

I chose 'steal', so I get to keep all the money. Now turn to p.289 to find out what this is all about.

What's in a Face? #4: Face-Off

OK, so you didn't make it past the interview as a prison guard (see **Be on Your Guard**), but I've sorted out another job for you, and this one's a real knock-out: mixed martial arts fighter.

I've lined up five possible opponents for your first fight. Please pick the one who you think you're most likely to beat (or – more realistically – who will hurt you the least).

A   B   C   D   E

ANSWER

As your manager, I hope that you picked Fighter A, who has the least aggressive-looking face. For your own sake, I'm praying that you didn't pick Fighter C.

Least aggressive   Average   Most aggressive

A   D   B   E   C

But isn't this all just prejudice? For all we know, people who look like Fighter A might be lean mean killing machines, while people who look like Fighter C are gentle giants, right?

Actually, no. A group of researchers asked participants to rate fighter photographs (originals, not the composites that you rated*) for aggressiveness. These ratings significantly predicted the proportion of fights won by each fighter.† So it's not just a cliché: people who look like tough fighters generally are. The evolutionary benefits of being able to figure out who looks like they'd be handy in a fight are obvious. What is less obvious is exactly how we make these judgements.

The researchers found that the more aggressive-looking – and more successful – fighters generally had larger noses, deep-set eyes and prominent eyebrows. Though, from looking at the

---

* Each composite was generated from photographs of many different professional fighters with the relevant aggressiveness ranking. For example, Pictures A and C were generated by averaging across photos of the fighters who were rated as looking the least aggressive and the most aggressive respectively.

† A related study found that fighters who smile in their weigh-in photos are more likely to lose, presumably because, from an evolutionary perspective, a smile is a sign of weakness and submission.

photos above, it is clear that the most obvious difference is a wider face. Many other studies have shown that men with wider faces, relative to face height, are more aggressive in both real-life settings – one study looked at ice hockey matches – and laboratory experiments. For example, in money-earning games, men with wider faces frequently press a button that deducts money from a (fictitious) opponent, at no benefit to themselves. But it's not just trivial things like hockey and tiny sums of money; face-width can literally be a matter of life and death. One study found that men with wider faces were less likely to be stabbed, strangled or bludgeoned to death (this finding – like all of those discussed in this section – applies only to men, and not women).

So if you see someone who looks like Fighter C, I'm sure he's a nice guy and everything, but if he suggests joining your ice hockey game, you might be best advised to decline, *ever so politely*.

If you don't, you might find yourself experiencing . . .

The Psychology of Pain

All pain is psychological: pain has no existence other than in its subjective experience in the brain. So if you've broken a limb but feel no pain – for example, because you're high on adrenaline – then there *is* no pain. Conversely, if you genuinely feel in pain, then you *are* in pain, even if no doctor can find any physical injury.

An interesting consequence of the fact that pain is 'all in the mind' is that the way that you think about pain actually seems to affect the level of pain that you experience. You can learn more about the way you think about pain by completing the questionnaire below.

Everyone experiences painful situations at some point in their life. Such experiences may include headaches, tooth pain, joint or muscle pain. People are often exposed to situations that may cause pain, such as illnesses, injury, dental procedures or surgery.

We are interested in the types of thoughts and feelings that you have when you are in pain. Below are thirteen statements describing different thoughts and feelings that may be associated with pain. Using the following scale, please indicate the degree to which you have these thoughts and feelings when you are experiencing pain.

0 – not at all; 1 – to a slight degree; 2 – to a moderate degree; 3 – a great deal; 4 – all the time;

When I'm in pain. . .

1. I worry all the time about whether the pain will end. ....
2. I feel I can't go on. ....
3. It's terrible, and I think it's never going to get better. ....
4. It's awful, and I feel that it overwhelms me. ....

5. I feel I can't stand it any more. ....
6. I become afraid that the pain will get worse. ....
7. I keep thinking of other painful events. ....
8. I anxiously want the pain to go away. ....
9. I can't seem to keep it out of my mind. ....
10. I keep thinking about how much it hurts. ....
11. I keep thinking about how badly I want the pain to stop. ....
12. There's nothing I can do to reduce the intensity of the pain. ....
13. I wonder whether something serious may happen. ....

ANSWERS

- Add up all your answers to find your total *pain catastrophising* score. This reflects the degree to which you experience 'an exaggerated negative mental set' when undergoing (or just anticipating) pain. The average score is around 20. If you scored 30 or above, you are in the top 25 per cent of pain catastrophisers (i.e., those who catastrophise the most). Although absolute cut-off points are not always particularly meaningful, those who score 30 or above are often classified as 'pain catastrophisers'. If you scored 10 or below, you are in the bottom 25 per cent of catastrophisers (i.e., among the most stoical). You should bear in mind that all of the average scores listed here are taken from a group who had experienced soft-tissue back injury serious enough to warrant an average of seven months off work. So if you have never experienced similar pain, you might find your scores somewhat out of line.
- Add up your answers to questions 8, 9, 10 and 11 to find your *rumination* score. This reflects the degree to which you keep thinking about and going over the pain. The average score is around 8. A score of 11 or above – or 3 or below – would put you in the top/bottom 25 per cent of pain ruminators.
- Add up your answers to questions 6, 7 and 13 to find your *magnification* score. This reflects the degree to which you build

up the pain. The average score is around 3. A score of 5 or above would put you in the top 25 per cent of pain magnifiers (to come in the bottom 25 per cent, you need to score 0).

- Add up your answers to questions 1, 2, 3, 4, 5 and 12 to find your *helplessness* score. This reflects the degree to which you feel that you can do nothing to reduce or cope with the pain. The average score is around 8. A score of 13 or above or 3 or below would put you in the top/bottom 25 per cent with regard to the helplessness that you experience in the face of pain.

But this isn't just about putting labels on people for the sake of it. Levels of pain catastrophising, as measured by this questionnaire, are a great predictor of the pain that people experience, and the likelihood of a successful recovery. For example, one recent review found that patients with higher levels of pain catastrophising not only rate their pain as more intense but also . . .

- experience increased levels of disability following knee surgery.
- are more likely, following injury at work, to experience chronic long-term pain (as opposed to short-term pain that ends when the physical injury has healed).
- experience higher levels of depression.
- take more painkillers.
- stay longer in hospital.

This is the case for both adults and children as young as seven, and does not seem to depend on the particular type of pain experienced, whether this is caused by surgery, arthritis, tissue injury, dental procedures, headaches or even psychology researchers.

Yes, this really happens. Researchers' favourite ways of inducing pain, while leaving no lasting damage, are to shine lasers onto the skin and to have participants hold their hand in a bucket of ice water. I tried this last one for myself while taking part in a study of a new painkilling drug. All I can say is that I was either a member of the placebo control group (the group that receives a dummy pill as opposed to the painkiller) or a pain catastrophiser. It *hurt*.

If catastrophising makes pain worse, can we reduce patients' pain by encouraging them not to catastrophise? Happily, the answer seems to be yes. For example, in one recent study with sufferers of whiplash, all patients were given physical therapy, but only half were additionally given psychological therapy designed to reduce pain catastrophising. This therapy not only successfully reduced patients' scores on the pain-catastrophising scale (as compared with the control group) but also reduced their rated pain levels and increased their chances of going back to work.

Another way to reduce catastrophising, and hence reduce pain, is to distract patients: for instance, with a joke. For example, have you heard the one about the man who went into the baker's asking for some *pain*? It turned out he had been studying French.

Further Reading
Ben Goldacre's *Bad Science* – one of my favourite popular science books – has an interesting section on how all pain is 'all in the mind'.

A Sinister Questionnaire

Historically, left-handed people have had a bad press, thought of as awkward, clumsy, unlucky or downright evil: one famous left-hander, according to many medieval paintings, was the devil himself. This prejudice is built into many languages, including French, where left (*gauche*) also means 'awkward' or 'clumsy', and Latin, where left (*sinister*) also means unlucky. Both *gauche* and *sinister* have similarly negative connotations in English; *right*, on the other hand (ho, ho), also means 'correct' or 'proper'.

Many older left-handers will remember being told that they were 'wicked' – often by their class teachers – and forced to use their right hand. Sadly, such discrimination against a minority for little more than its own sake seems to be a very common psychological trait (see Literacy Test).*

Recently, though, things have been looking up for lefties, particularly in the West, where they are widely believed to be more creative. We will find out shortly whether or not this reputation is deserved.

First let's measure your own handedness. Many people are neither entirely left-handed nor entirely right-handed, but show different preferences depending on the activity or object in question. Indicate your preferences by ticking the relevant boxes in the following table:

---

* The relationship between left-handedness and homosexuality (non-right-handers are roughly 40 per cent more likely to be gay) may well have contributed to this discrimination, given the almost universal prejudice against homosexuality that existed until relatively recently.

	Always left	Usually left	Both equally	Usually right	Always right
Writing					
Throwing					
Toothbrush					
Spoon					

ANSWERS

To calculate your handedness score, add together the four numbers that correspond to the boxes you ticked, and divide by 4.*

	Always left	Usually left	Both equally	Usually right	Always right
Writing	-100	-50	0	50	100
Throwing	-100	-50	0	50	100
Toothbrush	-100	-50	0	50	100
Spoon	-100	-50	0	50	100

For example, I ticked 'Always right' for 'Writing', 'Throwing' and 'Toothbrush' and 'Usually right' for 'Spoon'. Adding up these numbers gives 350 (100 + 100 + 100 + 50 =350), which I then divide by 4 to arrive at a handedness score of 87.5.

- If your handedness score is larger than 80 (forgetting about any minus sign), then you are defined as *consistent-handed*.
- If your handedness score is smaller than 80 (forgetting about any minus sign), then you are defined as *inconsistent-handed*.

---

* Some readers may doubt that a four-item questionnaire is sufficient for measuring handedness. In fact, the study in question found that this short questionnaire is a better measure of handedness than seven- and ten-item questionnaires, as these longer versions often contain items that are either ambiguous (e.g., 'opening a box' and 'using a broom', for which most people use both hands) or redundant (e.g., if a questionnaire includes 'writing', there is no point also including 'drawing' as people virtually always give identical answers for the two).

Incidentally, 63 per cent of women are consistent-handed, while men are split almost exactly 50/50 between *consistent-* and *inconsistent-handedness*. Also, left-handers are more than twice as likely as right-handers to be *inconsistent-handed* (though it's not clear whether inconsistent left-handers are born this way or become inconsistent-handed as a result of pressure to use their right hand for some tasks).

What does your score say about you? It turns out that degree of preference for one hand (whether the left or the right) is a significant predictor of many characteristics relating to intelligence, memory and much more besides.

One recent review found that, when compared with consistent right-handers,* people who are inconsistent-handed . . .

- . . . have better memories, whether recalling lists of words, events from their own lives (including early childhood), dreams, faces or passages of text.
- . . . are more subject to anchoring effects (see Anchors Away), placebo effects (see YOU Are the Psychologist) and effects of cognitive dissonance (see St Valentine's Day: Massacred?) and experience more reversals with visual illusions such as the Necker Cube.
- . . . are more open to persuasion, more gullible and more likely to believe in magic.
- . . . have a greater preference for obscure musical genres (see Stereo Types).
- . . . are more likely to believe in evolution, and less likely to believe in creationism.
- . . . are more *loss-averse* (i.e., consider avoiding losses more important than making gains; see Can't Stand Losing You) but better able to avoid *sunk cost* effects (e.g., throwing good money after bad when gambling; see That Sinking Feeling), at least when it is clear that doing so will definitely avoid a greater loss.

---

* Consistent left-handers are hard to find, presumably because they are encouraged by others to use their right hand for at least some tasks.

- . . . are better at taking other people's perspectives and less likely to have right-wing political views.
- . . . are less likely to show brand loyalty in studies of consumer choice.
- . . . get to sleep faster.

What do these traits have in common? Most – even the less positive ones, such as gullibility and openness to persuasion – seem to reflect some kind of flexibility of thinking. But just why do people with inconsistent handedness show this flexibility?

The answer seems to be that these traits are a consequence of having a brain where the two hemispheres talk a lot to each other, rather than working more in isolation. Because the left hemisphere of the brain controls the right hand – and vice versa – inconsistent-handedness is just one more consequence of having a brain with high levels of this *hemispheric interaction*.

So overall, there is good evidence that inconsistent-handers enjoy some cognitive benefits over consistent-handers. When you put this fact together with the fact that inconsistent-handedness is more common among left-handers than right-handers, we can see that the 'myth' of the particularly creative or intelligent left-hander – like many myths – actually contains a grain of truth.

The 'I's Have It

Below are two emails. One was written by a person with high social status (e.g., a company boss or professor), the other by someone with lower status (e.g., an employee or student). Which is which?

From: XXX, XXX [mailto:XXX@XXX.XXX]
Sent: 03 August 2014
To: XXXXX
Subject: Meeting

Dear XXXX

I was wondering if I could meet up with you to talk about the project we discussed. I am free on Thursday from around 10am, but I will have to leave by 12 as I have another appointment.

Thanks
XXXX

From: XXX, XXX [mailto:XXX@XXX.XXX]
Sent: 03 August 2014
To: XXXXX
Subject: Meeting

Dear XXXX

It would be great to meet up to talk about the project we discussed. How about Thursday from around 10am – though there's something else happening at 12.

Thanks
XXXX

ANSWER

You probably spotted the clue in the title: the 'I's have it. Yes, the key is in the number of uses of 'I' in each email.

You might think that high-status people are more self-important and so use 'I' more often. Actually, a study of emails sent between professors and students at the University of Texas found that the opposite was true. It was the students who tended to use 'I' in their emails much more frequently than the professors.

The reason for this apparently paradoxical finding seems to be that people who feel insecure and self-aware are more focused on their own thoughts (*I was wondering*), behaviour (*I will have to leave*), situations (*I have another appointment*) and feelings (it would have given the game away too much here, but – in real life – many students start their emails with *I'm sorry to bother you . . .*). In fact, people who are suffering from depression also show increased use of 'I'. High-status people such as professors and bosses, on the other hand, rarely feel self-conscious.

Similar findings were observed when the researchers looked at letters sent between Iraqi soldiers of different ranks, or even when they randomly allocated 'leader' status to one member of a pair of students having a getting-to-know-you chit-chat. Yes, even though the 'low status' assigned to the non-leaders was transparently arbitrary, these participants still felt sufficiently self-conscious to increase their rate of 'I' use, as compared with the leaders.

But it's not just about your use of 'I'. A recent analysis of 700 million words culled from the messages of 75,000 Facebook users uncovered a whole host of interesting titbits, including . . .

- Men are more likely to talk about '**my** wife/girlfriend' than women are about '**my** husband/boyfriend' (though bear in mind that all of the gender differences discussed here, including this one, are of the tiny **Men Are from Mars** . . . variety).
- Women are more likely than men to talk about negative (but not positive) emotions.

- Men talk more than women about work and money.
- Men swear more than women, but there are no gender differences in talk about sex.
- Old people use 'I' less than younger people (maybe because they tend to enjoy higher status) and make less use of the past tense (perhaps surprisingly, given that they have more past to talk about).

The following relate to the traits discussed in Your Personality Profile:

- As you might expect from the above, frequent use of 'I' and 'you' predicts high and low neuroticism respectively.
- People who use 'you' a lot tend to be more extroverted.
- People who use 'we' a lot tend to be more agreeable.
- People who use a lot of negatives (*no, not, none* etc.) tend to be less conscientious ('No, I've not done my assignment yet. No, none of it').
- People who score high on the personality trait of openness tend to use fewer pronouns of all kinds (*I, we, you, him, her, it* etc.).

The website below includes some interactive games and exercises that let you further explore your own use of pronouns. Why not give them a try?

I would.

Web Link
Find out all about pronouns (those little words like *I, we, you, him, her, it*, etc. . .) at: www.secretlifeofpronouns.com

Write Stuff or Write-Off?

Having investigated your handedness and your writing style, let's put the two together and investigate your handwriting. Both psychologists and employers have long used graphology – the scientific analysis of handwriting – as a handy (sorry!) way of measuring personality and potential.

So, let's try it. Copy the following passage into the box below:*

The quick brown fox jumps over a lazy dog. Xylophone wizard begets quick jive form. Fred specialized in the job of making very quaint wax toys.

---

* This passage contains three *pangrams* – sentences that contain every letter of the alphabet.

ANSWER

Look at the passage you have written, and tick off all the characteristics that apply.

Overall style	angular = dynamic, energetic			rounded = creative, sympathetic, easily dominated
Slant	left = cold			right = warm
Pressure	hard = confident, aggressive, selfish			soft = quiet, kind, considerate
Crossing of t	heavy = weak-willed			light = purposeful
	long = upbeat and active			short = irritable
Dotting of i	right of stem = carefree, thoughtless			left of stem = careful, deliberate
	no dot = lacking attention to detail			
	horizontal dash instead of dot = lots of energy			
a and o	open loop = Talks a lot, straight-talking			closed loop = secretive
m and n	angular = enthusiastic, sociable			rounded = poor at observation, creative
CAPITALS	large = big ego			small = shy
Loops	large = imaginative, intelligent			small = lazy

What do you think? Was the analysis accurate for you?

In fact, although many people believe that graphology has a strong scientific basis, the truth is that countless studies have found absolutely no relationship at all between handwriting and personality (as measured by questionnaires such as the one you completed for Your Personality Profile).

Why, then, is the graphology myth so persistent?

One reason is that graphology is often confused with *forensic document examination*: the process of scrutinising a handwritten document or signature to try to prove who wrote it – for example, when a will is suspected of being a forgery. Most forensic document examiners will have nothing to do with graphology, but some blur the boundaries by offering both services.

Two further reasons are more interesting, because they are common to many different types of popular misconception and pseudoscience. The first is that graphology just *feels* so plausible. It seems simply common sense to assume that someone with small, neat writing is well organised, intelligent and self-controlled, while someone with a gigantic spidery scrawl is disorganised, thoughtless and chaotic. Indeed, one study found that participants with no training in graphology instinctively used the same links as 'experts': people already think – for example – that big writing equals big personality. Graphology feels so plausible because it simply tells us what we already (mistakenly) think we know.

The second is the so-called *Barnum effect* (named after the famous circus owner, who boasted about having 'something for everyone'). As any palm-reader, astrologer, fortune-teller, psychic, paranormalist or spiritualist won't tell you, if you throw out enough vague and general statements, at least a couple of them will stick (see **Horoscope Horror Show?**). Confirmation bias (see **Card Trick**) will then do the rest of the work for you. Look again at the personality traits above. Even though quite a few are opposites, you can make pretty much any of them fit, simply by choosing to remember situations where you were – for example – *weak-willed*, on the one hand, or *purposeful*, on the other.

In spite of all this, a number of presumably well-intentioned employers continue to use graphology as part of their hiring-and-firing decisions, even if only informally. So if a potential employer demands a handwritten application, you should be very suspicious. And, if you're feeling brave enough, ask them to have a look at the review articles listed in the reference section. The message is clear:

Graphology is a write off!

Can Psychology Save the World?: You Chose 'Steal'

I also chose 'steal', so we both leave with nothing. Now turn to p.289 to find out what this is all about.

YOU Are the Psychologist

Many of the sections in this book (A Trivial Pursuit, Anchors Away, The Tea Test, The Radiologist, Horoscope Horror Show?, What a Shape Tastes Like) have encouraged you to turn psychologist and run studies on your friends and family. We've also touched on some of the pitfalls that psychologists encounter when designing and interpreting studies (e.g., The Fool Hath Said in His Heart, 'There Is No God', Spare the Rod and Spoil the Child?, Video Gains?). So I think you're now ready for what is perhaps the most difficult test of all: designing your *own* study.

An enterprising teacher has come up with a new and exciting method for teaching basic maths in primary school, and many schools and teachers have already begun to use it. The Department for Education is considering formally incorporating this new method into the curriculum, but first want to evaluate it. This is where you come in. You have been asked to design a study that investigates whether or not this new method is more successful than current approaches. Take a few minutes to think about how you would design this study, making a few notes in the box below.

ANSWER

The obvious answer is simply to find some teachers who are using the new method and to ask them whether they think it is working better than the old method.

If this was your answer, then, sorry, but zero points. This experimental design is almost guaranteed to produce misleading results, and so is arguably worse than conducting no study at all. Let's go through the problems with this design, and see how we can fix them.

First, this design is likely to yield an *expectancy effect*. Because the teachers who adopted the new method expect to see better performance among their children, they probably will, either because the teachers are kidding themselves about the improved performance or because they are subconsciously working harder in order to fulfil their own prophecy. In one famous study, experimenters reported that rats that had been labelled as 'bright' were faster at escaping from a maze than a 'dull' group. In fact, the study was a set-up: the rats didn't differ in intelligence at all, and the finding was caused solely by expectancy effects. Presumably the experimenters somehow treated the 'bright' rats better, or were more inclined to give them the benefit of the doubt when measuring their performance.

If the children know they are getting some fancy new teaching method, we are likely to also see a particular type of expectancy effect known as a *Hawthorne effect*. Researchers working at Western Electric's Hawthorne Plant in Illinois found that, whatever changes they made to factory conditions – longer breaks, shorter breaks, more lighting, less lighting – productivity increased, apparently as a result. In general, whenever a change designed to boost performance is put in place, the participants feel 'special' and want – probably subconsciously – to show that it has been a success, and so up their performance.*

---

* Ironically, although the Hawthorne effect is a robust phenomenon, there may not have been one at the Hawthorne plant. Having uncovered the original

To overcome these problems, we need two things: a *placebo control group* and *blinding*. In drug trials, half of the participants get the new would-be wonder drug, while half a get a sugar pill with no active ingredient (the placebo). If the drug group respond to the treatment better than the placebo group, we know that we are seeing an effect of the drug, rather than an expectancy or Hawthorne effect. We need the same thing here. Half of the children (the test group) get the new teaching method for real, while the other half (the placebo control group) get all the trappings of the new teaching method – shiny new workbooks and a teacher who talks excitedly about the 'new' way of learning – but, under the surface, nothing changes. If the test group still outperforms the control group, this suggests that the method works.

But who decides whether or not the test group is outperforming the control group? If we want to avoid expectancy effects, it can't be the teachers. This is where blinding comes in. Whoever assesses the children afterwards must not know which children were in the test group and which the control group; i.e., they must be 'blind' to the teaching that each child received. We now have a *double-blind* study, where neither the experimenter (i.e., the assessor) nor the participants (i.e., the children) know who is in which group.*

Our study is still lacking one crucial ingredient: *randomisation*. If we create our test group by recruiting schools that are already using the new method and our control group by recruiting schools that are still using the old method, we introduce all kinds of con-

---

documents, Steven Levitt (co-author of *Freakonomics*) found that – as in most factories – productivity was greatest on a Monday and declined gradually throughout the week. Since all experimental changes were instigated on a Sunday, apparent productivity increases may have been caused simply by the normal ebb and flow of the working week.

* Ideally, the people who deliver the intervention (i.e., the teachers) should also be blind to each child's group. This would obviously be very difficult in this case, but not necessarily completely impossible. For example, we could train experimenters with no prior knowledge or experience of teaching to deliver either the old or the new method, without telling them which was which.

founds. (If you've forgotten what a confound is, please look back to Quoth the Raven's, 'What's My Score?' and The Fool Hath Said in His Heart, 'There Is No God' for an explanation.) The schools that have spontaneously decided to use a new teaching method are likely to be more forward-thinking and better resourced, with highly motivated pupils and teachers. An under-performing school that is already lurching from crisis to crisis has enough on its plate without trying to introduce new teaching methods, even if it could afford the new textbooks. Consequently, even if the new teaching method is no better than the old one, the schools who adopted it will probably show better performance than those that didn't.

To eliminate these confounds, we need to assign particular schools or classes – or, even better, individual children – to the test group and the control group *completely at random*. Provided we have enough schools and children on board, this will ensure that overall levels of teacher motivation, school financial resources etc. are equal across the two groups (an alternative to blinding is to try your best to match the two groups on each of these factors, though this is more difficult as you then need to be able to measure them).

So how did you get on? Score 1 point if you included a control group, 1 if you used blinding, and 1 if you used random (or matched) groups. Score another point if you mentioned comparing the performance of the groups using a statistical test (see The Tea Test). You may like to try this test on any friends you have who are teachers, researchers or psychology students. How many got 4/4?

The answer, I hope, is 'most of them'. This is basic stuff, covered in the first year of any undergraduate psychology degree. So you'd be forgiven for assuming that real-life government policies in education, business, transport, the environment, culture and so on are evaluated using *randomised double-blind placebo control trials* of the type that we have knocked up in a few minutes here.

As if. In reality, these types of trials are almost never used to evaluate government policy (although they are standard practice in medicine). Why not? First, governments are probably scared that voters who did not get the new programme (i.e. the control group) would be outraged and punish them at the ballot box. Although this isn't a particularly rational response – the programme may be useless, or even actively harmful – it's an understandable one. How would you feel if the government spent millions of pounds of taxpayers' money on an initiative that is offered to your neighbour but not to you? Second, it seems unlikely that any government would be brave enough to admit that its new initiative had 'failed'. Better to avoid running a trial altogether, and provide anecdotal evidence of its success ('When I speak to voters on the doorstep, they tell me . . .'). Finally, the generally accepted view seems to be that political leaders should make decisions on the basis of their convictions, their values, what they know in their bones to be true, and that to do otherwise is a sign of weakness. Can you imagine a party leader saying, 'Well, this policy may be the opposite of everything we stand for, but it produced the best outcome in a trial'?

Now that you've run several studies on other people, and even designed one yourself, you should be starting to get a pretty good idea of what it feels like to be a psychologist. If you like this feeling, and have been inspired to consider a career as an academic research psychologist for real, then take a look at the final section (Continuing Your Psych-Odyssey) for some tips on how to get started. For me, what's so great about this career is the fact that psychology can be used to provide a scientific and objective answer to almost any of life's big questions.

Continuing Your Psych-Odyssey

Well, that's it. I hope you've enjoyed your voyage of discovery to the four corners of the psychological globe, and that you've boosted your 'Psy-Q' by learning a great deal about both your own personal psychology and psychology in general.

I hope also that you will see this not as the end of your journey but as the beginning, that this book has inspired you to seek out psychology's answers to all of the questions that life throws up every day, from the most profound to the most trivial.

So where should you go from here? The easiest place to start is the list of references on the opposite page. Pick a section that particularly captured your interest, find the original study in the reference section, then try to track down a PDF of the full journal article online. Although some will be hidden behind paywalls, many are freely available and can be found by searching for the title or the names of the author(s) using Google Scholar (http://scholar.google.com), a search engine that is restricted to academic journal articles. Most authors post articles on their university web pages or on sites such as www.academia.edu and www.researchgate.net. If all else fails, it's fine to send the first author a polite (but short!) email asking for a copy. At worst, he or she will ignore the email; most likely, you'll get the article in a day or two, along with a pleasant note thanking you for taking an interest. Once you've read the article, consult its reference section to find an interesting-looking related article, and consult its reference section for another. And so on *ad infinitum*.

Ultimately, I hope that at least some of you will be sufficiently inspired to apply to study psychology at university or – if you are already doing so – to get a PhD and become a psychology researcher yourself. There's an ocean of knowledge out there, and we've barely skimmed the surface. Dive in.

References

The Raw Shark Test

Exner, J., Levy, A., Groth-Marnat, G., Wood, J. M., & Garb, H. N. (2008). *The Rorschach: A Comprehensive System*, vol. 1: *The Rorschach, Basic Foundations and Principles of Interpretation*. London and New York: Wiley and Sons.

Lilienfeld, S. O., Wood, J. M., & Garb, H. N. (2000). The scientific status of projective techniques. *Psychological Science in the Public Interest*, *1*, 27–66.

Shaffer, T. W., Erdberg, P., & Haroian, J. (1999). Current nonpatient data for the Rorschach, WAIS-R, and MMPI-2. *Journal of Personality Assessment*, 73(2), 305–36.

http://www.csicop.org/si/show/rorschach_inkblot_test_fortune_tell ers_and_cold_reading/

Your Personality Profile

Goldberg, L. R. (1999). A broad-bandwidth, public domain, personality inventory measuring the lower-level facets of several five-factor models. In I. Mervielde, I. Deary, F. De Fruyt, & F. Ostendorf (Eds.), *Personality Psychology in Europe*, vol. 7 (pp. 7–28). Tilburg, The Netherlands: Tilburg University Press.

Goldberg, L. R., Johnson, J. A., Eber, H. W., Hogan, R., Ashton, M. C., Cloninger, C. R., & Gough, H. C. (2006). The International Personality Item Pool and the future of public-domain personality measures. *Journal of Research in Personality*, *40*, 84–96.

International Personality Item Pool: A Scientific Collaboratory for the Development of Advanced Measures of Personality Traits and Other Individual Differences (http://ipip.ori.org/).

It's All Chinese to Me

Monahan, J. L., Murphy, S. T., & Zajonc, R. B. (2000). Subliminal mere exposure: Specific, general, and diffuse effects. *Psychological Science*, *11*(6), 462–6.

Hepper, P. (1988). Fetal 'soap' addiction. *The Lancet*, *331*(8598), 1347–8.

Zajonc, R. B. (2001). Mere exposure: A gateway to the subliminal. *Current Directions in Psychological Science*, *10*(6), 224–8.

Professional Psychopaths

Board, B. J., & Fritzon, K. (2005). Disordered personalities at work. *Psychology, Crime & Law*, *11*(1), 17–32.

Hare, R. D. (2003). *The Psychopathy Checklist,* revised, 2nd edn. Toronto: Multi-Health Systems.

I Just Can't Wait

Koffarnus, M. N., Jarmolowicz, D. P., Mueller, E. T., & Bickel, W. K. (2013). Changing delay discounting in the light of the competing neurobehavioral decision systems theory: A review. *Journal of the Experimental Analysis of Behavior*, 1–26.

Mischel, W., & Ebbesen, E. B. (1970). Attention in delay of gratification. *Journal of Personality and Social Psychology*, *16*(2), 329.

Lerner, J. S., Li, Y., & Weber, E. U. (2013). The financial costs of sadness. *Psychological Science*, *24*(1), 72–9.

Take It or Leave It?

Jensen, K., Call, J., & Tomasello, M. (2007). Chimpanzees are rational maximizers in an ultimatum game. *Science*, *318*(5847), 107–9.

Milinski, M. (2013). Chimps play fair in the ultimatum game. *Proceedings of the National Academy of Sciences of the United States of America* *10*(6), 1978–1979.

Henrich, J., Heine, S. J., & Norenzayan, A. (2010). The weirdest people in the world. *Behavioral and Brain Sciences*, *33*(2–3), 61–83.

Are You Stupider than a Monkey?

Inoue, S., & Matsuzawa, T. (2007). Working memory of numerals in chimpanzees. *Current Biology*, *17*(23), R1004–R1005.

Cook, P., & Wilson, M. (2010). Do young chimpanzees have extraordinary working memory? *Psychonomic Bulletin & Review*, *17*(4), 599–600.

The Tragic Tale of Kitty Genovese

Manning, R., Levine, M., & Collins, A. (2007). The Kitty Genovese murder and the social psychology of helping: the parable of the 38 witnesses. *American Psychologist*, *62*(6), 555.

Fischer, P., Krueger, J. I., Greitemeyer, T., Vogrincic, C., Kastenmüller, A., Frey, D., & Kainbacher, M. (2011). The bystander-effect: A meta-analytic review on bystander intervention in dangerous and non-dangerous emergencies. *Psychological Bulletin*, *137*(4), 517.

The Necker Cube

Franks, C. M., & Lindahl, L. E. H. (1963). Extraversion and rate of fluctuation of the Necker Cube. *Perceptual and Motor Skills*, *16*(1), 131–7.

Christman, S. D., Sontam, V., & Jasper, J. D. (2009). Individual differences in ambiguous-figure perception: Degree of handedness and interhemispheric interaction. *Perception*, *38*(8), 1183.

Anchors Away

Tversky, A., & Kahneman, D. (1974). Judgment under uncertainty: Heuristics and biases. *Science*, *185*(4157), 1124–31.

A Shocking Experiment

Milgram, S. (1963). Behavioral study of obedience. *Journal of Abnormal and Social Psychology*, *67*, 371–8.

Milgram, S. (1965) Some conditions of obedience and disobedience to authority. *Human Relations*, *18*, 57–76.

Haslam, S. A., & Reicher, S. D. (2012). Contesting the 'nature' of conformity: What Milgram and Zimbardo's studies really show. *PLoS Biology*, *10*(11), e1001426.

Mission to Mars

Saffran, J. R., Aslin, R. N., & Newport, E. L. (1996). Statistical learning by 8-month-old infants. *Science*, *274*(5294), 1926–8.

Carrot or Stick?

Tversky, A., & Kahneman, D. (1974) Judgment under uncertainty: Heuristics and biases. *Science*, *185*, 1124–1131.

Liar, Liar

Aamodt, M. G., & Mitchell, H. (2006). Who can best catch a liar? A meta-analysis of individual differences in detecting deception. *Forensic Examiner*, *15*, 6–11.

Bond, C. F., & DePaulo, B. M. (2008). Individual differences in judging deception: Accuracy and bias. *Psychological Bulletin*, *134*(4), 477.

Wright, G. R. T., Berry, C. J., & Bird, G. (2012) 'You can't kid a kidder': Association between production and detection of deception in an interactive deception task. *Frontiers in Human Neuroscience*, 6:87. doi: 10.3389/fnhum.2012.00087.

Wright Whelan, C., Wagstaff, G. F., & Wheatcroft, J. M. (2013).

High-stakes lies: Verbal and nonverbal cues to deception in public appeals for help with missing or murdered relatives. *Psychiatry, Psychology and Law*, 1–15. doi: 10.1080/13218719.2013.839931

Vrij, A., Leal, S., Mann, S., Warmelink, L., Granhag, P., & Fisher, R. (2010). Drawings as an innovative and successful lie detection tool. *Applied Cognitive Psychology* 24(4), 587–94.

Lyer, Lyer

Fodor, J. A. (1983). *The Modularity of Mind: An Essay on Faculty Psychology*. Cambridge, MA: MIT Press.

Segall, M. H., Campbell, D. T., & Herskovits, M. J. (1966). *The Influence of Culture on Visual Perception*. Indianapolis, IN: Bobbs-Merrill.

Henrich, J., Heine, S. J., & Norenzayan, A. (2010). The weirdest people in the world. *Behavioral and Brain Sciences*, 33(2–3), 61–83.

Jahoda, G. (1971). Retinal pigmentation, illusion susceptibility and space perception. *International Journal of Psychology*, 6(3), 199–207.

The Line-Length Illusion

Asch, S. E., (1951). Effects of group pressure on the modification and distortion of judgments. In H. Guetzkow (Ed.), *Groups, Leadership and Men* (pp. 177–90). Pittsburgh, PA: Carnegie Press.

Perrin, S., & Spencer, C. (1981). Independence or conformity in the Asch experiment as a reflection of cultural and situational factors. *British Journal of Social Psychology*, 20(3), 205–9.

Bond, R., & Smith, P. B. (1996). Culture and conformity: a meta-analysis of studies using Asch's (1952b, 1956) line judgment task. *Psychological Bulletin*, 119(1), 111.

A Barking-Mad Test?

Levinson, B. M., & Mezei, H. (1973). The Draw-a-Dog Scale. *Perceptual and Motor Skills*, 36(1), 19–22.

Goodenough, F. (1926). *Measurement of Intelligence by Drawings*. New York: World Book Co.

Harris, D. B. (1963). *Children's Drawings as Measures of Intellectual Maturity*. New York: Harcourt, Brace & World, Inc.

Naglieri, J. A., & Pfeiffer, S. I. (1992). Performance of disruptive behavior disordered and normal samples on the Draw A Person: Screening Procedure for Emotional Disturbance. *Psychological Assessment*, 4(2), 156.

Your Perfect Partner

Buss, D. M. (1989). Sex differences in human mate preferences: Evolutionary hypotheses tested in 37 cultures. *Behavioral and Brain Sciences, 12*, 1–14.

Buss, D. M., Shackelford, T. K., Kirkpatrick, L. A., & Larsen, R. J. (2001). A half century of mate preferences: the cultural evolution of values. *Journal of Marriage and Family, 63*, 491–503.

Trivers, R. (1972). Parental investment and sexual selection. In B. Campbell (Ed.), *Sexual Selection and the Descent of Man: 1871–1971* (pp. 136–79). Chicago, IL: Aldine.

Lippa, R. A. (2007). The preferred traits of mates in a cross-national study of heterosexual and homosexual men and women: An examination of biological and cultural influences. *Archives of Sexual Behavior, 36*(2), 193–208.

Digital Love

Cacioppo, J. T., Cacioppo, S., Gonzaga, G. C., Ogburn, E. L., & Vander-Weele, T. J. (2013). Marital satisfaction and break-ups differ across on-line and off-line meeting venues. *Proceedings of the National Academy of Sciences 110*(25), 10135–10140.

St Valentine's Day: Massacred?

Laurin, K., Kille, D. R., & Eibach, R. P. (2013). 'The way I am is the way you ought to be': Perceiving one's relational status as unchangeable motivates normative idealization of that status. *Psychological Science, 24*(8), 1523–32.

Festinger, L., & Carlsmith, J. M. (1959). Cognitive consequences of forced compliance. *Journal of Abnormal and Social Psychology, 58*(2), 203–10.

The Tea Test

Fisher, R. A. (1925). *Statistical Methods for Research Workers*. Edinburgh: Oliver & Boyd.

Pearson, K. (1900). On the criterion that a given system of deviations from the probable in the case of a correlated system of variables is such that it can be reasonably supposed to have arisen from random sampling. *Philosophical Magazine, 50*, 157–75.

Yates, F., and Mather, K. (1963). Ronald Aylmer Fisher, 1890–1962. *Biographical Memoirs of Fellows of the Royal Society, 9*, 91–129.

Reading and Righting

Davis, C. J. (2010). The spatial coding model of visual word identification. *Psychological Review*, *117*(3), 713.

Hauk, O., Davis, M. H., Ford, M., Pulvermüller, F., & Marslen-Wilson, W. D. (2006). The time course of visual word recognition as revealed by linear regression analysis of ERP data. *Neuroimage*, *30*(4), 1383–1400.

Prelude or Requiem?

Rauscher, F. H., Shaw, G. L., & Ky, K. N. (1993). Music and spatial task performance. *Nature*, *365*(6447), 611.

Davies, P. J. (1984). Mozart's illnesses and death: 1. The illnesses, 1756–90. *The Musical Times*, *125*, 437–42.

Nantais, K. M., & Schellenberg, E. G. (1999). The Mozart effect: an artifact of preference? *Psychological Science*, *10*, 370–73.

Thompson, W. F., Schellenberg, E. G., & Husain, G. (2001). Arousal, mood and the Mozart effect. *Psychological Science*, *12*, 248–51.

http://www.guardian.co.uk/culture/2003/jan/10/artsfeatures.shopping

The Surgeon

Coleman, L., & Kay, P. (1981). Prototype semantics: The English word *lie*. *Language*, 26–44.

Troppmann, K. M., Palis, B. E., Goodnight Jr, J. E., Ho, H. S., & Troppmann, C. (2009). Women surgeons in the new millennium. *Archives of Surgery*, *144*(7), 635.

Christian Lynge, D., Larson, E. H., Thompson, M. J., Rosenblatt, R. A., & Hart, L. G. (2008). A longitudinal analysis of the general surgery workforce in the United States, 1981–2005. *Archives of Surgery*, *143*(4), 345.

The Doctor

Duncker, K. (1945). On problem-solving. *Psychological Monographs*, *58*(5), 1–113.

The Radiologist

Neisser, U. & Becklen, R. (1975). Selective looking: Attending to visually specified events. *Cognitive Psychology*, *7*, 480–94.

Simons, D. J., & Chabris, C. F. (1999). Gorillas in our midst: Sustained inattentional blindness for dynamic events. *Perception-London*, *28*(9), 1059–74.

Drew, T., Võ, M. L. H., & Wolfe, J. M. The invisible gorilla strikes again: Sustained inattentional blindness in expert observers. *Psychological Science*. 10.1177/0956797613479386

Dalton, P., & Fraenkel, N. (2012). Gorillas we have missed: Sustained inattentional deafness for dynamic events. *Cognition*, *124*(3), 367–72.

The Health Minister

Tversky, A., & Kahneman, D. (1981). The framing of decisions. *Science*, *211*, 453–8.

Mandel, D. R. (2001). Gain-loss framing and choice: Separating outcome formulations from descriptor formulations. *Organizational Behavior and Human Decision Processes*, *85*(1), 56–76.

Kühberger, A. (1998). The influence of framing on risky decisions: A meta-analysis. *Organizational Behavior and Human Decision Processes*, *75*(1), 23–55.

Marteau, T. M. (1989). Framing of information: Its influence upon decisions of doctors and patients. *British Journal of Social Psychology*, *28*(1), 89–94.

Red or Black?

Gilovich, T., Vallone, R., & Tversky, A. (1985). The hot hand in basketball: on the misperception of random sequences. *Cognitive Psychology*, *17*(3), 295–314.

Gershenson, C., & Pineda, L. A. (2009). Why does public transport not arrive on time? The pervasiveness of equal headway instability. *PloS ONE*, *4*(10), e7292.

Track the Attacker

Snook, B., Taylor, P. J., & Bennell, C. (2004). Geographic profiling: The fast, frugal, and accurate way. *Applied Cognitive Psychology*, *18*(1), 105–21.

http://www.newyorker.com/reporting/2007/11/12/071112fa_fact_gladwell

Canter, D., & Hammond, L. (2006). A comparison of the efficacy of different decay functions in geographical profiling for a sample of US serial killers. *Journal of Investigative Psychology and Offender Profiling*, *3*(2), 91–103.

Alison, L., Bennell, C., Mokros, A., & Ormerod, D. (2002). The personality paradox in offender profiling: A theoretical review of the processes involved in deriving background characteristics from crime scene actions. *Psychology, Public Policy, and Law, 8*(1), 115.

Morality Play

Hall, L., Johansson, P., & Strandberg, T. (2012). Lifting the veil of morality: Choice blindness and attitude reversals on a self-transforming survey. *PloS ONE, 7*(9), e45457 doi: 10.1371/journal.pone.0045457.

Haidt, J. (2001). The emotional dog and its rational tail: a social intuitionist approach to moral judgment. *Psychological Review, 108,* 814–34.

Mercier, H., & Sperber, D. (2011). Why do humans reason? Arguments for an argumentative theory. *Behavioral and Brain Sciences, 34,* 57–74.

The Arts Critic

Lebuda, I. & Karwowski, M. (2012). Tell me your name and I'll tell you how creative your work is: Author's name and gender as factors influencing assessment of products' creativity in four different domains. *Creativity Research Journal, 25*(1), 137–42.

Card Trick 1 and 2

Wason, P. C. (1966). Reasoning. In B. M. Foss, (Ed.), *New Horizons in Psychology*. Harmondsworth: Penguin.

Ernst, E. (2010). Homeopathy: what does the 'best' evidence tell us? *Medical Journal of Australia, 192*(8), 458–60.

'All I Have To Do Is Dream'

Walker, M. P., Brakefield, T., Morgan, A., Hobson, J. A., & Stickgold, R. (2002). Practice with sleep makes perfect: Sleep-dependent motor skill learning. *Neuron, 35*(1), 205–11.

Mednick, S. C., & Alaynick, W. A. (2010). Comparing models of sleep-dependent memory consolidation. *Journal of Experimental & Clinical Medicine, 2*(4), 156–64.

Debarnot, U., Castellani, E., Valenza, G., Sebastiani, L., & Guillot, A. (2011). Daytime naps improve motor imagery learning. *Cognitive, Affective, & Behavioral Neuroscience, 11*(4), 541–50.

Yáguez, L., Nagel, D., Hoffman, H., Canavan, A. G. M., Wist, E., & Hömberg, V. (1998). A mental route to motor learning: Improving trajectorial kinematics through imagery training. *Behavioural Brain Research, 90*(1), 95–106.

Coffman, D. D. (1990). Effects of mental practice, physical practice, and knowledge of results in piano performance. *Journal of Research in Music Education, 38*, 187–96.

The Interpretation of Dreams

Freud, S. (1899). *Die Traumdeutung* [*The Interpretation of Dreams*]. Leipzig: Franz Deuticke.

The March of Time

Boroditsky, L. (2001). Does language shape thought? Mandarin and English speakers' conceptions of time. *Cognitive Psychology, 43*(1), 1–22.

Berlin, B., & Kay, P. (1969). *Basic Color Terms*. Berkeley, CA: University of California Press.

Heider, E. (1972). Universals in color naming and memory. *Journal of Experimental Psychology, 93*, 10–20.

Levinson, S. C. (1997). Language and cognition: the cognitive consequences of spatial description in Guugu Yimithirr. *Journal of Linguistic Anthropology, 7*(1), 98–131.

It Feels So Right

Frederick, S. (2005). Cognitive reflection and decision making. *The Journal of Economic Perspectives, 19*(4), 25–42.

Men Are from Mars, Women Are from Venus

Hyde, J. S. (2005). The gender similarities hypothesis. *American Psychologist, 60*(6), 581.

Hampson, E. (1990). Variations in sex-related cognitive abilities across the menstrual cycle. *Brain and Cognition, 14*, 26–43.

Hausmann, M., Slabbekoorn, D., Van Goozen, S. H., Cohen-Kettenis, P. T., & Güntürkün, O. (2000). Sex hormones affect spatial abilities during the menstrual cycle. *Behavioral Neuroscience, 114*(6), 1245.

Focus on Your Knitting

Unsworth, N., Heitz, R. P., Schrock, J. C., & Engle, R. W. (2005). An automated version of the operation span task. *Behavior Research Methods, 37*(3), 498–505.

Sanbonmatsu, D. M., Strayer, D. L., Medeiros-Ward, N., & Watson, J. M. (2013). Who multi-tasks and why? Multitasking ability, perceived multitasking ability, impulsivity, and sensation seeking. *PloS ONE*, *8*(1), e54402.

Mäntylä, T. (2013). Gender differences in multitasking reflect spatial ability. *Psychological Science*, *24*(4), 514–20.

Buser, T., & Peter, N. (2012). Multitasking. *Experimental Economics*, *15*(4), 641–55.

Stoet, G., O' Connor, D. B., Conner, M., & Laws, K. R. (2013). Are women better than men at multitasking? *BMC Psychology*, *1*(1), 1–18.

Quoth the Raven's 'What's My Score?'

Duckworth, A. L., & Seligman, M. E. (2005). Self-discipline outdoes IQ in predicting academic performance of adolescents. *Psychological Science*, *16*(12), 939–44.

Strenze, T. (2007). Intelligence and socioeconomic success: a meta-analytic review of longitudinal research. *Intelligence*, *35*(5), 401–26.

Batty, G. D., Deary, I. J., & Gottfredson, L. S. (2007). Premorbid (early life) IQ and later mortality risk: Systematic review. *Annals of Epidemiology*, *17*(4), 278–88.

Hauser, R. M. (2002). *Meritocracy, Cognitive Ability, and the Sources of Occupational Success*. Center for Demography and Ecology Working Paper 98–07. Madison, WI: University of Wisconsin. (Thanks are due to Robert M. Hauser for generously making available to me a spreadsheet summarising the data reported in the paper.)

Zimmerman, Paul (1984). *The New Thinking Man's Guide to Pro Football*. New York: Simon and Schuster. p. 416.

Conversion table: http://www.us.mensa.org/AML/?LinkServID=5A1CE 69C-C4DD-6B70-EE32B45588243A22

http://www.shortlist.com/shortlists/10-surprisingly-clever-celebrities

http://www.businessinsider.com/the-smartest-people-in-the-world-2011-3?op=1

http://www.onlygoodmovies.com/blog/movie-news/celebrity-iq-scores/

Sulloway, F. J. (2007). Birth order and intelligence. *Science*, *317*, 1711–12.

Devlin, B., Daniels, M., & Roeder, K. (1997). The heritability of IQ. *Nature*, *388* (6641), 468–71.

Dickens, W. T., & Flynn, J. R. (2001). Heritability estimates versus large environmental effects: the IQ paradox resolved. *Psychological Review*, *108*(2), 346.

The Fool Hath Said in His Heart, 'There Is No God'

Zuckerman, M., Silberman, J., & Hall, J. A. (2013). The relation between intelligence and religiosity: a meta-analysis and some proposed explanations. *Personality and Social Psychology Review* 17(4), 325–354.

Lynn, R., Harvey, J., & Nyborg, H. (2009). Average intelligence predicts atheism rates across 137 nations. *Intelligence*, 37(1), 11–15.

Idiocracy?

Woodley, M. A., te Nijenhuis, J., & Murphy, R. (2013). Were the Victorians cleverer than us? The decline in general intelligence estimated from a meta-analysis of the slowing of simple reaction time. *Intelligence*, 41(6), 843–850.

Flynn, J. R. (2007). *What Is intelligence?: Beyond the Flynn Effect*. Cambridge: Cambridge University Press.

Daley, T. C., Whaley, S. E., Sigman, M. D., Espinosa, M. P., & Neumann, C. (2003). IQ on the rise: The Flynn effect in rural Kenyan children. *Psychological Science*, 14(3), 215–19.

Carr, N. (2008). Is Google making us stupid? *Yearbook of the National Society for the Study of Education*, 107(2), 89–94.

Flynn, J. R., (2012). *Are We Getting Smarter?: Rising IQ in the Twenty-First Century*. Cambridge: Cambridge University Press.

Jensen, A. R. (2011). The theory of intelligence and its measurement. *Intelligence*, 39(4), 171–7.

Visscher, P. M., Hill, W. G., & Wray, N. R. (2008). Heritability in the genomics era – concepts and misconceptions. *Nature Reviews Genetics*, 9(4), 255–66.

Stereo Types

Rentfrow, P. J., & Gosling, S. D. (2003). The do re mi's of everyday life: The structure and personality correlates of music preferences. *Journal of Personality and Social Psychology*, 84, 1236–56.

Rentfrow, P. J., & Gosling, S. D. (2006). Message in a ballad: The role of music preferences in interpersonal perception. *Psychological Science*, 17, 236–42.

Rentfrow, P. J., & Gosling, S. D. (2007). The content and validity of music-genre stereotypes among college students. *Psychology of Music*, 35, 306–26.

Rentfrow, P. J. & Gosling, S. D. (2003). Norms for the Short Test of Music Preferences. Unpublished data, University of Texas at Austin.

Horoscope Horror Show?

Weber, G. W., Prossinger, H., & Seidler, H. (1998). Height depends on month of birth. *Nature*, 391(6669), 754–5.

Davies, G., Welham, J., Chant, D., Torrey, E. F., & McGrath, J. (2003). A systematic review and meta-analysis of northern hemisphere season of birth studies in schizophrenia. *Schizophrenia Bulletin*, 29(3), 587–93.

Gavrilov, L. A., & Gavrilova, N. S. (2011). Season of birth and exceptional longevity: Comparative study of American centenarians, their siblings, and spouses. *Journal of Aging Research*, http://dx.doi.org/10.1061/2011/104616.

Thompson, D. (1971). Season of birth and success in the secondary school. *Education Research*, 14(1), 56–60.

Brewer, J., Balsom, P. D. and Davis, J. A. (1995). Seasonal birth distribution amongst European soccer players. *Sports, Exercise and Injury*, 1, 154–7.

Skirbekk, V., Kohler, H. P., & Prskawetz, A. (2004). Birth month, school graduation, and the timing of births and marriages. *Demography*, 41(3), 547–68.

Forer, B. R. (1949). The fallacy of personal validation: A classroom demonstration of gullibility. *Journal of Abnormal and Social Psychology*, 44, 118–23.

Are You a Conspiracy Theorist?

Lewandowsky, S., Oberauer, K., & Gignac, G. E. (2013). NASA faked the moon landing – therefore, (climate) science is a hoax: an anatomy of the motivated rejection of science. *Psychological Science*, 24(5), 622–33.

What a Shape Sounds Like

Ramachandran, V. S., & Hubbard, E. M. (2001). Synaesthesia – a window into perception, thought and language. *Journal of Consciousness Studies*, 8(12), 3–34.

Maurer, D., Pathman, T., & Mondloch, C. J. (2006). The shape of boubas: Sound–shape correspondences in toddlers and adults. *Developmental Science*, 9(3), 316–22.

Coulter, K. S., & Coulter, R. A. (2010). Small sounds, big deals: Phonetic symbolism effects in pricing. *Journal of Consumer Research*, 37(2), 315–28.

What a Shape Tastes Like

Gallace, A., Boschin, E., & Spence, C. (2011). On the taste of 'Bouba' and 'Kiki': An exploration of word–food associations in neurologically normal participants. *Cognitive Neuroscience*, 2(1), 34–46.

Spence, C., & Ngo, M. K. (2012). Assessing the shape symbolism of the taste, flavour, and texture of foods and beverages. *Flavour*, 1(1), 12.

Spence, C., & Gallace, A. (2011). Tasting shapes and words. *Food Quality and Preference*, 22(3), 290–95.

Hanson-Vaux, G., Crisinel, A. S., & Spence, C. (2013). Smelling shapes: Crossmodal correspondences between odors and shapes. *Chemical Senses*, 38(2), 161–66.

What's in a Name?

Oliver, J. E., Wood, T., Bass, A. (2013). *Liberellas versus Konservatives: Social Status, Ideology, and Birth Names in the United States.* Paper presented at the annual meeting of the Midwestern Political Science Association.

What's in a Face?

Perrett, D. I., Burt, D. M., Penton-Voak, I. S., Lee, K. J., Rowland, D. A., & Edwards, R. (1999). Symmetry and human facial attractiveness. *Evolution and Human Behavior*, 20(5), 295–307.

DeBruine, L. M., Jones, B. C., Unger, L., Little, A. C., & Feinberg, D. R. (2007). Dissociating averageness and attractiveness: Attractive faces are not always average. *Journal of Experimental Psychology: Human Perception and Performance*, 33(6), 1420.

DeBruine, L. M., Jones, B. C., Smith, F. G., & Little, A. C. (2010). Are attractive men's faces masculine or feminine? The importance of controlling confounds in face stimuli. *Journal of Experimental Psychology: Human Perception and Performance*, 36(3), 751.

Perrett, D. (2012). *In Your Face: The New Science of Human Attraction.* London: Palgrave Macmillan.

Tips for Dancers?

Miller, G., Tybur, J. M., & Jordan, B. D. (2007). Ovulatory cycle effects on tip earnings by lap dancers: Economic evidence for human estrus. *Evolution and Human Behavior*, 28(6), 375–81.

Havlíček, J., Dvořáková, R., Bartoš, L., & Flegr, J. (2006). Non-advertized does not mean concealed: Body odour changes across the human menstrual cycle. *Ethology*, *112*, 81–90.

Roberts, S. C., Havlicek, J., Flegr, J., Hruskova, M., Little, A. C., Jones, B. C., et al. (2004). Female facial attractiveness increases during the fertile phase of the menstrual cycle. *Proceedings of the Royal Society of London Series B, 271*(S5), S270–S272.

Hitler's Sweater

Lindeman, M., Heywood, B., Riekki, T., & Makkonen, T. (2014). Atheists become emotionally aroused when daring God to do terrible things. *International Journal for the Psychology of Religion*, *24*(2), 124–32.

Nemeroff, C., & Rozin, P. (1994). The contagion concept in adult thinking in the United States: Transmission of germs and of interpersonal influence. *Ethos*, *22*(2), 158–86.

Getting All EmotIQnal

Goleman, D. (2000). Leadership that gets results. *Harvard Business Review*, *78*(2), 78–93.

Landy, F. J. (2005). Some historical and scientific issues related to research on emotional intelligence. *Journal of Organizational Behavior*, *26*(4), 411–24.

Schutte, N. S., Malouff, J. M., Hall, L. E., Haggerty, D. J., Cooper, J. T., Golden, C. J., & Dornheim, L. (1998). Development and validation of a measure of emotional intelligence. *Personality and Individual Differences*, *25*(2), 167–77.

Be on Your Guard

Haney, C., Banks, C., & Zimbardo, P. (1973). A study of prisoners and guards in a simulated prison. *Naval Research Review*: September, 1–17. Washington, DC: Office of Naval Research.

Zimbardo, P. (2007). *The Lucifer Effect: Understanding How Good People Turn Evil*. New York: Random House.

Haslam, S. A., & Reicher, S. D. (2012). Contesting the 'nature' of conformity: What Milgram and Zimbardo's studies really show. *PLoS Biology* 10(11): e1001426. doi:10.1371/journal.pbio.1001426.

Carnahan, T., & McFarland, S. (2007). Revisiting the Stanford prison experiment: Could participant self-selection have led to the cruelty? *Personality and Social Psychology Bulletin*, *33*, 603–14.

What's in a Face? #2: The Talking Dog

Ambridge, B., Pine, J. M., Rowland, C. F., & Young, C. R. (2008). The effect of verb semantic class and verb frequency (entrenchment) on children's and adults' graded judgements of argument-structure overgeneralization errors. *Cognition*, 106(1), 87–129.

Ambridge, B. (2011). Paradigms for assessing children's knowledge of syntax and morphology. In E. Hoff (Ed.). *Guide to Research Methods in Child Language*. London: Blackwell-Wiley (pp. 113–32).

Literacy Test

Greenwald, A. G., McGhee, D. E., & Schwartz, J. L. K. (1998). Measuring individual differences in implicit cognition: the Implicit Association Test. *Journal of Personality and Social Psychology*, 74, 1464–80.

Perrett, D. (2012). *In Your Face: The New Science of Human Attraction*. London: Palgrave Macmillan.

Baron, A. S., & Banaji, M. R. (2006). The development of implicit attitudes evidence of race evaluations from ages 6 and 10 and adulthood. *Psychological Science*, 17(1), 53–8.

Kelly, D. J., Quinn, P. C., Slater, A. M., Lee, K., Gibson, A., Smith, M., & Pascalis, O. (2005). Three-month-olds, but not newborns, prefer own-race faces. *Developmental Science*, 8(6), F31–F36.

Tajfel, H., Billig, M. G., Bundy, R. P., & Flament, C. (1971). Social categorization and intergroup behaviour. *European Journal of Social Psychology*,1(2), 149–78.

Hamlin, J. K., Mahajan, N., Liberman, Z., & Wynn, K. (2013). Not like me = bad: Infants prefer those who harm dissimilar others. *Psychological Science*, 24(4), 589–94.

Lebrecht, S., Pierce, L. J., Tarr, M. J., & Tanaka, J. W. (2009). Perceptual other-race training reduces implicit racial bias. *PLoS ONE*, 4(1), e4215.

Roll Play

Poretz, M., & Sinrod, B. (1989). *The First Really Important Survey of American Habits*. New York: Price Stern Sloan.

Kimberly-Clark (27 January 2010), How does America roll? Cottonelle brand teams with Tori and Dean to end the age-old debate: Over or under? (press release), *PR Newswire*.

Widdicombe, B. (8 June 2004), Butler serves up more dirt on Diana, *New York Daily News*, 38.

http://www.drgilda.com/

A Trivial Pursuit

Dijksterhuis, A., & Knippenberg, A.V. (1998). The relation between perception and behavior, or how to win a game of trivial pursuit. *Journal of Personality and Social Psychology*, 74(4), 865–77.

Bargh, J. A., Chen, M., & Burrows, L. (1996). Automaticity of social behavior: Direct effects of trait construct and stereotype activation on action. *Journal of Personality and Social Psychology*, 71, 230–44.

Doyen, S., Klein, O., Pichon, C., & Cleeremans, A. (2012). Subliminal behavioral priming: It is all in the brain, but whose brain? *PLoS ONE*, 7(1), doi: 10.1371/journal.pone.0029081.

Bargh. J.A., (2012). http://www.psychologytoday.com/blog/the-natural-unconscious/201205/priming-effects-replicate-just-fine-thanks

Eder, A., Leipert, C., Musch, J., & Klauer, K. (2012). Failed replication to prime intelligent behavior. Retrieved 3 April 2013 from http://www.PsychFileDrawer.org/replication.php?attempt=MTIo

Roberts, M. S., Crooks, W., Kolody, T. J., Pavlovic, T., Rombola, K. J., & Standing, L. G. (2013). No effect on intelligence from priming. Retrieved 3 April 2013 from http://www.PsychFileDrawer.org/replication.php?attempt=MTQz

What's in a Face? #3: Brown-Eyed Girl

http://www.bbc.co.uk/news/uk-england-24112067

Kleisner, K., Priplatova, L., Frost, P., & Flegr, J. (2013). Trustworthy-looking face meets brown eyes. *PLoS ONE*, 8(1), e53285.

At My Wick's End

Duncker, K. (1945). On problem-solving. *Psychological Monographs*, 58(5), i–113.

Weisberg, R., DiCamillo, M., & Phillips, D. (1978). Transferring old associations to new situations: a nonautomatic process. *Journal of Verbal Learning and Verbal Behavior*, 17(2), 219–28.

Under Pressure

Clandra, A. (1968). Angels on a pin. *The Saturday Review*, 21 December, p. 60.

Spare the Rod and Spoil the Child?

Ferguson, C. J. (2013), Spanking, corporal punishment and negative long-term outcomes: A meta-analytic review of longitudinal studies. *Clinical Psychology Review*, 33,196–208.

Nobes, G., Smith, M., Upton, P., & Heverin, A. (1999). Physical punishment by mothers and fathers in British homes. *Journal of Interpersonal Violence*, 14(8), 887–902.

Video Gains?

http://vgsales.wikia.com/wiki/Video_game_industry

http://www.apa.org/about/policy/interactive-media.pdf

Anderson, C. A., Shibuya, A., Ihori, N., Swing, E. L., Bushman, B. J., Sakamoto, A., & Saleem, M. (2010). Violent video game effects on aggression, empathy, and prosocial behavior in eastern and western countries: a meta-analytic review. *Psychological Bulletin*, 136(2), 151.

Ferguson, C. J. (2010). Blazing angels or resident evil? Can violent video games be a force for good? *Review of General Psychology*, 14(2), 68.

Oei, A. C., & Patterson, M. D. (2013). Enhancing cognition with video games: A multiple game training study. *PloS ONE*, 8(3), e58546.

Rosser Jr, J. C., Lynch, P. J., Cuddihy, L., Gentile, D. A., Klonsky, J., & Merrell, R. (2007). The impact of video games on training surgeons in the 21st century. *Archives of Surgery*, 142(2), 181.

Franceschini, S., Gori, S., Ruffino, M., Viola, S., Molteni, M., & Facoetti, A. (2013). Action video games make dyslexic children read better. *Current Biology*, 23(6), 462–6.

Ferguson, C. J. (2007). The good, the bad and the ugly: a meta-analytic review of positive and negative effects of violent video games. *Psychiatric Quarterly*, 78(4), 309–16.

Shut Your Face(book)?

Clayton, R. B., Nagurney, A., & Smith, J. R. (2013). Cheating, breakup, and divorce: Is Facebook use to blame? *Cyberpsychology, Behavior, and Social Networking*, 16(10), 717–20.

Cake Addicts

Koo, J. W., Mazei-Robison, M. S., Chaudhury, D., Juarez, B., LaPlant, Q., Ferguson, D., ... & Nestler, E. J. (2012). BDNF is a negative modulator of morphine action. *Science*, 338(6103), 124–8.

Field, M., & Cartwright-Hatton, S. *Psychological Disorders*. London: Sage.

Davis, C., & Carter, J. C. (2009). Compulsive overeating as an addiction disorder: A review of theory and evidence. *Appetite*, 53(1), 1–8.

Bulik, C. M., Sullivan, P. F., & Kendler, K. S. (1998). Heritability of binge-eating and broadly defined bulimia nervosa. *Biological Psychiatry*, 44(12), 1210–18.

Lilenfeld, L. R., Ringham, R., Kalarchian, M. A., & Marcus, M. D. (2008). A family history study of binge-eating disorder. *Comprehensive Psychiatry*, 49(3), 247–54.

http://www.psychiatry.org/addiction

Heyman, G. M. (2009). *Addiction: A Disorder of Choice*. Cambridge, MA: Harvard University Press.

Koffarnus, M. N., Jarmolowicz, D. P., Mueller, E. T., & Bickel, W. K. (2013). Changing delay discounting in the light of the competing neurobehavioral decision systems theory: a review. *Journal of the Experimental Analysis of Behavior*, 99(1), 32–57.

Anokhin, A. P., Golosheykin, S., Grant, J. D., & Heath, A. C. (2011). Heritability of delay discounting in adolescence: a longitudinal twin study. *Behavior Genetics*, 41(2), 175–83.

Geier, A., Wansink, B., & Rozin, P. (2012). Red potato chips: Segmentation cues can substantially decrease food intake. *Health Psychology*, 31(3), 398.

http://news.bbc.co.uk/1/hi/business/7490346.stm

That Sinking Feeling

Arkes, H. R., & Blumer, C. (1985). The psychology of sunk cost. *Organizational Behavior and Human Decision Processes*, 35(1), 124–40.

Arkes, H. R., & Ayton, P. (1999). The sunk cost and Concorde effects: Are humans less rational than lower animals? *Psychological Bulletin*, 125(5), 591.

Can't Stand Losing You

Kahneman, D., Knetsch, J. L., & Thaler, R. H. (1991). Anomalies: the endowment effect, loss aversion, and status quo bias. *Journal of Economic Perspectives*, 5(1), 193–206.

Genesove, D., & Mayer, C. (2001). Loss aversion and seller behavior: Evidence from the housing market. *Quarterly Journal of Economics*, 116(4), 1233–60.

Stick or Switch?

Redelmeier, D. A., & Tibshirani, R. J. (1999). Why cars in the next lane seem to go faster. *Nature*, *401*(6748), 35.

http://hpyblg.wordpress.com/2010/12/31/why-does-the-other-lane-always-seem-to-go-faster/

Mind over Matter

Hood, B., Gjersoe, N. L., & Bloom, P. (2012). Do children think that duplicating the body also duplicates the mind? *Cognition*, *125*(3), 466–74.

Your Memory Is Limitless

Shepard, R. N. (1967). Recognition memory for words, sentences, and pictures. *Journal of Verbal Learning and Verbal Behavior*, *6*(1), 156–63.

Standing, L. (1973). Learning 10,000 pictures. *Quarterly Journal of Experimental Psychology*, *25*(2), 207–22.

Bonin, P., Peereman, R., Malardier, N., Méot, A., & Chalard, M. (2003). A new set of 299 pictures for psycholinguistic studies: French norms for name agreement, image agreement, conceptual familiarity, visual complexity, image variability, age of acquisition, and naming latencies. *Behavior Research Methods, Instruments, & Computers*, *35*(1), 158–67.

Do Humans Dream of Electric Sheep?

Kay, K. N., Naselaris, T., Prenger, R. J., & Gallant, J. L. (2008). Identifying natural images from human brain activity. *Nature*, *452*(7185), 352–5.

Mitchell, T. M., Shinkareva, S. V., Carlson, A., Chang, K. M., Malave, V. L., Mason, R. A., & Just, M. A. (2008). Predicting human brain activity associated with the meanings of nouns. *Science*, *320*(5880), 1191–5.

Horikawa, T., Tamaki, M., Miyawaki, Y., & Kamitani, Y. (2013). Neural decoding of visual imagery during sleep. *Science*, *340*(6132), 639–42.

Kassam, K. S., Markey, A. R., Cherkassky, V. L., Loewenstein, G., & Just, M. A. (2013). Identifying emotions on the basis of neural activation. *PLoS ONE*, 8(6) e66032.dot:10.1371/journal.pone.0066032.

Soon, C. S., Brass, M., Heinze, H. J., & Haynes, J. D. (2008). Unconscious determinants of free decisions in the human brain. *Nature Neuroscience*, *11*(5), 543–5.

Prescient Palmistry?

Fink, B., Manning, J. T., & Neave, N. (2004). Second to fourth digit ratio and the 'big five' personality factors. *Personality and Individual Differences*, 37(3), 495–503.

Bailey, A. A., & Hurd, P. L. (2005). Finger length ratio (2D: 4D) correlates with physical aggression in men but not in women. *Biological Psychology*, 68(3), 215–22.

Schneider, H. J., Pickel, J., & Stalla, G. K. (2006). Typical female 2nd–4th finger length (2D: 4D) ratios in male-to-female transsexuals – possible implications for prenatal androgen exposure. *Psychoneuroendocrinology*, 31(2), 265–9.

What's in a Face? #4: Face-Off

Třebický, V., Havlíček, J., Roberts, S. C., Little, A. C., & Kleisner, K. (2013). Perceived aggressiveness predicts fighting performance in mixed-martial-arts fighters. *Psychological Science*, 24(9), 1664–72.

Carré, J. M., & McCormick, C. M. (2008). In your face: Facial metrics predict aggressive behaviour in the laboratory and in varsity and professional hockey players. *Proceedings of the Royal Society B: Biological Sciences*, 275(1651), 2651–6.

Stirrat, M., Stulp, G., & Pollet, T. V. (2012). Male facial width is associated with death by contact violence: Narrow-faced males are more likely to die from contact violence. *Evolution and Human Behavior*, 33(5), 551–6.

Kraus, M. W., & Chen, T. W. D. (2013). A winning smile? Smile intensity, physical dominance, and fighter performance. *Emotion*, 13(2), 270.

The Psychology of Pain

Sullivan, M. J., Bishop, S. R., & Pivik, J. (1995). The pain catastrophising scale. *Development and Validation: Psychological Assessment*, 7(4), 524–32.

Sullivan, M. J. L., Adams, A., Rhodenizer, T., et al. (2006). A psychosocial risk factor targeted intervention for the prevention of chronic pain and disability following whiplash injury. *Physical Therapy*, 86, 8–18.

A Sinister Questionnaire

Lalumière, M. L., Blanchard, R., & Zucker, K. J. (2000). Sexual orientation and handedness in men and women: A meta-analysis. *Psychological Bulletin*, 126(4), 575.

Veale, J. F. (2013). Edinburgh handedness inventory–short form: A revised version based on confirmatory factor analysis. *Laterality: Asymmetries of Body, Brain and Cognition, 19*(2), 164–77 .

Prichard, E., Propper, R. E., & Christman, S. D. (2013). Degree of handedness, but not direction, is a systematic predictor of cognitive performance. *Frontiers in Psychology, 4*(9), 1–6.

Hardyck, C., Petrinovich, L. F., & Goldman, R. D. (1976). Left-handedness and cognitive deficit. *Cortex, 12*(3), 266–79.

Westfall, J., Jasper, J. D., & Christman, S. D. (2012). Inaction inertia, the sunk cost effect, and handedness: Avoiding the losses of past decisions. *Brain and Cognition, 80*, 192–200.

McManus, I. C. (2004). *Right Hand, Left Hand: The Origins of Asymmetry in Brains, Bodies, Atoms, and Cultures*. Cambridge, MA: Harvard University Press.

The 'I's Have It

Kacewicz, E., Pennebaker, J. W., Davis, M., Jeon, M., & Graesser, A. C. (2013). Pronoun use reflects standings in social hierarchies. *Journal of Language and Social Psychology*, 10.1177/0261927x13502654.

Schwartz, H. A., Eichstaedt, J. C., Kern, M. L., Dziurzynski, L., Ramones, S. M., Agrawal, M., & Ungar, L. H. (2013). Personality, gender, and age in the language of social media: The open-vocabulary approach. *PLoS ONE, 8*(9), e73791.

Write Stuff or Write-Off?

Tett, R. P., & Palmer, C. A. (1997). The validity of handwriting elements in relation to self-report personality trait measures. *Personality and Individual Differences, 22*(1), 11–18.

King, R. N., & Koehler, D. J. (2000). Illusory correlations in graphological inference. *Journal of Experimental Psychology: Applied, 6*(4), 336.

Driver, R. W., Buckley, M. R., & Frink, D. D. (1996). Should we write off graphology? *International Journal of Selection and Assessment, 4*(2), 78–86.

Neter, E., & Ben-Shakhar, G. (1989). The predictive validity of graphological inferences: A meta-analytic approach. *Personality and Individual Differences, 10*(7), 737–45.

YOU Are the Psychologist

Rosenthal, R., & Fode, K. L. (1963). The effect of experimenter bias on the performance of the albino rat. *Behavioral Science, 8*(3), 183–9.

Rosenthal, R. &. Jacobson, L. (1963). Teachers' expectancies: Determinants of pupils' IQ gains. *Psychological Reports, 19*, 115–18.

Levitt, S. D., & List, J. A. (2011). Was there really a Hawthorne effect at the Hawthorne plant? An analysis of the original illumination experiments. *American Economic Journal: Applied Economics, 3*(1), 224–38.

Can Psychology Save the World?

Flood, M. M. (1958). Some experimental games. *Management Science, 5*(1), 5–26.

Hardin, G. (1968). The tragedy of the commons. *Science, 162*, 1243–8.

http://www.theguardian.com/environment/2011/mar/11/kyoto-protocol

http://www.theguardian.com/environment/2012/mar/28/uk-greenhouse-gas-emissions

Credits